American Foreign Policy

The Lost Consensus

George H. Quester

PRAEGER SPECIAL STUDIES • PRAEGER SCIENTIFIC

Library of Congress Cataloging in Publication Data

Quester, George H.
    American foreign policy.

    Bibliography: p.
    Includes index.
    1. United States—Foreign relations—20th century—
Historiography. 2. United States—Foreign relations—
20th century. I. Title.
E744.Q47   327.73   82-616
ISBN 0-03-061666-2   AACR2
ISBN 0-03-061664-6 (pbk.)

Published in 1982 by Praeger Publishers
CBS Educational and Professional Publishing
A Division of CBS, Inc.
521 Fifth Avenue, New York, New York 10175 U.S.A.

© 1982 by Praeger Publishers

23456789 145 987654321

Printed in the United States of America

For My Mother

Acknowledgments

An author always owes more debts than he can remember to acknowledge. A great number of students and colleagues contributed to this book, in some cases more unwittingly by enlisting on opposing sides of the very debate of which the book is a part, in other cases by explicitly taking the time to read portions of the early drafts. None of these people is accountable for the final version as presented by the author here, for it is in no way meant to be a summary of consensus, but rather, as its title suggests, a description of absence of consensus.

The book was written while I was teaching at Cornell University and U.C.L.A. Among the faculty colleagues who were especially helpful in responding to drafts of the argument, I would have to list Robert Jervis, Peter Katzenstein, Stephen Krasner, and Richard Ullman. Arline Blaker and Lynn Ashworth carried the burden of typing the various drafts.

A portion of the book appeared as an article in the Fall, 1980 issue of *Foreign Policy*.

Special thanks go to my wife, who made it all more fun.

Contents

1
Introduction

American foreign policy went through a traumatic change in the Vietnam War at the end of the 1960s; it saw a turning inward about which academic analysts can hardly agree, a turning inward that makes predictions about the future very difficult.

The election of Ronald Reagan as president has been seen by some as ending whatever abdication of international responsibilities might have afflicted the United States after Vietnam, but the evidence offered by the 1980 election is hardly conclusive in this regard. The willingness of the American people and Congress to commit economic and human resources as in the days of the cold war remains very much in doubt; the American public in the 1980s remains confused, and deeply divided, about the goals it wishes to serve in the world. As the cold war—for whatever explanation—was replaced by detente, detente is now being replaced by something else again, a process about which academics and the American public can not yet settle on any definitions or explanations.

The foreign policy of the United States has of course turned inward and outward before. An analysis by Frank Klingberg in 1952 suggested a very regular oscillation about American foreign policy, with periods of inward and outward orientations averaging 21 and 27 years, as follows:

Inward	Outward
1776–98	1798–1824
1824–44	1844–71
1871–91	1891–1919
1919–40	1940–(67?)
(1967–88?)	

The remarkable feature of the Klingberg analysis was[1] that it almost exactly predicted the American disillusionment with Vietnam—for 1967.

Yet can we now definitely count upon such a new U.S. turn outward by 1988? ("Hold on, fellows, the Yanks are coming.") What if the United States does not turn outward again, ready to defend? We must consider the possibility that this most recent U.S. aversion to military engagements is too complicated to be timed simply for another seven years. We must ask whether the inward turn since the end of the 1960s is not unique for the history of American foreign policy.

The intention of this book is thus to examine the past and present of American foreign policy, so as to sort out what can be expected for the future. It will begin by discussing three distinct interpretations of all American foreign policy.

The first interpretation, a "power politics" approach, is basically that the United States is no better and no worse than other countries, i.e., no different, as it has been engaged in the normal pursuit of power that characterizes all international dealings everywhere.[2]

The second interpretation is rather what might be advanced by Marxist and other radical analysts, that the United States has indeed been worse than other countries in the amount of trouble it causes for the international system, precisely because it has been more capitalist in its basic economic system.[3]

The third interpretation of the "American liberal" would then finally be that the United States has in fact been better than other countries in having a more generous and altruistic outlook toward the rest of the world. Perhaps this is because it has been more successful at home, and thus has been more in the mood to share what it felt contributed to happiness.[4]

Having outlined these three contending views, the book will then apply them to the emergence of the United States as a major power through the world wars, then in the analysis of the cold war, and finally to whatever has emerged since the cold war. It will relate U.S. post-Vietnam trauma precisely to the debate about these interpretations of American foreign policy, contending that a major complication about the future of the United States stems from an internal soul-searching since 1967 about the nature of its past. What was previously a general consensus about the goals of American foreign policy, accepting the third view, may be a consensus no longer, as a large number of Americans (in effect accepting the second view noted above) now doubt the relevance or sincerity of earlier American feelings on this subject. Even if such doubt is not well-founded on the basis of the facts of the past, it is important in its own right; when large numbers of Americans are now unsure of themselves in foreign policy, where before they felt quite confident about the goals they were seeking to serve, this by itself amounts to a major turning point in such foreign policy. The United States is less committed now than it was before 1967 to becoming involved in a military defense of the "free world," and this change is a large part of what this book is trying to explain.

One form of power politics interpretation (the first view) of this change might have been relatively more reassuring, suggesting simply that there was much less need to deploy military force now for the spread of Communist political control to be restricted (or "contained"). In this view, an elementary balance-of-power mechanism might have taken hold whereby Communist states fell to quarreling with, and checking, each other, viz. China and the USSR, or Vietnam and Cambodia, as the ability of the Soviet Union to make gains in Africa would never match its hold on Eastern Europe. This then was a view that the United States was only appearing less resolute about resisting communism because there was really much less to resist, as the balancing of expansive tendencies in the world can now take care of itself.[5]

Such an explanation of the cooling of any American ardor for plunging into the jungles of Angola is not so satisfying, however. To be sure, advantages have been gained from the internal divisions of the Communist world, as "the monolith" is gone. Yet, what if technology makes the USSR still the one Communist power that matters for many areas, the only one able to deploy ships and troop-carrier aircraft and rocket launchers in quantity? The balance-of-power mechanism does not solve so much of the problem in Africa when the Russians can fly in thousands of Cubans, and the Chinese cannot fly in comparable numbers of North Koreans or Cambodians to check them. Cambodia and Vietnam did not check each other in Southeast Asia for very long. The Chinese or Rumanian press criticism of Soviet foreign policy is amusing to read, but it may not support a hope that the classical American problem of defending political democracy against attack by Communist states will now take care of itself.

A less reassuring explanation of lowered American foreign policy vehemence must thus be pursued here, namely that the American people have since 1967 gone through a very confusing reexamination of what they want to accomplish in the outside world, a reexamination of what previously had been a consensus, and is now no longer, about what is good in the world. The United States lost more than a minor war and a minor piece of territory in Vietnam. It may have lost an important and special aspect of its foreign policy, a consensus it felt about core issues.

This author (the reader should be warned) may still find most plausible the third view noted above that American foreign policy has mainly been driven by generous impulses toward the outside world; but a great number of students, and of Americans in general, no longer accept this view, with many of them instead endorsing the second view, blaming international problems on the selfishness of American capitalism. As younger Americans no longer trust in the generosity of their own country, they may no longer feel much of such generosity themselves, or at least may be very much in disagreement about the forms any generosity should take.

Rather than thus assuming that Americans have only become less willing to make military preparations because there was less menace to prepare against (consistent with the power politics view that nations never change, as only opportunities and situations change), it may rather be that Americans are less willing to undertake such preparations because they are now confused.

Regardless of what side of the current debate we might adopt, one must agree that debate has now replaced consensus. Sorting out this debate will be crucial to sorting out the future.

NOTES

1. Frank Klingberg, "The Historical Alternation of Moods in American Foreign Policy," *World Politics* 4, no. 2 (January 1952): 239-73.

2. As an example of what could surely be labeled a power politics approach, sees Hans Morgenthau, *Politics Among Nations* (New York: Knopf, 1967).

3. See, for an example among many others, Gabriel Kolko, *The Roots of American Foreign Policy* (Boston: Beacon Press, 1969).

4. A good illustration of this perspective, which would be contended to have once been the dominant American view, can be found in Frank Tannenbaum, *The American Tradition in Foreign Policy* (Norman: University of Oklahoma Press, 1955).

5. An application of a relatively reassuring balance-of-power analysis with regard to events in Angola might be found in Gerald Bender, "Angola, the Cubans, and American Anxieties," *Foreign Policy*, no. 31 (Summer 1978), pp. 3-30.

2
Power Politics: The United States the Same as Other Countries

The first view of American foreign policy to be considered is that of power politics, sometimes also referred to as realpolitik or political realism, a view which would expect most or all of the nations of the world to behave basically the same. States are predictable, by this view, in that they seek after power (just as individual firms in economic analysis are rendered predictable and understandable in their behavior when one assumes that they always seek after monetary profit).

This, to repeat, would be a view by which the United States was no worse and no better than any other country in its foreign policy, simply seeking to guard itself against the military, economic, social, and political strengths of others, exploiting its own power opportunities as they arise in each of these areas. Such pursuit of power would sometimes thus dictate an interventionist activism, and at other times would instead counsel a more restrained and patient or "isolationist" attitude.[1]

The tone of the power politics approach is ideal for guarding students against naivete and disappointment about foreign policy. Generous and altruistic goals are not to be expected in others, and are not to be pursued for ourselves. Power is the capital upon which depends anything else one would want to do in life, and the advice here is always to keep an eye on power. We should not be so gullible as to expect that European and other foreign states will be after anything else; indeed some of the confusions and mysteries of such foreign countries' behavior sort themselves out nicely when the power focus is applied. We should also not be so hypocritical as to assume anything more noble than this in ourselves.

In addition to serving as an antidote to hypocrisy, this realpolitik approach cautions against any presuppositions that morality will be practical in the anarchic international arena, against any hope that the good things in life will always go together. Peace may not necessarily be compatible with democracy abroad, and neither may be compatible with economic prosperity.

The radical and liberal interpretations of international politics, which shall be discussed later, both tend to conclude instead that progress can be made on many fronts of human affairs at the same time, that what advances the morally good society on the home front will do so as well for international relations. Accustomed to a certain "success" in their domestic society, most Americans might quite naturally have assumed that problems can also be solved for the international system. But the realpolitik view would caution very much against such optimism, as "the necessity for choice" and "the art of the possible" become continuously relevant.

Instead of endorsing the "normal morality" of domestic dealings, by which one should be honest and aboveboard, avoid violence, and adhere to agreements, the power politics analyst would thus present a substantially different moral imperative, whereby all the diplomats and soldiers and functionaries of any government, including the American government, simply have a duty to their own country; in the words of Stephen Decatur, "my country, right or wrong." In what is strikingly analogous to the lawyer-client relationship, American foreign policy makers (by this view), are supposed to be deceitful in dealing with others, whenever their country would come out stronger thereby. What is more, a realpolitik interpretation of American foreign policy would be that this is exactly what has happened all along, as Theodore Roosevelt or John Foster Dulles behaved no differently than Bismarck or Clemenceau.

International dealings thus differ from domestic politics in many ways, by the realpolitik view, so much that these really amount to two different subjects. International politics depends much more on military force and the threat of force. It depends much less on law and concepts of ordinary social morality. International politics lacks any real sense of total community, of all striving for the good of all (a community that might well be attained *within* countries). Hence, international politics begins with competition, with cooperation being the counterpoint, while domestic politics is just the reverse.

It has to be noted (a point to which we shall return often) that Americans have not accepted such a picture of themselves in the past. Wrongly or rightly, they have rather seen their own foreign policy behavior as distinctive, placing moral concerns above the pursuit of power. Yet the typical image that Europeans have held of the United States, at least since 1890 and the American decisions to invest in a fleet and go to war against Spain, has rather been to see the United States just as the realpolitik analyst would, as an ordinary country, behaving just as Germany or France or the Soviet Union would have behaved.[2]

An appearance of hypocrisy can indeed be annoying in its own right. Just as some Americans would today find protestations of international morality irritating when they come from Indian diplomats (for example, after the seizure of Goa or after the detonation of an Indian "peaceful nuclear explosive"), much of the world must in the past have seen such American self-appraisals as hypocritical self-delusions. Once the United States began to deploy fleets instead of sticking to its earlier isolation, the diplomats of Europe would stop thinking of it as a different kind of country. And even the earlier isolation would be interpreted, by many, as nothing more than an astute exploitation of opportunity by the rules of power politics.

EXPLANATORY POWER: ISOLATION?

The appeal of power politics theory (just as the appeal of classical economic theory for describing the behavior of the firm) stems importantly from its ability to predict state behavior, to sort out what might otherwise be viewed as paradox. If such an approach could explain every shift in American foreign policy, it would be not only psychologically appealing as a theory, but also intellectually convincing.

Any theory will attempt to prove its validity by how it relates the background changes (the "independent variables") to the twists and turns of the foreign policy we must explain (the "dependent variable"). But what about the years for which such wide twists and turns cannot be recalled, the years Americans remember as "isolation"? The inward and outward turnings noted by Klingberg for the earlier nineteenth century may be real, but few would deny that the shifts after 1890 dwarf these in magnitude and significance.*

---

*Historians might also challenge Klingberg's coding and definition of some of the earlier periods. For example, how can one call the American Revolution a period of introversion, when the years of the U.S. Civil War are classified as extroversion? Both in effect were civil wars for Americans, wars in which attention was primarily directed to domestic questions, with foreign alliances and entanglements viewed as accessory to such questions. The U.S. Civil War indeed almost saw a suspension of the Monroe Doctrine, as French forces were allowed to occupy Mexico.

Since the turning outward of 1891 was more profound than any that had occurred before, the years before 1890 thus indeed largely merit the "isolation" label. But what do these years then say about the validity of the power politics interpretation?[3]

Quite a few analysts would see such isolation as a valuable illustration of a correct American power politics approach, as a time when the United States naturally and safely put its own material interests first. Advocates of a "new isolationism" at the end of the Vietnam War thus sometimes based their case on the alleged irrelevance of distant struggles between Communists and anti-Communists to the natural power interests of the United States.[4] Isolationism, for these observers, is remembered as selfish, as illustrating the application and the merits of an exercise in realpolitik.

A part of the American isolationism of the nineteenth century could thus be interpreted as a simple and straightforward defensive exploitation of the balance-of-power mechanism. Just as Great Britain behaved toward the continent, the United States could behave toward all of Europe, including Great Britain. As long as these units of the old system remained divided, they checked each other, and thus reduced the threat of any projection of their military or naval power into the United States. At the same time, the powers on the continent of Europe looked so strong and powerful that it would be pointless to try to project American military power into their territory.

The new American republic could avoid committing itself to any prearranged alliances with any of these powers. In many ways, this was nothing more than what British policy has also been toward alliances with any continental state, a simple and straightforward application of balance-of-power strategy, freeing the United States to spend less on military and naval appropriations.[5]

The relative isolationism of American foreign policy before 1890 can thus be made consistent with a realpolitik outlook, but the problem is that it may be equally consistent with some other outlooks. Some Americans would today instead remember a tradition of altruistic isolationism, staying out of international power conflicts not so much because this would serve the national interests of the United States, but rather because this was the best that could be done to serve the cause of liberal democracy abroad and at home.

As we shall discuss, liberals feel in general that the United States should foster politically democratic regimes at home and abroad, regimes of government by the consent of the governed, regimes where the incumbent in office is checked by the scrutiny of a free press, and by the knowledge that he cannot prevent opposing candidates from running against him in the next election. While liberals more recently might have felt that it was appropriate to intervene abroad to serve these ends, we also must take note of an older tradition of opposition to intervention grounded precisely on the fear that such interventions will always backfire.[6]

To put the problem quite starkly, the exportation of political democracy may always threaten political democracy back home. To be persuasive in supporting freedom abroad, one may have to expand one's army and navy; yet armies and navies historically have been menaces to freedom. To be persuasive abroad, one may have to become imperious and high-handed; but such imperiousness and high-handedness may make the United States more like Spain or Great Britain, in the very process of displacing Spain or Great Britain. Perhaps the best that the United States can do to support political democracy abroad is thus to be sure to practice it at home, to continue to offer the example first set after the American Revolution. Everything else will backfire.

A genuinely altruistic isolationist argument here is thus often stated almost as an "iron law," a "limit to what we can do," which might have sounded just as plausible in the 1860s as it was to sound in the 1960s agony of Vietnam.[7] This would be a view that the Watergate scandal could never have happened, if it had not been for the very active American foreign policy of the 1950s and 1960s, demonstrated dramatically by the Watergate involvement of the Central Intelligence Agency, nominally an externally directed part of the government. The broader weakening of the role of Congress, as compared with the "imperial presidency," might similarly never have developed, but for U.S. foreign policy commitments.

As Figure 2.1 suggests, the years of U.S. isolationism thus do not prove per se either a liberal or a power politics outlook. Just as "realistic" advocates of power politics will alternate between advocating isolation or intervention, depending on the facts of the current inter-

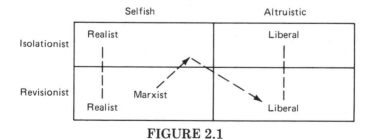

FIGURE 2.1

national situation, some liberals will feel constricted by "iron laws" directing them toward isolation, while others will not.

To put things in perspective, radicals, as will be noted in the next chapter, would advocate isolationsim as things stand at the moment, since they distrust the causes for which American power is currently being deployed, but they would oppose isolation, and advocate intervention, once they had seen the United States establish a proper regime at home.

Some liberals would thus have advocated isolationsim therefore as the most generous posture possible for the outside world. Others will insist that generosity requires a departure from isolation. Looking once more at the years before 1890, we must note Klingberg's outward turnings, however minor, and remember that the United States was not isolationist for every corner of the world. If the United States practiced physical isolation and nonintervention vis-à-vis Europe, it did not do so in the Pacific; and there was American participation of sorts even in Europe.

While avoiding alliances, and avoiding the expense of military forces, the United States was not above expressing preferences or lending encouragement to those developments in Europe of which it approved. By letting the European regimes balance each other, while implicitly or explicitly questioning all of their legitimacies, serving as a sanctuary for all those who rebelled and failed in the revolutions, the United States might have reason to feel that it was making a close to optimal contribution to what could be done to improve that part of the world.[8]

In the Pacific and the Far East, the American pattern was instead to dispatch naval squadrons, and indeed to lodge objections to the maintenance or extension of European colonial presences in the region. A great deal of the apparent American fixation with places away from Europe in the nineteenth and early twentieth centuries can thus be explained by simple opportunity. The interface of interventionist impulse and practical opportunity here simply produced a different result. However much Americans might identify with Greeks or Hungarians or others in their desires for liberty, the European regimes looked too well equipped with armies and navies in these sections to be susceptible to an American challenge. By contrast, Asia, Latin America, and the Pacific were theaters where an injection of American influence might deliver much more in the way of returns.

Asia did not look capable of holding its own against European encroachment in the same manner as Austria might hold against Russia and vice versa. It would therefore be a place where American power could be effectively deployed, and needed to be deployed, if the chance of self-government and republican political democracy was to be preserved. One thus sees deployments of American forces to open Japan, to try to preserve a non-European regime in Samoa, and to try to do the same in China.[9] China and Japan were not comparable enough in power to the European states to suggest that some sort of balancing of power was likely; rather than sitting back to let military influences check each other, the United States would have to deploy some military influence of its own.

Yet the motive might indeed have been much the same, to offer Asians, as much as possible, the option of coming ultimately to adopt the American political and economic example. Rather than having to salute or bow to the English queen, how much better if Asian peoples could come to be electing their own presidents. Rather than any artificial and traditional restrictions on trade, how much better for all concerned if the economic decisions of buying and selling were left to each individual, along with decisions on what to read and decisions on whom to vote.

Looking south, instead of east or west, would one have styled American policy toward Latin America as "isolationist" in these years? The stereotypical answer would have been "of course, no," for the general tone of American foreign policy is seen to have been to separate the Western Hemisphere from the rest of the globe, and, as in the Monroe Doctrine, to accept being involved in Latin America as the price of this.[10]

One indeed sees a certain "ratchet effect" about American commitments to foreign self-government, blending the liberal impulses with practical realism. As stated in the Monroe Doctrine, but as also applied for Liberia and Samoa and China, the United States would threaten military action to preserve self-government—where it had already come into being. Where this had not yet come into being, where colonial and imperial rule still held sway, the American policy was to be more patient, encouraging and advocating self-rule, but not threatening any military deployment to further it.

EXPLANATORY POWER: THE MOVE
TO INTERVENTION?

European diplomats and newspaper editors might thus have been more willing to see the United States as an unusually peaceful nation in the isolationist years before 1890, when a great deal of steel was produced in Pittsburgh and almost none of it went into warships.

After 1890, however, after the Spanish-American War, they surely tended to see the United States as just another power-minded country. As fleets were built and deployed, battles were fought, and overseas positions were occupied, the identifiable twists and turns would be present now to draw out a power politics analysis more fully. The radical interpretation of American foreign policy (to be discussed in the next chapter) will attach a great significance of its own to the outward turning after 1890. Yet does the American decision at this point to invest in a fleet have to say very much about any special defects of the United States? Rather than using this to indict the capitalist United States as a particularly imperialistic and troublemaking country, can one not instead still extract an interpretation of the United States as behaving here in a very ordinary manner?

What will follow is an outline suggesting how the American move into world politics at the outset of the twentieth century might simply be derived instead from the threats and opportunities of power, leading to no particular indictment of the United States.

The British fleet that so much dominated the oceans in the nineteenth-century days of sail had not needed onshore bases, since sail power gave it a virtually total range. The same British fleet that controlled the English Channel could thus sail to attack any coast in the world. Much of this then changed in the later 1800s when steam-powered fleets replaced the sailing ship as the most effective combat arm.

First, it would be necessary now to seek bases and coaling stations, since the range of such ships was not unlimited. Second, because of the need for such nearby onshore bases, and because the new technology of steam might allow some other industrialized state to outbuild Britain, British naval power might not go anymore unchallenged all around the world.

The British, for their own reasons, had supported causes not so odious to the United States. The United States did not so much mind British naval dominance, when this dominance did not require tampering with the onshore sovereignty of the world. Or if it did mind such dominance, there was little that could be done about it. But if the new technology now made it possible for the United States to run the race with Great Britain more closely, then the United States might enter. And it would particularly do so if a race for coaling stations were begun around the coasts of the world, or if other European nations, less content with the simple onshore balance of power, were to enter the naval race.

The United States thus may have seized naval bases between 1890 and 1914 simply because the new determinants of sea power made this the best way to satisfy traditional American goals, and at the same time because their seizure preempted the other states who would now have liked to seize them also. In contesting Great Britain, the previous master of the seas, the United States was in this way matching the behavior of Germany, Japan, France, and the Russian Empire.[11]

We shall later come back to consider in much greater detail the further process of U.S. emergence onto the world power scene in the first four decades of the twentieth century, and then the cold war, and then after.

For the moment, in outlining more of the general nature of a power politics interpretation of U.S. foreign policy, we might simply continue the stress on changes in opportunity, rather than changes in goals, for explaining changes in American posture. World War I was a threat to American trade, to all of civilization, and to the British domination of the high seas to which Americans had grudgingly been accustomed. But it was also an opportunity, as the United States could choose in 1916 (and did choose) to try to build "a navy second to none," and could exert an influence on Europe in 1918 because its regimes had exhausted themselves in that war. With American troops on the Rhine in 1919, and an American president drafting the outlines of a future world system, who could fault the Europeans for seeing this as an American indulgence in power politics?

The subsequent retreat from power, and explicit turn toward isolationism in 1920, reflected too much of a nostalgia for the easy power relationships of the past, when two wide oceans had so long ensured the United States against military threats. But when the Japanese penetrated too far into China in the 1930s, and when Hitler's Germany then grew too fast as a threat to the globe, the American response again made sense in power terms, heading off the threat of a very hostile Fascist hegemony, seizing the opportunity to establish an American hegemony in its place.

Analysts of power politics would thus criticize Wilson's idealism at Versailles, and the naiveté of the subsequent grasping for isolationism. As exemplified by Hans Morgenthau, they would regard American foreign policy as close to the rational optimum of power pursuit from 1890 to 1917, and then again from 1940 to 1960, with the Vietnam War as another mistake.[12] Yet mistakes are made as power is pursued. The dominant theme, which the realpolitik commentators would find more inevitable than in need of being recommended, is that every state is largely guided by the opportunities and threats of world power.

It may have been folly for the United States, by this yardstick, to try to keep troops in Vietnam, for this was an attempt at overreaching practical opportunity, just as it would have been folly for the United States to try to deploy troops to Europe in the nineteenth century. But it was not folly to grab the opportunities as they arose in the Caribbean at the start of the century, or in Europe or the Far East in the late 1940s.

How does the power politics interpretation then fit for the events of American foreign policy after Japan and Nazi Germany were defeated in 1945? The power politics approach is a useful antidote to disappointment and naivete in the analysis of international politics. It is an antidote as well to anger and indignation, for the emphasis it places on the opportunities of the international system, as the explainer of all that happens (since nations are morally all the same in their appetites), leaves us a little more in the mood to be sympathetic to our adversary. Rather than the perfidy and aggressiveness of others, it would therefore tend to trace the outbreaks of conflict to changes in the international arena, changes that suddenly reward aggressiveness on either side, after a prior state of the arena would have rewarded restraint and moderation instead.

Just as one does not wish to feel gullible about the international system, one does not wish to feel moral outrage, if the facts of the matter would instead support a more resigned and understanding attitude. Some of this psychologically soothing impact of the power-politics model shows up again when it is applied to what still often grips us today—the outbreak of the cold war.

The cold war, by this view, may have begun as something like what game theory calls a "prisoners' dilemma," a situation where neither side could trust the other once the common enemy of Nazi Germany had been defeated, where the two sides as a result had to make virtually simultaneous hostile moves, because each distrusted the other, and each would have come out worse if it waited for the other to strike the first blow.

No matter what the intentions of any state, it will have to be *somewhat* concerned to shepherd its own power, and to contain the power of the possible adversaries whose own selfish or generous motives might run in different directions. When states have to fear each other, the machinations of the international arena then take on a life of their own. Hobbes suddenly begins to look more relevant than Locke, as one reads the political philosophers. If this is a "psychological" explanation of mutually unwanted behavior, it is nonetheless an explanation that does not say very much negative about the particular phobias or neuroses or traumas of the two societies

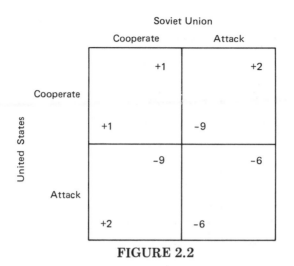

Soviet Union

FIGURE 2.2

involved, but which rather sees them as victims of the uncertainties of the international situation itself.

In the matrix of game theory, the choices of each side are pictured in Figure 2.2. The Soviets must conclude, simply because of the dictates of the international system, that they are better off opposing the United States no matter what the United States does. And U.S. decision makers similarly conclude that antagonistic moves toward the USSR are appropriate no matter what the other side does. Yet the bizarre result is then that both sides are dragged down to a solution that is worse than if each had stayed on the cooperative path.[13]

The "common sense" feeling that there has to be "blame" for the cold war, that this entire period of American foreign policy was somehow a pathology, stems from a perception that money and lives and effort could have been spared, could have been devoted to more satisfying purposes, if the clash of wills with Moscow had not erupted. But the clash was perhaps unavoidable.

The pure prisoner's dilemma situation outlined above suggests that each side would indeed have liked to attack the other, even if the other had not been on the attack. Closer to the theory that the cold war was largely a misunderstanding (perhaps a necessary misunderstanding?) would be the matrix shown in Figure 2.3. Here everything is the same as before, except that neither Moscow nor Washington would really have liked to engage in political or military contests, if each had only been sure that the other side felt the same. The pathology here is thus doubled, in that each side would be bet-

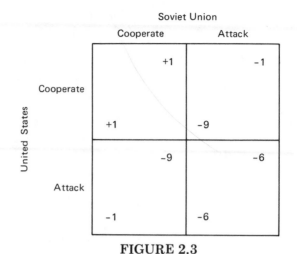

FIGURE 2.3

ter off in the cooperative box, and each side slides out of this box only because it *mistakenly* thinks that the other side has aggressive intentions. Yet such mistakes may also have been unavoidable. What could have headed off such counterproductive behavior? Looking to the international arena, the likelihood of counterproductive conflicts under "prisoners' dilemma" are reduced when each side is assured of more advanced warning before the other side could make any significant move; this is assured when there are fewer power vacuums (the aftermath of World War II produced them in abundance), or when there are third and fourth and fifth parties that can intervene to deny an aggressor total victory, and to shield the victim of attack against total defeat.

The impact of strong defensive barriers is to slow down the possibilities of attack, and thus to make each side less tempted and less worried by such attack. The influence of outside observers (as with the U.S. technicians deployed today between the Israelis and Egyptians in the Sinai Desert) is to do the same. Nature is sometimes so kind as to provide such reassurances naturally against preemptive attack. At other points, it turns in the opposite direction. When the turn is toward situations inducing greater alarm and precautionary moves, the result is to pull nations into confrontations with each other, and this could easily enough suffice as an explanation for the cold war.

What would anyone in the past have expected to happen after the collapse of a major power, regardless of the ideology or world view or intentions of the powers that remained? The predictions of the old balance-of-power model would have been straightforward enough, that the wartime coalition of allies would cease to get along, as soon as their common enemy was eliminated.

Does this amount to saying that the cold war was inevitable? It comes close, being entirely comparable to the reappearance of British-Russian tension after the defeat of Napoleon, or of British-American tension after the German surrender in 1918. At its most simple-minded form, this sometimes gets presented as a kind of iron law by which "all power vacuums get filled," by which nations are bound to conflict when they have no common enemy to bind them together into alliances. In this view if Hitler had been able to gird the Germans for more prolonged resistance, the cold war would have been postponed; failing this, it was bound to break out.

As it stands, the power politics approach can thus claim to explain and predict an interesting fraction of the twists and turns of American foreign policy. By forcing us to concentrate on power as the most important variable, it reinforces its case that power is the only variable worth caring about.

Yet can this approach explain all of the choices Americans have made, all the backs and forths between intervention and isolation? Power is an important variable, but is it really the only goal Americans have pursued? Has it ever been a goal they have pursued as an end in itself? Has power not been rather a means to other ends, something which therefore gets pursued only as it tends to serve those ends?

THE LOGICAL FLAWS OF REALPOLITIK

Rather than debating whether it is an altruistic concern for the political freedom of others that shapes U.S. foreign policy, or instead a pursuit of markets for capitalists, the "realist" would insist that it is the inherent need then to be concerned about maintaining national power. The power politics view argues that the United States is an "ordinary country," exerting power where it can, staying out of the middle of the fray where this is instead the best it can do. It argues that it is the changes of opportunities and threats here that explain the ins and outs of U.S. foreign policy, just as they would explain much of any country's foreign policy.

The power politics view of course is not totally wrong, for changes of opportunity are always important for explaining policy choices, as has just been demonstrated in the previous pages. The United States must be somewhat concerned about power, regardless of what else it cares about, for without power it can serve no other goals. Yet the difficulty with this realpolitik approach is precisely that it does not explain enough, thereby misleading someone trying to track all the ins and outs of foreign policy. Americans, like other peoples, may be interested in power because it contributes to certain goals, but one must ask what these goals are, and whether they have indeed been the same as the goals of such more traditional global powers as Great Britain and France.

If the pursuit of power advocated by the realpolitik analysts boils down logically to a concern only for the material well-being and military security of the American homeland, the evidence is then hardly clear that most Americans have accepted this as the dominant consideration for the bulk of their history. As they have debated intervention versus isolation, people on both sides of the argument have been influenced by more generous considerations. The radical and the liberal analyses of foreign policy, to be discussed in the next two chapters, both place other considerations ahead of the simple pursuit of power. While differing about what is the appropriate form of a moral concern for the welfare of others, they would agree that such a moral concern is not impossible, or even unusual, in this world.

One portion of the realpolitik message has been incontrovertible, namely that the United States has to watch its budget of power and influence when developing a foreign policy, and that serving one goal may get in the way of serving another. Yet such a discussion of means and opportunities, however unassailable, does not then substitute for a fuller discussion of ends, and does not entitle the "realist" commentator to legislate such ends for other Americans. Astuteness about opportunities has nothing to do, logically, with astuteness about ends. To present a tough-minded "old hand" analysis of the nature of diplomacy is in no way to generate any substantively valid insights about whether it is more appropriate to fight for power, or for political democracy, or for economic justice.

Some of the realpolitik analysis indeed implies than it is improper to care about anything but power, improper for Woodrow Wilson to immerse himself in the supposed welfare of East Europeans, or for Lyndon Johnson to commit himself to a certain picture of the happiness and welfare of Vietnamese. Yet the realists are then pushed into something of a logical quandary. Is their message that all states inherently *must* pursue power? Then there is absolutely no point in *advocating* such pursuit, since it takes care of itself. Could it be however that Americans or others have been abnormal in seeking after something other than power? If so, it is unclear again why the realpoliticians have any call to insist on a shifting of tastes here.

All human beings "pursue" oxygen. It is useful for us to know this, and there is no *need* to urge people to adhere to this pursuit. But some human beings pursue chocolate ice cream, while others pursue vanilla. Some pursue power, while others pursue freedom or justice for others. Here there is no *basis* for urging one or the other.

If the realpoliticians think it appropriate to lust after power, let them do so themselves, but can they tell me that I may not instead lust after economic justice or political freedom?

The "realist" might explore one way out of this logical dilemma, of course, by contending that Americans have not been guilty of abnormality as a nation, but only of hypocrisy. If the United States, like other nations, has in fact been pursuing power all these years, then it has simply been kidding itself in feeling more high-minded; this is a minor form of error of analysis, perhaps, but still trouble-some, as well as irritating.

What the realist often imputes to American foreign policy is thus indeed what European observers imputed, in particular as the United States became more active in international affairs at the end of the nineteenth century. If Americans remember themselves defending the open door in China and the League of Nations, other states saw this all as facade, assuming that the United States was simply pursu-ing the normal gains of power and wealth and glory that had pulled other states into the international arena in the past.[14]

But who was deluding himself there? Was it American hypocrisy to have assumed higher goals for ourselves or was it self-delusion on the part of German, British, and French commentators to have missed the differences about the United States? The selfish in this world are not resentful only of hypocrisy in others; they are often just as resentful of any genuine generosity for the awkwardness of the comparisons that must follow.

Have Americans simply been hypocritical, in actuality behaving just as any European power would have behaved? Or have they been naive, unaware of the realities of the international system? Or have they been aware of such realities, and at the same time generous, trying to do good in the world? The last possibility continues to be baffling to the realist in Europe, or in the United States itself.

Naiveté and foolishness can always be attacked. Someone bur-dened by it will get the opposite of what he expects. But generosity may be much harder to criticize, for it is the generous nation's own business to decide.

In its more properly modest form, a "realistic" interpretation would thus be only a discussion of opportunities, rather than goals, and would be in no way contradictory to the values of either the liberal or the Marxist. Regardless of whether Americans were concerned mainly with the maintenance of free elections or of economic justice, they would have to resign ourselves to some inherent limits to U.S. power, and would have to recognize some situations that are inherently more likely to ensnare all sides in counterproductive conflict. The power politics analyst here would merely be warning one and all against being too optimistic about what can be achieved in the outside world, and against any naive assumptions that foreign powers will agree with U.S. values.

In summary, the realists are thus on the safest ground in urging us to be better informed about the actual possibilities we are dealing with, and the real linkages of actions to consequences. If it is difficult to question preferences and values, it is much easier to question any policy based on factually incorrect premises, for foolish policy would be endorsed by no one.

Since the American people were able to escape a more active involvement in the world for long periods of history, the cost of this could have been a loss of familiarity with the harsh constraints of the international system. As a result of having pursued (perhaps very astutely and wisely) a policy of isolation and balance of power, could Americans in the process have become unusually unaware of their surroundings?

The theories of political realism are particularly well tuned to international politics, to the anarchy described by Hobbes for situations without a centralizing government; such theories may conversely be badly tuned to domestic politics in a nation like the United States that experiences no coups or threats of coups. U.S. politics may satisfy Americans as all that domesticated politics should have to offer, while the wilder realm of international politics is something much more unpleasant to contemplate.

AN ASIDE: THE CLOSING OF THE FRONTIER

Before turning in the next chapter to the more serious radical critique that the United States, for economic reasons, might actually be unusually troublesome as an international actor, we might close this section on power political analysis with a short digression into a view that would indict the United States for being *unusually power-oriented*, unusually keen to deploy military force, because something noneconomic about history and sociology makes it particularly inclined to violence. This would be to hold to the political and social dimensions by which Americans typically have most tended to measure themselves; but it would come out with the opposite of our normal nostalgic self-compliments.

The next chapter will discuss how the American move outward after 1890, conjoined in time with the pacification of the western frontier, can be argued to show a capitalist tinge to our foreign policy. But what else might it show?

One can indeed develop a noneconomic theory linking the frontier's closing with an expansion of American foreign policy effort. Rather than discussing unemployment, such a theory might seem a little more straightforward and simpleminded, namely that the Indian frontier had provided the United States with a necessary outlet for adventure and violence, for which it now needed a replacement in places like Cuba, the Philippines, and China.

Are Americans unusually violent as a people? Periodic self-indictments have emerged after each failure of the Congress to pass adequate gun-control laws, after each urban riot or assassination attempt. Given that we are discussing the sources of foreign policy, a basically very violent form of public policy, we might well pause and ask whether this is not the most important attribute of Americans to assess, ahead of leanings toward altruism or isolation. Is violence indeed "as American as apple pie"?[15]

The question of violence is of course closely linked to the frontier. We remember the frontier as a violent place. The violent Hollywood movies go back to this setting again and again. Was it thus "no accident" that the U.S. navy was expanded as soon as the frontier had been tamed? What role did the frontier actually play here, given that no such feature affects the political style of places like Great Britain and Germany and Sweden and Italy? Was it an outlet for violence? Or was it an incubator for it, whetting appetites for gunplay and military campaigns, so addicting the United States to violence that it finally brought about the bombings of the jungles in Vietnam?

Yet such an assumption, that the United States has a tradition of violence, could all be barking up the wrong tree, for the Old West may have been very atypical of the country as a whole. The frontier for many Americans was a place to be steered clear of, a place where one would encounter troubles one did not need. There were times in the late nineteenth century when life insurance policies would become void if one passed west of the line enclosing states admitted to the Union.

Even with regard to the violent nature of the West itself, historians disagree among themselves about how bad the situation was. The movie industry surely exaggerates the phenomenon, for violence generally provides more interest on the screen than could be found in the humdrum daily peaceful existence of a town that had achieved law and order. And if Americans show something about themselves today by their liking for violent movies, this would hardly be a comment only on Americans, for the same films are shown to full houses in Scandinavia, Japan, Pakistan, and South America.

In any event, the days of the frontier did not see the world expecting the United States to be a violent power, but rather saw it as an unusually unarmed country, given its industry and manpower. The United States before 1890 was the marvel of the world for how small its navy and army were. The stereotype of the American in these decades was of a nation of shopkeepers, of democrats (and perhaps also of criminals and murderers), of undisciplined individualists, unsuited for training as soldiers. The change after 1890 was not that the United States was thereafter unusually well-equipped with military forces; even in the years up to World War I, it was below the world average in warships per capita, or in the fraction of its GNP that was spent on defense. It was rather that before 1890 the United States had been so far behind everyone else.

Whatever the history, however, there will be critics who could fairly contend that the United States stands out in today's reality as an unusually violent and criminal place. What about its murder rates, which are higher than most of the countries it identifies with? What about its obstinate failure to pass gun-control laws?

American visitors to Asia are usually amazed to discover how little risk of crime there is on the city streets of Tokyo, Bangkok, Hong Kong, or Kuala Lumpur. Elementary poverty causes some risk of burglary, and doors must therefore be locked. Yet American businessmen and diplomats feel no anxiety about letting their teen-age sons and daughters walk home by themselves at night, for the likelihood of violent crime against persons is far less than one encounters at home. Unhappily, there is indeed one significant exception to this pattern in the Far East, the Philippines, ironically the one Asian state governed for any long period of time by the United States (but also the only one governed for such a duration by Spain).

Yet the pattern again hardly provides so simple and clear-cut an indictment of the United States, once one looks away from Asia. Countries around the globe seem to develop idiosyncracies about their attitudes on all such matters. Germans, like other Europeans, are much stricter and more sensible about gun control, but seem stubbornly unable to accept speed limits on their highways. Higher rates of violent crime show up all through Latin America, raising again the issue of whether Spanish or American influence is to blame in the Philippines (or whether any outside influence is to blame). But Latin America additionally has been characterized by relatively few wars and arms races, such that the supposed link between domestic violence and violent foreign policy becomes even more muddled.

If the Philippines have been much more plagued with shootings and crime than Malaysia and Indonesia, does this then correspond with any real differences in the foreign policies of these nations? The differences that emerge would seem to be much more determined by the particular circumstances of the foreign threats and opportunities they have faced.

NOTES

1. Among the important works applying such a power-oriented analysis would have to be counted Hans Morgenthau, *Scientific Man vs. Power Politics* (Chicago: University of Chicago Press, 1944); Edward Hallett Carr, *The Twenty Years' Crisis* (New York: St. Martin's, 1939); Harold and Margaret Sprout, *Foundations of National Power* (New York: Van Nostrand, 1951); Kenneth W. Thompson, *Realism and the Crisis of World Politics* (Princeton: Princeton University Press, 1960); and Robert H. Tucker, *The United States in the World* (Washington, D.C.: Potomac Associates, 1976).

2. For a discussion of European views questioning whether the United States was particularly liberal or non-power-oriented in its foreign policy, see Edward W. Chester, *Europe Views America* (Washington, D.C.: Public Affairs Press, 1962), pp. 88–97, and Max Silberschmidt, *The United States and Europe* (London: Harcourt Brace Jovanovich, 1972).

3. A good general discussion of isolationism can be found in Selig Adler, *The Isolationist Impulse* (New York: Abelard-Schuman, 1957).

4. One advocate of a renewed conscious isolationism was Robert W. Tucker, *A New Isolationism: Threat or Promise?* (New York: Universe Books, 1972).

5. The balance of power mechanism is well analyzed in Ernest B. Haas, "The Balance of Power: Prescription, Concept, Or Propaganda?," *World Politics* 5, no. 4 (July 1953): 442–77.

6. For a good statement of liberal and other motives for isolationism, see Hans Kohn, *American Nationalism* (New York: Macmillan, 1957), pp. 178–80, and Alexander DeConde, ed., *Isolation and Security* (Durham: Duke University Press, 1957).

7. For what comes close to such an iron law analysis, by which intervention abroad is bound to corrupt what is held dear at home, see Harold Stearns, *Liberalism in America: Its Origin, Its Temporary Collapse, Its Future* (New York: Boni and Liveright, 1919).

8. That the United States was indeed intervening in Europe, at the maximum level of which it was capable, is suggested in the analysis of Gordon Craig, "The United States and the European Balance," *Foreign Affairs* 55, no. 1 (October 1976): 187–98.

9. For a more general analysis of the U.S. commitment to intervention in Asia, see Foster Rhea Dulles, *America in the Pacific* (Boston: Houghton Mifflin, 1932).

10. A very comprehensive history of the Monroe Doctrine can be found in Dexter Perkins, *Hands Off* (Boston: Little, Brown, 1941).

11. The American decision to expand into a role as a naval power is analyzed in Harold and Margaret Sprout, *Toward a New Order of Sea Power* (Princeton: Princeton University Press, 1943).

12. See Hans Morgenthau, *In Defense of the National Interest* (New York: Alfred A. Knopf, 1952), pp. 28–33.

13. The sad consequences of a prisoners' dilemma situation as analyzed in game theory are laid out clearly in Anatol Rapoport and A. M. Chammah, *Prisoner's Dilemma: A Study of Conflict and Cooperation* (Ann Arbor: The University of Michigan Press, 1965).

14. For further European commentary on American motives, see James Burnham, ed., *What Europe Thinks of America* (New York: John Day, 1953), and Henry Steele Commager, ed., *America in Perspective* (New York: Random House, 1947).

15. For a more general inquiry into whether violence might be distinctively American, see Richard Hofstadter and Michael Wallace, eds., *American Violence: A Documentary History* (New York: Alfred A. Knopf, 1970).

3

The Radical Critique: The United States Worse than Other Countries

This chapter turns to the second explanation for all of American foreign policy. Rather than considerations of power, or of steering the outside world toward happiness, can it be that U.S. foreign policy is really explained by the demands and weaknesses of the U.S. domestic economy?

We will be considering theories here that thus expect a pathology, expect that *defects* of U.S. domestic economic order will be closely linked to *defects* of U.S. foreign policy, to interventions that only worsen the lot of foreigners, rather than "liberating" or improving them. These are, above all, theories of capitalism, theories arguing that there is indeed something special about American foreign policy that distinguishes it from the foreign policy of India or the USSR or China or Kenya, but that the "something special" is that the United States is so much a part of the capitalist world.

Coming in a great variety of forms, accepted by a great many analysts outside the United States, especially in the Communist bloc and in the economically underdeveloped Afro-Asian world, such radical, or "revisionist," or Marxist interpretations of American foreign policy would not view U.S. motives as altruistic, but rather as the needs and drives of a pathological form of capitalism.[1]

American foreign policy is not to be explained by the generosity of Americans as a whole in this view, but rather by the selfishness of a privileged portion of Americans. The masses of Americans may indeed be generous (most radical interpretations of U.S. foreign policy would avoid any conclusion that *all* Americans are at fault, that all together could be exploiting the outside world); yet the vested interest that constitutes the most privileged class of Americans is not so generous but rather pursues its own particular interests, to the detriment of the mass of Americans as well as of foreigners.

25

The general prescription for a change in American foreign policy here would thus tend to begin with a change at home, an elimination of the special capitalist nature of the United States that allegedly leads us to cause trouble abroad. The United States in this view is not special in being more liberal or high-minded than other nations. It behaves like any other mature capitalist economy, in seeking markets and investment opportunities abroad, to relieve its problems of unemployment at home. The United States is special, but it is only so because it is the most capitalist country in the world.

SOME MINOR VARIETIES OF CRITICISM

There are a great number of forms of such economic explanation for foreign policy, and sorting them is not always easy, as one must watch for subtle distinctions in their development. One straightforward approach might be to look at degrees of scale, at how much of the economy is involved as we contemplate the explanation of particular foreign policy choices.

We can begin with a very small-scale, nonsystemic form of explanation in typical news reports of alleged "special interest." Some men are richer than others. Some richer men depend on foreign policy favors to maintain or to expand their wealth, or to indulge their personal choices, and some of such richer men then get such favors, as the policy process overall is corrupted.

We will not dwell very long on this type of theory. Columnists such as Jack Anderson regularly present allegations of such corruption. With regard to serious impact on general policy, such theories were advanced as a possible explanation for U.S. entry into World War I, as munitions manufacturers who had sold weapons on credit to Great Britain and France became fearful that their bills would not be paid if the Entente lost, and thus subsidized a campaign of intensive propaganda for American entry into the war against Germany.[2] More recently, the influence of ITT and other corporations on American decisions to oppose the Allende regime in Chile has been cited as an example of such a special interest corruption of what American foreign policy should have been.[3]

Yet the significance of the propaganda by the "merchants of death" prior to 1917 has now been substantially debunked again, and the centrality of ITT's interests to U.S. policy on Chile is also in question. (American corporations have not typically been given back their holdings by the military regime that succeeded Allende.)

Many radical critics would indeed steer away from such examples, as penny-ante cases, as the kind of instances that produce a naive "reformism" when the public uncovers them. The reformer simply advocates tighter rules against bribery and conflict of interest, and then concludes that the problem has been disposed of. A Marxist analyst of American foreign policy would instead contend that only a total rearrangement of the economic processes of the United States could change such political outcomes. The petty briberies of special interest, in such a Marxist view, are thus not the problem, but merely a superficial symptom of a much deeper problem.

A second form of analysis then moves somewhat up on the scale, to treat the entire government as a congeries of selfish and independent bureaus, no more wedded to the national interest than the individual firms of the "private sector." While individual business firms openly maximize profit, the bureaus of the government pretend to be maximizing the national interest, but actually bend domestic policy and foreign policy so as to expand their own budgets, or their manning documents, or their share of the power in making decisions.

This form of "bureaucratic politics" analysis, which became very fashionable in the 1960s, shares with the Marxist approach an assumption that there is a basic and deep pathology about American foreign policy choices, so that the policy which emerged is not the best that one could do in relating national means to national ends in a very uncertain world, but is far less than this.

The bureaucratic politics approach would not so necessarily have to endorse the radical indictment of capitalism, for much of what it finds at fault is occurring entirely within the government.[4] Analysts of this persuasion would indeed be inclined to apply the same kind of analysis to the Soviet and Chinese and other governments, except that the "inside dope" and interview materials are not available to make the accounts of pathology so lively and credible. Because the detailed case studies cannot be constructed for the Communist states, the subliminal tendency of the bureaucratic politics analyst is however to find fault nonetheless most often with his own country's policy process, and perhaps thus to conclude that the capitalist world we know best is the portion of the globe that disturbs tranquility the most.

When the analysis is applied in particular to the "military-industrial complex," the ties to an indictment of capitalism become strong again, as profit-hungry businessmen at General Dynamics conspire with the promotion-hungry admirals and generals who want new military gadgets to play with. As an analysis of why the American defense budget is allegedly too high, this form of analysis thus begins to converge with the radical critique, as wars become more likely because American industry is intent on keeping itself fully employed, as unneeded missiles and warships are then procured, when the funds could have been better (and more peacefully) spent on schools and transit systems.

MACROECONOMICS AND UNEMPLOYMENT

The major form of economic interpretation of American foreign policy does not linger so long, however, at the level of special interests, or of the military-industrial complex, but rather sees the entire capitalist economy as a sick economy, dependent on foreign aggressions as a way of somehow overcoming its internal deficiencies.

We can catalog various ways in which an economy could be defective in terms of the domestic requirements of society. An economy might be unable to produce enough of the foodstuffs and other goods needed for the good life; this has not typically been the American problem. If an economy instead produces enough in total, the distribution of such production might be very uneven; this has indeed been more of an American problem, as the poorest in the United States surely are worse off than the poorest in Scandinavia (and, radicals would argue, worse off than the poorest in the USSR or Bulgaria).

A third form of domestic defect for an economy, in the end perhaps the most important for the radical analysis, is that it could be prone to unemployment, generating a great dissatisfaction and rebelliousness among the workingmen who are denied the elementary psychological assurance and dignity of being able to sell their services.

The radical analysis of capitalism has used several different theories of unemployment, with the more profound critics being fully conscious that such theories can contradict each other, while the less profound simply bundle them all together.

The straightforward explanation of unemployment presented by Karl Marx himself was that capital would increasingly have to replace labor as an economy matured, diminishing profits and driving the capitalists themselves into anxiety (since only labor could really be a source of profits), at the same time diminishing unemployment opportunities and driving the proletariat to rebellion (since capital could not be generated rapidly enough to mate up with all the available supply of labor, given the continually increasing necessary ratio of capital to labor).

This purely Marxist form of explanation for unemployment has historically been difficult to confirm in the advanced industrial societies, as capital has still delivered profits to those owning it and has indeed been generated fast enough to absorb all available labor, and then some. One only has to point to the chronic shortages of labor in today's Japan (where industrialists go about lamenting the drop in the birthrate after World War II) or the chronic reliance of West German industry on labor imported from Italy, Yugoslavia, and Turkey.

Marx's theory of unemployment paradoxically has fit much better for the kinds of societies to which Marx never expected it to apply—industrially underdeveloped areas such as India and Southeast Asia.[5] A good illustration of this comes with the impact of the Green Revolution on the production of food in these areas, as the new agricultural techniques that are desperately needed to feed a growing population at the same time cause major social problems; these more productive methods are more capital-intensive than traditional agricultural methods, leaving a portion of the agricultural labor force redundant, driving them into the cities to look for work, to look for the capital with which to mate in the production process, capital that as yet does not exist.

If Marx's prediction of a link between American-style advanced industrial capitalism and unemployment was thus doomed to be wrong in its specification of its causal link, there are nonetheless other forms of radical theory that might fill the gap, arguing that a connection is still here, even if it is of a different form.

One non-Marxist approach here would point instead to a lack of aggregate demand, as the uneven distribution of income leaves some of us with more than we can spend on consumption goods and the opportunities for investment become so unrewarding that investment spending can no longer absorb all of savings at a level of full employment.

John Maynard Keynes, whom one normally associates with liberal and nonrevolutionary forces in the British and American political spectrum, thus might supply a better reinforcement for the radical argument than Marx could. The Keynesian tie to theories of imperialist foreign policy is not really so farfetched, moreover, for an important forerunner to Keynes had appeared already before World War I in J. A. Hobson,[6] who contended that the European investment in a naval arms race and competition for colonies had arisen simply because of a lack of aggregate demand at home, a lack that could easily be remedied by a redistribution of income toward the poor; the poor had enough unsatisfied material needs to keep any economy fully employed.

A short discussion of the fundamentals of a Keynesian argument may be in order here. The science of economics explains a great deal by assuming an urge to earn money, but it does not assume any particular use for the money after it has been earned. Why would we then choose to save money, rather than to spend it on goods? Perhaps we are simply guarding against future needs. Perhaps we relish the social or political power that such savings might supply. Perhaps we have come to enjoy money for its own sake.

Having left unexplained why men might work to earn a potential to consume, when they do not consume, economics can only (as Keynes noted) ensure an equilibrium at full employment if all the savings (the earnings not allocated to consumption) are spent instead on investment goods. Presumably one would prefer to earn a percentage return on one's savings by such investments, rather than missing such a return.

A problem arises, however, if profitable investment opportunities decline so much that no significant interest could be paid for all of the savings at hand, such that the holders of savings then would come to prefer to retain their unconsumed earnings in a liquid form. Such an absence of sufficient investment opportunities could thus cause an imbalance by which it was impossible for the economy to remain at the full-employment level, and the result would be widespread unemployment and unhappiness, with political consequences that might ultimately produce a revolution. The direct cause of such unemployment under capitalism would thus be quite different from what Marx contended, not a shortage of capital to mate up with labor, but rather a surplus of savings, because of the uneven distribution of income through society. Yet the results would be the same—either unemployment, or the bending of state policy to avoid such unemployment in some more artificial way, to leave intact the privileges and inequities of capitalism.

The tie with foreign policy then emerges quickly enough, in that the investment opportunities required to pay meaningful rates of interest, and thus to generate the necessary demand for the production of machinery and capital goods, might be found abroad, if one can only extend the power of the United States to make sure these opportunities remain open.

The military power of the United States must thus be deployed over at least two time periods. Such power is required to pry such investment areas open in the first place, to allow American entrepreneurs to purchase the mining concessions or plantations or oil leases involved, overcoming the opposition of any local government (or other capitalist government) that might have tried to forbid such purchase. Second, U.S. military operations will thereafter be periodically required to protect any such investments already made against seizure and confiscation, for if the precedent of confiscation were allowed, American investors would lose confidence in all such ventures, and the gap in aggregate demand would reappear.

What would be the response here of most of the economic analysts who style themselves Keynesians? Their normal answer would be that there is no need to send the Marines to Vietnam or to Angola or to Latin America to win an exemption from unemployment here, since a liberal public works program within the United States could generate the extra demand to absorb the labor that was unemployed. Hobson's proposals, after all, were not for the abolition of all of capitalism, but rather for a simple "reformist" Social Democrat approach of redistributing income by means of state action. The capitalist system of the United States or Great Britain in the earlier third of the twentieth century may not have understood the arguments of Hobson or Keynes, and thus may have lacked an easy escape from the unemployment problem (although there were forerunner programs of public works that may have been applying the correct solution here, without understanding why). But the contemporary capitalist system surely can generate as much aggregate demand as it requires, without accepting any additional risks abroad, disturbing international peace, or otherwise reshaping its foreign policy. If the capitalist system incorporates an understanding of Keynes, it should, in short, be capable of behaving in international politics just as a Socialist country would behave, in no way driven by a search for markets.

Yet one could still envisage a radical counter to this, within the Keynesian context, and it might run as follows. The privileged and ruling classes in a capitalist economy will understand the Keynesian option, but will be reluctant to apply it in a liberal way, for fear of setting a bad precedent for their own position—for fear, that is, of beginning some major income redistribution that might not be curtailable any more when the simple needs for an increase in aggregate demand had been satisfied.

The upper middle class of the United States would thus presumably approve "public works" of the form of the Kennedy Center in Washington, D.C., and the Space Program, and the various other projects that really amount to the channeling of consumption back to itself. But it would balk at spending great sums on the alleviation of poverty, or on the rebuilding of slums, or on the improvement of health and educational services it was not itself utilizing.

Since the list of possible middle-class-oriented public works programs is short, the ruling interests of the United States thus would still presumably prefer to avoid the kinds of public spending that can become an opening wedge for antipoverty programs that will enormously raise their tax bills; they would instead prefer to invest in missiles and tanks (defense spending also augments aggregate demand, but without setting the dangerous precedent of economic leveling) and in foreign investment opportunities, the opportunities that the missiles and tanks will be used to protect.

When one gets into intention, rather than mere capability, therefore, one finds here at least something of a case that the American form of capitalism has not yet found an alternative to an active foreign policy ("active" meaning warlike) as the solution to its difficulties with unemployment.

The Keynesian form of the explanation for unemployment in our
society is more persuasive than the Marxist. The Keynesian form at
first glance seems to offer a way out, sparing the capitalist economy
any need to mortgage its foreign policy. But this way out may not
work, once the concerns about income distribution are taken into
account.

The possibility that wealthier Americans might be objecting to
domestic applications of the Keynesian model, because of the precedents it sets on income redistribution, is hardly to be dismissed.
Liberal Democrats used to laugh at Eisenhower and his fellow Republicans for being too ignorant to understand Keynes, as the
Republicans returned repeatedly to the obtuse theme that deficit
spending by the government was inherently immoral and irresponsible, that "you couldn't run a business that way." Yet the Republicans may have understood more than they admitted, since in politics,
domestic or international, it is not always so wise to show how much
you know. By pretending that Keynesian economics was somehow
inherently counterintuitive and irresponsible, the Republicans succeeded in delaying its acceptance by the American political public
at large for as much as a decade.

The American capitalist, by this accusation, is in a trap where
he must choose one corner of the triangle shown in Figure 3.1, and
in the end opts for the corner of steering American foreign policy
into overseas adventure.

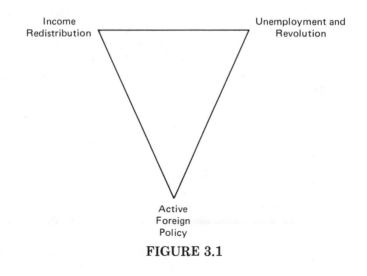

FIGURE 3.1

SOME GROUNDS FOR SKEPTICISM
ABOUT THE RADICAL CHARGE

Yet does this then produce such an airtight case about the misman-agement of American foreign policy? Before concluding that the radical critique of American foreign policy is well founded, because the ruling classes somehow are caught with no other choices but un-employment, income redistribution, or a warlike foreign policy, one must consider whether this kind of a constraint really has been in effect for much of the American history we have been surveying (or indeed for any of it).

If the vested interests of the United States could (by this radical analysis) find any way other than war to avoid unemployment and income leveling, they would surely choose it, for war is not particu-larly healthy for the wealthy either. The experience of World War I, and of wars prior to this and wars since, has surely been that armed conflict is dangerous for the established order, introducing disre-spect for property and greater government intervention in the daily lives of citizens. Wall Street never showed any enthusiasm about the war in Vietnam, and it is questionable whether the business interests of the United States were at all enthusiastic about the imperialism shown in the Spanish-American War; Andrew Carnegie certainly is a very visible example of the "business pacifism" that viewed navies and military preparations as a great obstacle to normal trade, rather than a support for it.[7]

Even if one stipulates that the problem of the Keynesian aggre-gate demand shortage is real, nature may well offer ways out. The re-visionist interpretations of American foreign policy themselves tend to fall back on this, given their need to account for the remarkably *low* level of American naval and military spending in the years before 1890. The open frontier is alleged then to have supplied an abundant array of investment opportunities that would have made expendi-tures on foreign investments or on navies unnecessary for the pur-poses of stabilizing the economy. While a few radical analysts of the American system thus paint American foreign policy as *at all times* warped by the dictates of an economy inclined toward selfish capital-ism, the cleaner form of the argument sees the bulk of such warping coming only with the turning out of American foreign policy after 1890 (an analysis which thus deprecates the significance of Kling-berg's earlier periods of extroversion).[8]

But was the open frontier in the West the only hope of generat-ing the investment opportunities necessary to keep the economy in balance? Indeed not. In the years after World War II, for example, the simple pent-up purchasing power accumulated during that war combined with the "baby boom," together with technological break-throughs in consumer items ranging from ballpoint pens to television sets, to deliver all the purchasing power needed, and more than was needed. Just as the technological forward march of advanced in-dustrial societies largely upset Karl Marx's prediction that a capital shortage would necessarily generate unemployment, so the opening up of new technological areas has renewed the supply of investment opportunities.

Where such investments have to be developed abroad, moreover, the trend of technology has been to steer them more and more to-ward parts of the world less troubled in any day-to-day fashion by the risks of revolution and confiscation, or the risk of war, thus re-quiring less of a harnessing of American foreign policy to any special interests here.[9]

Finally, if state action still proves indispensable for bolstering aggregate demand in times of slump, the vested interests may become progressively more ingenious at finding public works to shape such expenditures to reinforce their own well-being, going well beyond the Kennedy Center. Radical commentators have indeed noted that much of the spending that is intended to redistribute wealth down-ward in the United States is speedily perverted to do just the reverse. If this is a sad commentary on the chances for a domestic redistri-bution of economic well-being, it nonetheless suggests that the link to an allegedly warlike foreign policy does not have to be so binding.

HISTORICAL COINCIDENCE?

And what about the evidence of the historical record? Proving the causes of events is always difficult. One sometimes tries to make a causal explanation more plausible by finding a link in timing of input and output, of cause and effect. The radical interpretation thus at-tempts to do a great deal with a link after 1890 between the closing of the frontier and the onset of active foreign policy, or "imperial-ism." This school would contend that the open frontier in several ways offered the U.S. capitalist system a "safety valve" before 1890, given our tendency toward unemployment, but that the elimination of this frontier safety valve then forced the United States to become engaged in a bellicose foreign policy thereafter.

Before the closing of the frontier, the profit returns on the virgin lands, and on the railroads and other accessories needed to develop them, presumably sufficed to offer enough investment opportunities to absorb savings, and thus to keep the economy close to its optimal state. When the business cycle somehow nonetheless still produced periodic depressions and unemployment, the ability of the unemployed worker to move himself and his family west additionally provided a buffer then against the political discontent or proclivity to revolution that otherwise would have followed.

If the U.S. economy had a need for violent expansion before 1890, in this view, the need was satisfied by the happy accident of an empty continent (empty that is, except for perhaps a million native American Indians, with whom no organized political power of the international scene had yet chosen to identify).

The drives of capitalism thus could stay unconnected with foreign policy, since the conquest of the Indians was treated as domestic policy (although it indeed tied up much of the U.S. Army, just as the protection of American investments around the Caribbean would later tie up much of the U.S. Marine Corps). In retrospect we do not so very much discuss the American conquest of the continent as "imperialism," just as we do not use this phrase very much with regard to the Russian push into Siberia. Imperialism is rather usually taken to refer to the seizures of sovereignty over pieces of land that are not contiguous and are inhabited (and remain inhabited) by populations very different in ethnic makeup from the new governors.

How would the defender of American foreign policy then want to come back to rebut the causal argument thus being presented here? The strength of the radical case depends on the alleged evidence of American imperialism after 1890, but it also depends somewhat on an absence of such active American foreign policy before.

As noted, the case is sometimes already weakened from the radical side itself, by those who would have it that American foreign policy has always and all along been driven by economic pathologies at home. Causation is basically being inferred here from the chronology and proximity in time of two events; if the light goes on very shortly after I flick the switch, I feel justified in concluding that the flicking of the switch caused the light to come on. If we thus uncovered an abrupt change in the degree of militance in U.S. foreign policy just as investment opportunities within the United States itself declined, we would then have a similar kind of evidence in support of the causal link. But if the accusation is extended to suggesting that the United States was engaged in such militance even earlier ("the light was on all along"), then the evidence for a causal link becomes much less clear.

Leaving aside such radical weakenings of the radical argument here, the alleged American shift outward after 1890 as a consequence of the maturation of American capitalism might be challenged simply on a more detailed examination of all the American overseas involvements before 1890. The United States sent Decatur and a naval force to the shores of Tripoli from 1801 to 1805. It sent Perry to open Japan in 1854, all before the closing of the frontier. It also involved itself actively in the future of Samoa after 1880.[10]

The revisionist might brush these off simply as earlier occasions where the opportunities and safety valve of the Indian frontier were for the moment not sufficient to absorb American capital and energies; if there are too many of such earlier examples of American foreign policy activism, however, the link with capitalism becomes very diffuse, and other causal theories then again become much more convincing, not the least of which might be American liberal desire to do good in the world.

The sequence of the closing of the frontier somehow being followed directly by the eruption of American imperialism may thus be somewhat an artifact of high school history books, as the chapter on "The Frontier" fits in all too neatly before the chapter on "Imperialism." Even revisionist interpreters have had to acknowledge some forerunners of American interest in naval power before the 1890s. The first important round of enhanced American foreign policy activity here may thus indeed have emerged in the just-mentioned tensions throughout the 1880s about the future of Samoa, as the Germans and British were inclined toward an assertion of sovereignty by one advanced state or another, and the United States, as with the later pattern of China and the earlier pattern for Latin America and Liberia, instead pressed for the maintenance of Samoan independence.

The radical may thus not be able to prove so much by the coincidences of history. If the closing of the American frontier as a safety valve for eastern unemployment becomes a less proximate cause for the beginnings of an active American naval and foreign policy, it also thus becomes less convincing as the actual cause. Did the United States now enter the world arena because it had an increased need for markets, or because it saw British naval power waning, or because it felt a compassionate commitment to the self-government of others and now sensed an increased opportunity to do something useful in this line? The latter is what will be argued in this book.

If one wishes to dwell on the juxtapositions of historical events, a clear counterexample might come some 40 years later, when the United States plunged into the unemployment of the Great Depression. The first reaction of the United States government, under Hoover and then just as much so under Franklin Roosevelt, was hardly to look for overseas investments or overseas military adventures to eliminate the unemployment but rather through the first half of the 1930s to become all the more isolationist and opposed to international entanglements.[11]

Revisionists can point to the later 1930s, when Roosevelt, despite his apparent ignorance of the correctness of Keynes' argument, at last allowed military preparations to bring full employment and prosperity back to the country. Yet were China and Europe thus being used as a vehicle for the alleviation of American domestic economic ills here; or was it not rather that the objective geopolitical menace of Hitler, and the objective cruelty of the Japanese in China, now drove the United States, against its preference, to commit resources to military uses?

To return to the outward swing after 1891, the linkage here may be fuzzy rather than crisp. And even if there was some material connection between the frontier closing and the beginnings of a navy, there might be other plausible explanations of such a tie, which would leave the alleged economic drives of capitalism out of the picture altogether. It would hardly be surprising if a nation that had to tie up much of its army fighting Indians would be less interested in applying its influence to more distant theaters. An elementary consideration of power resources and power politics would thus convince some observers that they had all the explanation they needed here. The frontier in this view was not a safety valve but an enormous distraction.

THE ROOSEVELT COROLLARY

One can hardly deny that the new American involvement in the outside world at the beginning of the twentieth century dealt with economic questions. The issue is rather what made the issues important for Americans—the drives of the U.S. capitalist economy, or continuing concern for self-government, in Latin America and elsewhere.

The tendency of South American and Caribbean states to incur additional foreign debts after the 1890s had the price of increasing the temptation or likelihood of European intervention, an intervention that could then lead to a permanent assumption of sovereignty, or at least to the acquisition of naval bases. The enunciation of the 1904 Roosevelt Corollary to the Monroe Doctrine, historically so detested by Latin Americans for the U.S. armed interventions that it was used to justify, may thus have again been a much more liberal American response to a real problem.[12]

Attackers of the corollary condemn its apparent stress on the sanctity of debt, its apparent endorsement of the argument that un-paid debts could be a legitimate excuse for international use of force. Yet this was hardly a particularly American idea at the time, but was the consensus of the nations of Europe, i.e., of the nations that were capable of deploying naval power. Having lent out funds in good faith, on the promise that these funds would be repaid, such nations would regard it as an act of robbery if an irresponsible regime any-where on the globe were to refuse to make payments on schedule, and they would indeed be tempted to deploy force, or even to oc-cupy land in response.

In face of this consensus, the Roosevelt Corollary may not have been any amplification at all of the rights of property here, but rather the simple reconciliation of this to the additional requirement of the Monroe Doctrine that self-government in the Western Hemis-phere at no point be surrendered again to colonial government. With the decline of British monopoly dominance at sea, the threat of a race for competing naval bases in the hemisphere was all too clear.

GENERAL OVERSEAS INVESTMENT

If Americans thus agreed with Europeans that international debt was sacred, how much of a self-indictment of the U.S. capitalist system was this? The American endorsement of the claims of foreign credi-tors brings us at length to what may indeed be the most central irri-tant of international economic relations, that of foreign investment. How does it come to be that one country owns a great deal of prop-erty inside another? If this is not matched by a reciprocal degree of property ownership in the opposite direction, will this be tolerable and desirable in the long run? Why should there be so many tensions here? Why should Canadians object to ownership by companies based in New York, when citizens of Iowa do not object to the same New York ownership?

A part of the explanation is of course a simple unthinking sense of political stigma, which we encounter today in reverse, in the American resentment of Arab or other foreign investment within the United States. Foreign investment is somehow seen as a sign of being in debt, of having been less prudential or less efficient than one's neighbor in the past.

Second, we may be dealing with an elementary human resent-ment against so artificial an institution as property. Those who no longer have will always feel tempted to challenge the title of those who now have more. Yet this human tendency is of course substantially exacerbated where the title of ownership must extend across international boundaries. All of our notions of loans, savings, investments, and property depend on something else known as law, on the enforcement of sheriffs and constables and central authority, which makes one pay at a later time what one promised at the earlier. But international law is overwhelmingly weaker than domestic law, such that the certainty of enforcement of contracts will go down, so that the temptations of altering the status quo, and the irritations connected with the status quo, go up. Given the inherent temptation to try to erase the past, to declare that "property is theft," especially when the balance of debts becomes too one-sided between nations, the system will thus not function without some residual threat of force, the force which in the latter nineteenth century became gunboat diplomacy. This then produces still greater resentments, as the institution of foreign debt becomes associated with the prospect of foreign military attacks.

A third kind of objection would shift away from the temptations of debt erasure here, to the fear that international trade as reflected by foreign investment is actually bad for the developing countries of the world. What were entered into freely enough (or at times perhaps not so freely) by the recipient countries turned out to put them into a worse position than if no such foreign investment had occurred.

Could it thus simply be that trade per se is bad for one of the countries voluntarily engaged in it? The post-1945 discussion of "dependencia" has come up with a number of versions of such a conclusion,[13] but we could indeed easily enough find such feelings already in the protectionist arguments that led to the national tariff barriers in Europe and the United States at the end of the nineteenth century, and even earlier in various forms of mercantilist argument.

This hardly needs to be an argument that foreign investment is *intended* or designed to be bad for the host countries, but rather that it somewhat inadvertently works out that way. As each side to the transaction makes its choices with apparent regard to its own interests, one of them indeed is sabotaging its own long-term interest, as it buys from abroad what it should rather force itself to produce at home. Such "infant industry" arguments in effect are arguments for forcing one's self to save, forcing one's self to accept a lower standard of living for the short run, in hopes that this will induce the development of industries with high growth potential, thus assuring a much higher standard of living for the long run, for one's children and grandchildren.

If the United States or Great Britain knowingly saw continued trade as a way of stunting the industrialization and the emergence of trade rivals abroad, their strong historical support for free trade would then be indicted as a most ungenerous act. Far more likely, however, was that these producers, who had surged in front of the rest of the world in industrialization and manufactures, saw themselves as bringing a blessing to the world as a whole, letting anyone buy who wished to (anyone who did not wish to buy did not have to), so as to improve his life-style by importing something that worked better and cost less.

CHINA AND THE OPEN DOOR

Next to the Spanish-American War and the Roosevelt Corollary, and the southward investment waves that followed, radical interpretations of American foreign policy have been drawn perhaps most often to the American decision to resist Japanese entry into China, culminating ultimately in the Pearl Harbor attack and American participation in World War II.[14] While the American opposition to Hitler and European fascism might have to be credited to more generally humane motives, the American commitment to Asia is again sometimes portrayed as part of an endless competition over markets, as the United States was allegedly drawn into opposition to Japan simply by fear that American goods no longer would be allowed to be sold in areas under Japanese military rule.

Such an American commitment to the opening of markets on the Chinese mainland allegedly had been in effect continuously from the Spanish-American War itself, as the Philippine Islands were then seized as a base from which trade could be projected, and the United States demanded an open door in China, resisting Japanese encroachments after World War I and all through the 1920s and 1930s.

Yet again the economic interpretation of American foreign policy here paints U.S. policy too selfishly. On self-centered mercantile grounds alone, the United States would hardly have been so opposed to Japanese and other foreign incursions into China, since trade was often easier when foreign armies had restored law and order. The American merchant of the 1920s had much reason to fear the rise of Chiang Kai-shek, for one professed intention of the Kuomintang Chinese Nationalists was to deemphasize contacts with the West, and to curtail the foreign mercantile presence. The Chinese war lords of the 1920s were a nuisance for trade on simple predatory grounds, but the Kuomintang (KMT) promised to be a menace on ideological grounds. It would be a great mistake to assume that the

KMT of the 1920s and 1930s promised to be what KMT rule of Taiwan has been since 1950. The Nationalist regime on Taiwan, for its own reasons and needs, has kept the door very open to trade. The KMT proposal for the whole of China at the beginning of the Japanese attack was somewhat different.

It is thus no surprise that one saw some American as well as British businessmen welcoming the first Japanese invasions of Manchuria and Shanghai, seeing Japan as yet another "European" power entering upon the civilizing mission, establishing the law and order necessary for serious trade to follow in its wake. Japan would stamp out criminality, and also prevent bolshevism.

What then produced the American turnaround into such full support for the Chinese against Japan? Some of the turnaround was immediate, in simple loyalty to the Wilsonian League of Nations absolute injunction against the initiation of war and the resort to aggression. Just as the backward and barbaric Ethiopia, still tolerating a slave trade, had to be backed automatically when Mussolini launched a blatant aggression against it, so China had to be backed.[15]

The larger part of the turnabout then came with reports back to the United States of the behavior of the Japanese troops in China, reports of enormous and unusual atrocities against a defenseless civilian population as well as against Chinese prisoners of war. While the Japanese army had succeeded in behaving in a very "European" fashion during World War I (for example in its treatment of German war prisoners at Tsingtao), it reverted now to a very Asian style of military behavior in the war with China, venting its resentment for armed resistance by orgies of rape and murder, one of the more salient illustrations coming with the fall of the Nationalist Chinese capital at Nanking.

Believers in the theory that the United States acts only out of the selfish interests of predatory capitalism would claim that American opinion was now mobilized for China and against Japan simply because Japan was monopolizing the markets it seized. Yet the Japanese at times even showed a desire to attract American investments into the territories they had under their control. American businessmen might well have looked forward to a peace based on a Japanese conquest, for this would have produced the speediest opening of trade channels.

Rather what links more closely with the American turnaround is the flow of anguished press comment on the Japanese army's behavior, accompanied by a stream of letters from American missionaries to the same effect. The role of the missionary link between the United States and China can hardly be overstressed.[16] However misguided some later critics would find it to be, it personified the American assumption that the Chinese were potentially the same kinds of people as Americans, that their happiness would be raised by having access to American institutions and ways of living, that such an improvement in the quality of life in China was something good in its own right, something that made Americans happy for its own sake.

Americans were also now drawn into the China-Japan quarrel by analogies with Europe. As Hitler and Mussolini were now repeatedly showing the League of Nations ban on the use of military force to be an empty bluff, the analogy with Japanese behavior seemed all too clear. Revisionist interpretations of the 1930s too often insist on treating the Far East in isolation. But U.S. policy planners, and others, now saw it in a global perspective.

It is ironic that it was only in 1938 that Hitler's Germany made a definite commitment to an alliance with Japan in the war with China and on all other matters, until then toying with the idea of an alliance instead with Chiang Kai-shek's China. A German-Chinese partnership against Japan would surely have confused American and world attitudes about what was afoot here as a threat to world peace, preventing the simplifying assumption that Japan, like Germany and Italy, was a "Fascist" state.[17]

Revisionists who see Americans guided by economic motives here, rather than by fear of a worldwide Axis alliance, often also see Japanese aggressive behavior as equally economic. Japan and the United States are portrayed as two capitalist market-seekers, locked in a zero-sum conflict by which only one could possibly be content with its share of the China market.[18] Yet Japanese behavior is also more complicated than such a neo-Marxist model would suggest.

A portion of Japanese behavior, especially the portion that antagonized the United States, was not based on any rational economic selfishness of the Japanese business system, but rather the self-indulgence of the Japanese army. To repeat an ethnocentric generalization, the barbarism of the advance into Chinese cities may simply have seemed the more traditional behavior of victorious armies in an Asian context. The massacres following Japanese victories were a form of compensation for Japanese fighting men that surely slowed and obstructed the resumption of any normal flow of trade and profits back to Japan. It was militarism or racism pursued for its own purposes, rather than for any mercantile purpose.

Turning to the larger portion of Japanese behavior, which in the Greater East Asia Coprosperity Sphere was indeed centrally designed to bring economic benefits back to Japan, even this has to be viewed differently from the alleged normal business imperative in competing for markets. What looks like "economic imperialism" (in the revisionist perspective so indistinguishable from the American desire to win customers throughout Asia) might instead be classified as "plunder," the straightforward arrogation of economic advantages by the threat of military power.

Japan may have become aggressive in the 1930s because the traditional power of Great Britain or France in the region was in decline, distracted by the threat of Nazi Germany in Europe. This aggressiveness may moreover have been enhanced by peculiarities of the Japanese domestic tradition and situation, engendering a relatively greater militarism and willingness to go to war, comparable to that shown in Fascist Italy and Nazi Germany. When such considerations are added together, one indeed has more than the desire for markets in the normal workings of a capitalist system. The normal capitalist is indeed always glad to find "steady customers," but he is not normally willing or anxious to use force to coerce such customers. The real believer in free-market capitalism would indeed have an instinctive distrust for any process that lined up his customers in this way.

Because Japan indeed had economic difficulties in the 1930s, in the wake of the worldwide depression, and because the Japanese aggressors tended to coat their empire with the euphemism of a "coprosperity sphere," the notion survives that Japan's foreign policy here (and of course the American responses that were entangled with it) must be seen as "economic." Yet the simple greed and lack of scruple about the use of force that went into this raises what are more profoundly political questions about the Japanese domestic system, and about the international system of East Asia at the time.

What did Japan do that the British or Americans did not do, or would not have done? Is it only that Japan lost a world war, while the English-speakers won, so that the capitalism of their "free trade" is not condemned, while the capitalism of Japan's "coprosperity sphere" is relabeled "Fascist aggression"?

There are indeed important differences between the Japanese and American approaches to markets in 1937, just as there are very important differences between the Japanese market approaches of 1937 and 1977. Were the Japanese seeking employment relief, higher profits, and crucial raw materials in their push outward here? Very possibly they were seeking all of these. But the push outward in the Greater East Asia Coprosperity Sphere was to win markets at the point of a bayonet, rather than by the superiority of Japanese merchandise over any competition. The intuitive American feeling that "fair trade is no robbery" may in the end not be satisfactory for Filipinos or Malaysians, but these people would nonetheless recognize an elementary difference in that "robbery is robbery."

The United States became extremely enthusiastic about China and the KMT during the war against Japan, not because it was assumed that it would turn China into an economic asset for the United States, but because it might turn China into a happy nation. Americans of course felt that the delivery and sale of American goods to China would be conducive to Chinese happiness, but one should not confuse the means and the end here. Chiang Kai-shek published a book during World War II in effect outlining a Chinese return to Confucian traditions,[19] and a much lesser involvement in trade and contacts with foreigners. If this had worked to make China a happy place, many Americans would not have minded the de-emphasis on trade with the United States. Happiness was the end that mattered, and trade the means, a sequence quite different from what radical critics of American foreign policy would contend.

The Chiang with whom Americans came to identify between 1932 and 1944 thus looked a great deal like nationalistic leaders around the third world today, like a Nasser or a Sadat or a Sekou-Toure, using his own Communists when their help was needed, repressing or murdering them when they were not needed anymore, at all times very distrustful of foreign influences and investment. Chiang was not simply some sort of comprador or puppet. Americans would have liked him less if they had thought he was.

THE ECONOMICS OF THE COLD WAR

Leaping ahead then, the next illustration of a U.S. capitalist need for markets cited in the revisionist literature comes in the period immediately following the German surrender in Europe, when the United States was demanding and pressuring the Russians for the opening of Eastern Europe to a free trade with the outside world.[20]

Was this primarily or even importantly because the United States needed customers for the glut of production that was expected to come because of its capitalistic defects? Revisionist accounts repeatedly cite a few occasional snatches of speeches or congressional testimony by American officials, most prominently Dean Acheson, suggesting that the United States looked forward to dealing with these new markets. Yet such evidence would quickly become suspect if one did a word count on the frequency with which such arguments were introduced, compared to all the other considerations being brought to bear. As things stand, the few paragraphs here and there of such economically selfish arguments could easily have been inserted as boiler plate to win the support of a more isolationist congressman from Kansas City or a businessman from Cincinnati.

The hard facts are of course that the United States had conducted very little trade with Eastern Europe before World War II, while Western Europe had conducted a great deal. While American entrepreneurs might be looking always for new markets, old patterns often shape such things, such that any opening of Poland and Rumania to trade was likely to help French and British and German businessmen considerably more than American.

Analysts stressing the dictates of capitalism sometimes then jump to use such West European business interests as the lynchpin of their arguments, but even here this would beg the question. Why would Americans be anxious to enrich a potential trade rival in Western Europe by giving it the easy ride of time-tested customers in Eastern Europe?

The reality is that the actual American policy makes sense here only if one introduces political ends; economic policy served as the means to this end (rather than the reverse, as Marxist and other radical analysis would have it). The American government had developed a belief by the end of World War II that full trade among nations was crucial to preventing resumptions of Naziism and aggression. This was based heavily on the worldwide experience of the Great Depression, when nations had largely suspended free trade relationships to retreat into a policy of autarky, and military independence emerged as an important by-product, with the perceived costs of war for Hitler's Germany thus being lower since there were far fewer trade ties to break. Americans thus believed that depressions and tariff barriers tended to produce Hitlers and Mussolinis. The American pressure against tariff barriers was directed not only against Communist regimes in Eastern Europe, but also against the British Empire and other colonial barriers.

Did the United States want peace here to get trade, or much more importantly, trade to get peace? Each of these linkages undeniably had some impact, but the second, after the miseries of World War II, carried considerably more weight than the first.[21]

The U.S. demand for a lowering of trade barriers was not the only "economic" issue at the outset of the cold war. Revisionists note with sympathy that the Russians showed great signs of being upset at the abrupt failure of the United States to continue making lend-lease loans after the Germans had surrendered. This American abruptness might have been due to inadvertance, or to a deliberate intention to show disapproval for what the Russians had been doing in Poland, and to demand an opening to trade.

Yet can this show much about the economic workings of capitalism? At an earlier point, when testifying about the proposed loans, Ambassador Harriman had explained how loans should be viewed in the American interest, putting unemployed American machines and workers to work. (If Harriman was thus offering a seemingly Marxist statement of why the loan made sense here, this author would of course find such statements to be equally much boiler plate, again intended mainly to win over some isolationist congressmen or businessmen to a foreign policy project whose advantages they would not otherwise appreciate.) How would the revisionist attack on American cold war policy handle such "evidence" suggesting that the proposed American loan to the Russians was actually consistent with the pressing needs of capitalism? Which way was it then? Would giving the loan to the Russians have been more capitalist, or was denying it more capitalist? One fears being "damned if you don't" here, and "damned if you do."

SELF-INDICTMENT

One must always be very careful here about "proofs" of the economic cause of imperialism that are based straightforwardly on the public government statements of the time. Such statements have often enough amounted to nothing more than propaganda or window dressing for policies that were basically more political.

European states were thus fond of announcing that they were advancing into places like Morocco or China to protect their merchants (or their missionaries), where profit or religion indeed had little or nothing to do with the grasping for the naval base or colony in question. Rather than being pulled into Morocco by the self-interest of French merchants, the French government in fact had to bribe such merchants to risk their lives by going into such a region to merit this protection, and to excuse the entry of military forces thereafter.[22] Desires for cultural glory, and for checks to the military power of others, account for more of the European imperialism of the 1880s and 1890s than any need for markets.

Similarly, in the U.S. case, Americans were understandably intent on differentiating themselves from the ethnocentric and power-minded nationalisms of Europe, and thus were prone to stress the seemingly less-selfish economic intention of keeping the door open to trade, even in instances where the United States might indeed now have been indulging some ethnic nationalism of its own (contrary to the image it wished to have of itself), or was joining in the race for military positions that the Europeans had been running.

In short, some of the American dwelling on an economic view of foreign policy in the 1890s thus amounts to euphemism and self-congratulation, rather than to any sort of admission of guilt. The distinction is an important one.

Citizens of any country can be counted upon to distort the descriptions of their own behavior in a direction that makes them feel better, makes them look better abroad. Had the world already been sensitized to a Marxist interpretation of international politics in the 1890s, as it was to be after the 1940s, Americans would have been far less likely in their Fourth of July speeches to describe their foreign policy in the Far East or elsewhere as directed to making trade possible; this would now have been to invite attack, rather than to ward it off.

Like anyone else trying to prove a position, the radical analyst of American foreign policy wishes to have his cake and eat it here. When Lyndon Johnson claimed that the United States was fighting in Vietnam in order to maintain self-determination and a pluralistic political system, this was dismissed as euphemism and propaganda. When a U.S. senator in 1898 spoke of holding the Philippines as a way of opening China for trade with the United States, this is taken as an honest confession of motives. Yet why could not the earlier statement have been the propaganda, and the latter a statement of actual motive?

THE MARSHALL PLAN

If one wishes to sort out generous or selfish motives in economics here, how is one then to explain the Marshall Plan, the unprecedented unilateral transfer of some $12 billion of economic assistance from the United States to Europe after 1948?[23]

The donation very clearly was of benefit to the Europeans in helping them achieve a more speedy economic recovery from the ravages of World War II. If one insists on looking for selfish returns for the United States, however, one again has to move into what may be more politics than economics. At the political level, the United States surely did see such economic assistance as helping to prevent the spread of Communist regimes into Western Europe. An increase in the living standards of West Europeans presumably made it less likely that they would vote Communist. An acceleration of economic recovery in Great Britain and France and Italy and West Germany would let such countries develop a military defense against the Red Army, if such a defense should be needed.

At the economic level, however, the Marshall Plan may have turned out to be a somewhat self-damaging act by Americans, as the European economies that emerged have proven to be (and indeed might have been predicted to be) effective competitors for the very customers in world markets that American firms might have wanted to win. If the chronic problem of American capitalism were indeed the finding of markets for the disposal of gluts, without which Americans would face unemployment, then it would have been wiser to keep Europe in its relatively devastated state after 1945.

The revisionist analysis can thus not demonstrate that the United States wanted to keep Western Europe (or Eastern Europe for that matter) free of Communist rule simply because of an alleged need for markets. The Marshall Plan contributed to the prosperity of all, but it did not contribute to making it easier to dispose of future American surpluses.

A Marxist analyst could of course come back to argue that the United States faced an immediate problem of disposal of surpluses in 1948, and thus was simply dumping its gluts of agricultural and industrial output into Western Europe because its economy at home could find no other way out. Given the hunger and devastation of Western Europe, very few of the recipients of American aid were disposed to take this interpretation seriously. The Marxist problem here is illustrated interestingly in the debates in one of the West German *Länder* about agreeing to accept Marshall Plan aid, with only a solitary Communist Party (CP) legislator trying to rouse some opposition. The CP delegate gave an impassioned speech in which he predicted that "The Americans will dump all their surplus food and industrial production on you," to which the rest of the assembly responded by chanting "if only it were already so."

The most plausible explanation of the Marshall Plan is thus that it responded to U.S. national values ("ideology," if you will), rather than to U.S. economic needs. Americans slept better at night thinking that Europeans soon would no longer be cold or hungry. They also slept better feeling that Europeans would be able to retain the system of free elections that had been the prospect as Hitler's forces were driven back.

One cannot ignore the calculations of political power that made it now to the American national power interest to keep Western Europe from falling under Moscow's control, for the consolidation of all of Eurasia under Stalin would have seemed a threat to the safety and self-government of the United States itself. Yet one can also not ignore the fact that the United States had some important altruistic motives in mind here as well.

In retrospect, of course, the Marshall Plan's success was heavily dependent on the substantial infrastructure of human capital that was already in place in Europe as aid was delivered. While the machines of Western Europe had been destroyed, the people who knew how to operate them remained alive, and the increase of output was thus very likely to be abrupt after the addition of American assistance. Far less decisive and satisfactory results were to be obtained in later years when similar foreign assistance was delivered to places that had never experienced industrialization, where the trained manpower was simply not available.

The Marshall Plan may thus have been bothersome for American foreign policy in the years that followed, precisely because it misled Americans into expecting great successes by the delivery of economic assistance anywhere else in the globe. As in the broader political models we have been discussing, Americans after 1945 quite naturally and liberally assumed that whatever was appropriate for Europe would be appropriate for any other corner of the globe. Just as political democracy, government by the consent of the governed, made sense, so it also made sense that a nation could make more rapid economic progress if it were given some large amounts of grain or machinery to help it through its period of extreme need.

UNPROVEN CHARGES

Let us now try to summarize the dispute. There is an important school of radical analysis that would place heavy emphasis on economic factors for explaining the outward turns of American foreign policy after 1890. With the closing of the frontier and the maturing of capitalism, shortages of aggregate demand allegedly arose at home, which would have produced unemployment and unrest if foreign markets could not be found—so a condensed version of the argument would run. It was no accident, therefore, that the United States now at last decided to build a large navy, to take possession of Hawaii and the Philippines, and to participate actively in the affairs of much of the world.

The basic argument of this book is that there are too many problems with such interpretation. Americans have in truth favored trade at all times in their history, but for a *mixture* of selfish and altruistic reasons. Trade was indeed thought good because it generated more producer surplus; any additional customers anywhere are likely to raise the value and returns of what one is producing. Trade may have been additionally good because it seemed to relieve business slumps: any additional customers anywhere reduce one's chances of being unemployed. Yet trade was also good because the customers benefited; any additional seller anywhere increases the choice of products available to the consumer.

To seize simply on the unemployment fear in this mix, and to give it all the credit for driving foreign policy, is a distortion. It would have suggested that there should be a high correlation as well between prosperity and inward-looking foreign policies, and this cannot be found. Even to weigh the entire bundle of such economic factors as driving American foreign policy is a distortion, for the relevant bundle must include also the host of political factors described.

Where the same foreign policy ventures could plausibly serve to increase the national power of the United States in a military and general economic sense, to increase the profits of American capitalist corporations, and to increase the happiness of foreigners as perceived by Americans, can one then do anything the least bit scientific in sorting out the presumed priority of such motives in relation to each other? Is it any less tautological or unfalsifiable for the believer in American altruism to claim that this plays an important role in such situations, than it is for the Marxist to contend that all of policy here is explained by economic interests, or for the realpolitician to claim that it is all explained by the national quest for power?

The ideal cases for a test are of course those where these variables clearly move in different directions on a policy choice, but such clear "test cases" are not easy to isolate. For lack of them, one may be thrown back in the end on to one's intuition, asking himself as an American why he felt particularly pleased at the demise of the Gang of Four in China, or at the demise of Idi Amin in Uganda, or why he felt particularly distressed at the fall of Czechoslovakia to Communist rule in 1948. Did the Communist seizure of power in Prague bother Main Street in the United States because the threat to North America was heightened, or because investment opportunities were cut off? Or were these trivial in comparison to the loss of political liberty for the Czechs who had just escaped from another denial of such liberty by the Germans?

The most difficult question may thus hinge on whether the U.S. concern with free press and free speech and free elections simply masks a desire to spread capitalism, as a burning need for markets in China and Eastern Europe and Latin America makes the United States seek excuses to restrict the power of the state in all these areas. U.S. concern for political democracy, in the radical view, has never been sincere, but is merely a mask to frustrate economic democracy, to keep socialism of any form from emerging. The distinction is not trivial, of course, for if capitalism were the explanation, American foreign policy here would have been much less altruistic, much less explained by American treatment of others as ends in themselves, but would serve rather simply as the means to solving U.S. domestic unemployment problems.

Free speech and free trade do often go together, this is undeniable. The classic liberals of the Lockean mode tended to view restrictions on business practice with almost as much concern as restrictions on a free press (the press, after all, is also a business).

One can then attack the puzzle in several ways. To begin, the urgency of the American need for markets in China or Latin America or Eastern Europe is often overstated in the radical analysis. An application of Keynesian economics can relieve many or most of the difficulties that allegedly required overseas investments or defense spending or the imposition of capitalism abroad. Americans may like capitalism abroad for its own sake. Americans like steady customers abroad, for who does not like steady customers? Yet the *urgency* of such a liking does not really explain the Spanish-American War, or the American revulsion at the Japanese invasion of China, or the American revulsion at the suppression of pluralism in Czechoslovakia and Poland and the rest of Eastern Europe after World War II.

Americans felt urgently upset about the denial of multiparty elections in Eastern Europe after World War II because this made the war against Nazi tyranny seem pointless, if new tyranny was simply to replace the old. Compared to this, the urgency of American alleged need for markets in Poland (markets to which the United States had never sold much before 1939) becomes less striking.

A different approach to disentangling this question would be to hunt for societies that maintain their political democracy while going quite far on the control of the economic sector, and vice versa. Sweden, Denmark, and Norway would approximate the former, while Nazi Germany looks much like the latter. Hitler did not frighten Americans because he might tax away the profits of those American companies with affiliates in the Reich. He drove the United States into a war because of the threat he posed to the happiness and well-being of millions of Europeans. Conversely, despite the precedent the Scandinavian social democracies set of backbreaking taxation and bureaucratic regulation of the private economic sector, American foreign policy toward these countries has been extremely friendly, importantly because (as in the United States itself) there is no prospect of a compromise of their political democratic system.

But what of U.S. opposition to the government of Salvador Allende in Chile?[24] Defenders of the Allende regime note that it had been freely elected, and as yet had made no real move to undo the processes of political democracy. The special interests of American firms such as ITT, and the proclivities of the Nixon administration for secret and devious international activities, by a critical view thus amount to the explanation for the U.S. decision to intervene to "destabilize" the regime, in the end producing a military coup and the most blatant dictatorship in Chile's history.

Yet the picture is less simple than this. Allende's position was that a recourse to political democracy would be attempted *as long* as it had the prospect of achieving economic democracy. "We will not tamper with the liberal election process, as long as we can make progress toward socialism without it," was the gist of Allende's message. For this he was attacked by Fidel Castro and others on the Left who argued that progress toward socialism, i.e., toward economic democracy, could not be made in the framework of political democracy, of free elections, and what goes with them.

Yet such an Allende position was also bound to draw objection from an American perspective. If one cannot achieve socialism in an atmosphere of free elections, most Americans would have felt, it was "socialism" that would have to be dispensed with, and not free elections. Allegedly reassuring comments by Allende that he believed that his economic goals could be accomplished in the context of liberal democracy, and that he would thus "not yet" turn to other means, were thus an inherently threatening message of "we'll allow elections as long as they seem to be coming out our way," a message which no serious political party in the United States itself could propound.

An important part of the American opposition to Allende may therefore not have depended on the special interests of ITT, or the peculiar deviousness of Nixon, but rather on the contingent threat to political democracy that Allende was posing. Americans may or may not be foolish in believing that political democracy is more important for the Chileans than economic democracy, but the presumption was surely not mistaken that Allende believed the reverse.

Allende was thus *tolerating* political democracy, on a very *contingent* basis, rather than endorsing it without conditions, as one indeed normally expects of the parties to a process of free elections. If the republican political process made the leveling of economic returns possible, well and good. If it did not, it would have to be dispensed with.

Would the U.S. government and people not have turned against Allende if he had made a more real commitment to political freedom? History denies us the evidence for a fully convincing answer, but the drive of the argument here is that he would have drawn American approval rather than antagonism.

One should also thus recall the widespread American popular support for Fidel Castro's insurgency against the dictatorial Batista regime at the end of the 1950s.[25] Castro did not get his money nor his arms from the Soviet Union but from a more traditional exporter of revolution, the United States. Students today may miss the piquant irony of Castro's constant wearing of 1950s style U.S. Army fatigues, instead of Russian-style uniforms. Deliberately or otherwise, these uniforms of the Cuban armed forces serve as memorial to the original source of their support. Castro drew this support from individual American citizens, rather than the U.S. government, just as had the revolutionaries of the nineteenth century, drawing it on the promise of instituting free elections if he won. Without such support it is plausible that he would not have succeeded.

Castro's assent to power was followed by a repudiation of his commitment to free elections and the constitution Batista had suspended. It is no accident, it would be contended here, that his support in the United States disappeared with this change of commitment.

Such arguments will still most probably not satisfy the radical critic, who will remain convinced that it is U.S. capitalism that fools one into believing in free elections. The final argument here will then become a little more involuted and ad hominem, but quite closely related to the central subject of this entire book. The revisionist who sees American foreign policy as the defense and projection of capitalism, rather than of political freedom, will now have trouble explaining his own success in the 1970s and accounting for the fact that Americans have been going through the second thoughts we have been describing about American attachment to political freedom. Had the United States become any less capitalistic as it decided to bow out of challenging the Cubans in Angola? Or was it instead that it had become less altruistically attached to the idea of free speech in Angola as events had moved along to make Americans rethink whether this is "what the Angolans need"?

Would the revisionists who attacked the Vietnam War thus have expected the rest of detente, the American disinclination to get into military challenges to Communist moves? One can of course forge a link with visions of the people standing up and engaging in protest, as the campuses of the 1960s boiled over, but the campuses were quieter in the 1970s, and the leftist revolution within the United States has not happened.

The change is not in the U.S. domestic system, nor in its alleged needs, but in U.S. experience with the outside world. With regard to this world, Americans may be tired, but more importantly, they are confused.

The argument here is thus that the revisionist or radical position has been mistaken in its explanations of past American foreign policy, even though it is very much in step with changes of attitudes that have shaped such policy. It was not economic greed nor the defects of the capitalist system that made the United States build warships or send them abroad in the past. But many Americans after 1967 began feeling that the defects of the existing economic system abroad required that the United States cease to send out warships to defend political democracy.

NOTES

1. Some of the variety of Marxist and non-Marxist "radical" interpretations of United States foreign policy can be found in Richard J. Barnet, *Roots of War* (Baltimore: Penguin, 1973); D. F. Fleming, *The Cold War and Its Origins* (Garden City: Doubleday, 1961); Gabriel and Joyce Kolko, *The Limits of Power* (New York: Harper & Row, 1972); Carl Oglesby and Richard Schaull, *Containment and Change* (New York: Macmillan, 1967); and Ronald Steel, *Pax Americana* (New York: Viking, 1967).

2. For a book stating the interpretations found so plausible by the Nye Committee, see Walter Millis, *The Road To War* (Boston: Houghton Mifflin, 1935).

3. Discussions of the role of ITT in Chile can be found in Robert Moss, *Chile's Marxist Experiment* (New York: John Wiley, 1974), pp. 30-31.

4. Morton H. Halperin and Arnold Kanter, eds., *Readings in American Foreign Policy: A Bureaucratic Perspective* (Boston: Little, Brown, 1973) offers a good selection of bureaucratic politics interpretations of government behavior.

5. See Joan Robinson, "Marx and Keynes," in *Collected Economic Papers* (Oxford: Blackwell, 1951), pp. 133-45.

6. J. A. Hobson, *Imperialism: A Study* (London: Allen and Unwin, 1902).

7. The opposition of Andrew Carnegie and some of his colleagues to American military spending is outlined in Robert Beisner, *Twelve Against Empire* (New York: McGraw-Hill, 1968).

8. See Walter LaFeber, *The New Empire* (Ithaca: Cornell University Press, 1963).

9. See Benjamin J. Cohen, *The Question of Imperialism* (New York: Basic Books, 1973), pp. 136-38.

10. For details of the earlier U.S. naval activism, see Harold and Margaret Sprout, *The Rise of American Naval Power 1776-1918* (Princeton: Princeton University Press, 1939).

11. A good overview of the extent of American aversions to foreign entanglements in the 1930s can be found in Manfred Jonas, *Isolationism in America* (Ithaca: Cornell University Press, 1966).

12. The Roosevelt Corollary is analyzed in Dexter Perkins, *The United States and the Caribbean* (Cambridge, Mass.: Harvard University Press, 1947).

13. The theories of "dependencia" are outlined in Frank Bonilla and Robert Sirling, eds., *Structures of Dependency* (Stanford: Stanford University Press, 1973).

14. A radical interpretation of the American commitment to the defense of China against the Japanese can be found in William Appleman Williams, *The Tragedy of American Diplomacy* (Cleveland: World, 1959), chap. 5.

15. The influence of Wilsonian ideas here about support for self-government and opposition to aggression is discussed in Henry L. Stimson, *The Far Eastern Crisis* (New York: Harper, 1936).

16. The role of American missionaries in inducing American identification with the Chinese people is detailed in Paul A. Varg, *Missionaries, Chinese and Diplomats* (Princeton: Princeton University Press, 1958).

17. See O. Edmund Clubb, *20th Century China* (New York: Columbia University Press, 1964), pp. 193, 200, 218-19 for discussion of the role of the German military mission in China and the lateness of the jelling of the Axis alliance.

18. See Akira Iriye, *Across the Pacific: An Inner History of American-East Asian Relations* (New York: Harcourt Brace, 1967), especially pp. 83-110.

19. Chiang Kai-shek, *China's Destiny* (New York: Macmillan, 1944).

20. See Gabriel Kolko, *The Politics of War* (New York: Random House, 1968), chaps. 11-13.

21. See discussion in C. Fred Bergsten, Robert O. Keohane, and Joseph S. Nye, Jr., "International Economics and International Politics: A Framework for Analysis," in *World Politics and International Economics*, eds. C. Fred Bergsten and Lawrence B. Krause (Washington, D.C.: Brookings, 1975), pp. 4-6.

22. The real nature of the French move into Morocco is discussed in Edmund Burke III, *Prelude to Protectorate in Morocco* (Chicago: University of Chicago Press, 1976).

23. A very useful analysis of the Marshall Plan is to be found in Jesse Jones, *The Fifteen Weeks* (New York: Viking, 1955).

24. See Elizabeth Farnsworth, "Chile: What Was the U.S. Role—More than Admitted," *Foreign Policy*, no. 16 (Fall 1974), pp. 127-41, and Paul E. Sigmund, "Chile: What Was the U.S. Role?—Less than Charged," *Foreign Policy*, no. 16 (Fall 1974), pp. 142-56, for discussions of the U.S. involvement with the Allende regime in Chile.

25. American backing for Fidel Castro's insurrection against Batista regime is discussed in Hugh Thomas, *Cuba: The Pursuit of Freedom* (New York: Harper & Row, 1971), especially pp. 909-24.

4

The Old Consensus:
The United States Better
than Other Countries

We come then to the third interpretation of American foreign policy, distinguished easily enough from the two we have discussed. Rather than believing (as do the realists) that the United States is just like any other country in seeking after power, or (as do the radicals) that the United States is unusually troublesome for the world because of the demands of capitalism, this is the view that the United States has been an unusually altruistic and generous nation on the world scene, channeling much of its foreign policy energy into trying to increase the happiness of others.[1]

The central theme of this book is indeed that Americans used to share an implicit but deep consensus about such generosity, and about what was the best way to help other peoples around the globe, a consensus that prevailed until the Vietnam War, but a consensus that cracked at just about Klingberg's projected 1967 turning point. Lack of consensus in this area since then, the sense of crisis in self-evaluation, may then well account for the confusions of American foreign policy as the cold war became something else.

But what was this "lost consensus" all about? Skeptics could respond that they do not remember anyone at the time stating so very clearly any propositions upon which all Americans so much agreed.

THE APPLICABILITY OF THE AMERICAN MODEL

It will be argued here that the following was widely accepted before the Vietnam War, and now is not—that the political practice of the United States would, if adopted for any corner of the globe, add to the happiness of the people living there. Americans have, in effect, assumed that the political system of a place like Minnesota would also work well in Burma or Kenya or Cuba or Algeria.

The latest inward phase (by Klingberg's typology) of American foreign policy attitudes, presumably commencing at the 1967 peak of the American involvement in the Vietnam War, might thus have come in a very different form from all the others that preceded it. It was different, it will be contended here, because a large fraction of Americans had now for the first time come to doubt the moral desirability of implanting a duplicate of the American political system in foreign countries. They were thus not being turned into isolationists simply by the costs of having influence abroad, but by doubts as to the appropriateness of such influence.

We shall want to say something here about the context in which Americans may have developed these feelings about the outside world, and then some more about whether this all has somehow amounted to an "ideology."

Americans often tell themselves, rather lightheartedly, that they have been a revolutionary force in world events. The Voice of America constantly reminds Africans and Asians that Americans were the "first new nation." Americans speak of their Revolutionary War, and thus invested a great deal of enthusiasm in 1976 celebrating the bicentennial of their "revolutionary" Declaration of Independence.

Critics of Marxist or otherwise radical persuasion would of course view all this as hypocritical nonsense by which Americans delude themselves into seeing the United States as a force for beneficial change, while they actually are just smugly attached to the economic status quo. Yet is it so totally silly for Americans to remember themselves as "revolutionary"? Is it the most transparent of propaganda to tell other newly independent nations that we share some great heritage, a propaganda that could fool no one but ourselves? Perhaps it is not.

For much of its history, the United States has been an example of possible change, and indeed a supporter of such change. When all the rest of the world still lacked governments based on the consent of the governed, the United States openly served as an example of republican rule. The United States was openly supportive of the French Revolution after 1789,[2] and was enthusiastic about the Latin American declarations of independence from Spain. It became quite engaged with the prospects of Greek independence from Turkey after 1831, and accorded diplomatic recognition to the Frankfurt Assembly in Germany during the revolutions of 1848.[3]

When leaders of such revolutions had to flee Germany or Hungary, as the movements toward political democracy were suppressed, they fled to the United States. In some sense the United States was thus the Algeria or Cuba of its time, an irritating safe haven for troublemakers where legitimate political authorities could not catch up with them, a vocal sounding board for the grievances of those challenging the old legitimate order; by its very example it was, like Cuba today, a challenge to the idea that the old ways of doing things were the only way of doing things.

Such an exemplary role would obviously be shaped by what the world had insisted on remaining. What was Europe and the rest of the world like between 1776 and 1848, and then from 1848 to 1918? At the risk of broad oversimplification, the outside world for the first century of American independence was governed by an ascriptive authority based neither on nationalism nor liberalism. Hereditary authority continued to govern, irrespective of the languages that people spoke, irrespective of any desire such people might have to elect their own rulers.

The issue of ethnic nationalism played less of a role in the United States, where the process of the Atlantic crossing had tended to standardize most Americans on spoken English. The issue of republican government, by contrast, counted for a great deal.

The revolutions sweeping Europe in 1848 can be seen as demanding *both* republican rule and ethnic self-determination. In their aftermath, the accommodation made by Bismarck and Louis Napoleon and others in the 1860s was to satisfy the demand for ethnic national identity, without making the parallel concession of real political democracy, real government by the election of the governed. The masses of Europe were thus in effect bought off after 1848 with half the loaf of what they had been demanding, and precisely the opposite half from what Americans cared about, what the United States was exemplifying.

We could thus move from 1776 to 1848 to 1872 to 1918, and perhaps to 1945, with the record still largely intact that the American model was waiting to be tried for most of Europe, and all the more so for the overseas possessions of Europe that were denied all self-government. It is only in the years since 1945 that the American model gets widely tried and rejected. It is only in these years that what Americans find appropriate for themselves comes to be seen as something of the past in much of the world, rather than something of the future.

The post-1848 European mix of ethnic nationalism without real concession to republican rule was destined to draw mixed reactions from the United States. Some Americans saw something to emulate here, thinking that they perhaps should similarly take more pride in their ethnic identity, in particular the English language, but then also the flag, and other symbols of nationalism. It is in this period that one sees Americans in the Progressive movement becoming concerned about persuading all immigrants to learn English as soon as possible.[4] It is in this period that the white stripes of the American flag cease to be used as a background for grocery advertising, and the elaborate ritual emerges for the first time of "respect for the flag." A few Americans might at this point even have wished to emulate the nationalistic drives of Europeans for colonies; if France could take pride in converting the natives of Niger to Frenchmen, could not Americans extend their culture and ethnic national identity somewhere as well?

Yet the bulk of the American attitude was not to emulate the European stress on nationalism ahead of republicanism, but rather to scoff at it. If Europeans took pride in forcing Asians to salute Queen Victoria or Kaiser Wilhelm or the president of France, Americans told themselves that they were above this, being intent rather on offering Asians a model and an opportunity for *self*-government. Europeans sent out navies to color in the map, while the United States now would send out a navy to keep the map from being colored in.

ESSENCE OF THE MODEL: POLITICAL DEMOCRACY

A dominant theme of American foreign policy in all of the nineteenth century and in most of the twentieth century was thus that it was the American model of politics (and probably the associated model of economics) that would conduce to the happiness of peoples in other countries. Whatever the dissatisfactions in retrospect with the American system, one could argue that it left most Americans at the time with a sense of success on the political side, with the not surprising result therefore that Americans assumed the same constitutional rules could work as well to produce satisfaction and happiness elsewhere.

On the political side, this American model was of course that governments should be elected by the people, and should have to be reelected again and again by the people, with the closely tied requirements of multiparty elections, freedom of press and speech, freedom from arbitrary arrest, and so forth. We really run no great danger of self-delusion in suggesting that the United States was thus indeed at the forefront of what could be called "political democracy."

Yet *political* democracy should be compared here with what might today strike some readers as more relevant—social or *economic* democracy, the equalization of material wealth from citizen to citizen.

The economic part of the American system had surely *not* been geared to what could be called "economic democracy," toward any substantial equalization of results and success, but rather toward what was more often styled equal opportunity, in a freedom from state-imposed restrictions on individual success. Again, the result for most Americans has not been remembered as an unhappy one. Widespread inequality of economic returns was balanced by substantial prosperity and overall economic success, such that the rich get richer while the poor did not do so badly either, by the standards of the rest of the world.

For most of the nineteenth century, with doubts emerging about this in the twentieth century, the economic by-products and results of political democracy in the United States thus did not seem to upset satisfaction with this political system, and often enough indeed reinforced the satisfaction. A Lockean belief in the equality of individuals (individuals coming out of a state of nature to negotiate a social contract) underpinned the belief in free elections, and it also supported the laissez-faire economic notion that two individuals should largely be free to buy and sell from each other as they pleased. The restrictions on state intervention that preserved a free press and opposition political parties also preserved entrepreneurs who wished to pursue profits free of state regulation.

The United States of America in the nineteenth century thus served as a model for Europeans who wished to overturn the traditional and ascriptive hereditary systems with which they were still saddled. It similarly struck many Europeans as a country that had generated genuine economic opportunity for more of its citizens than had any European country, and in the process had produced wealth for all. Having seen their own prosperity become the envy of much of the world, Americans in the twentieth century might quite understandably have assumed that such economic by-products of political democracy were just as exportable and conducive to happiness abroad as the political system itself.

In summary, a major theme throughout this book will thus be that any U.S. inclinations toward introversion or extroversion, "isolation" or "intervention," have been importantly a function of how Americans have compared themselves with foreign units in terms of political and economic success.

For much of American history, the comparison and derived conclusions seemed all too clear. With a political democracy as its form of government, the United States could feel itself significantly ahead of what it saw in most or all of Europe and Asia. With significant material prosperity, Americans could moreover feel that no real sacrifices or prices had been paid for this in the economic sector, indeed that political democracy and the solution of economic problems went hand in hand. As admitted, there was little American concern for what would today be styled "economic democracy," i.e., relative equalization of economic well-being, but the expectation was that political democracy would at least produce "equal opportunity," if not "equal success," and that such opportunity would assure that even those of lower success would be quite well off.

For as long as the rest of the world was burdened with the blatant political inequalities inherited from the feudal and monarchical past, there was thus little need for Americans to question the across-the-board relevance of their own system as a model for emulation. Free elections and freedom of the press and free enterprise were a mixture from which the outside world would benefit, and which the world would most likely adopt once the traditional holders of power were toppled from their thrones.

If Americans had been asked whether they felt any doubts about the likely contribution to happiness in a spreading of political democracy, about whether such feelings might be only a parochial expression of a Western culture, they would have replied negatively. Who today would deny the value of literacy all around the globe? The American endorsement of free elections, before 1967, was just about as automatic as today's endorsement of the values of literacy.

But we must now begin confronting the charge that Americans have been mistaking the tail for the dog here. When the United States wished to see some area freed of European rule, was the concern for "self-determination" here not merely a device to open up more customers and markets to American trade? Did not the economic aspects of laissez-faire capitalism come ahead of concern for the export of American political successes? Were Americans not really more guided here by economic selfishness than by political altruism?

It would clearly be a mistake to deny that Americans have looked forward to their own benefits in increased trade since the nineteenth century. Everyone likes to have "regular customers," likes the producer surplus that comes when one can sell more of his product. Yet it also would be a mistake to overlook American perceptions here of the "consumer surplus" that would result. Americans at all stages have believed that foreign purchasers of American goods would be ahead of the game as a result of the transaction. "Fair exchange is no robbery"; a transaction without physical coercion on either side must be of advantage to both sides, otherwise one of the parties would not have agreed to it. When contemplating selling locomotives to the Chinese at the start of the twentieth century, or selling medical products to Bolivians in the 1950s, the average American, whether or not he is a businessman, would tend to see the logic of free trade along very much these lines.

Just as a free and voluntary exchange of goods and services was seen as a natural accessory in self-government among free men at home, it was seen as such a corollary on the world scene. Was the American capitalist attitude toward Samoa or China or Latin America thus no different from that of European capitalist countries? In two respects it was substantially different. Americans, like Europeans, liked to sell goods abroad. But Americans, unlike Europeans, only very reluctantly accepted political sovereignty and control over territories abroad, and much more generally supported the antithesis of this, namely self-government around the globe. And Americans, unlike Europeans, like to feel that their success at selling products abroad had run the gauntlet of the tests of competition, i.e., that such sales really reflected the consumer wishes of the buyers, rather than some artificial import restrictions that had been imposed at the point of a gun.

Revisionist interpretations of post–World War II American foreign policy tend to make a great deal of Henry Luce's American Century formulation, quite rightly assuming that the influence or representativeness of the views expressed in his publications was very great. Yet one has to be careful to be precise about what Luce and people of similar views about the postwar world were looking forward to with such zest. If one reads the statements in detail, it assuredly was not simple power in the sense of earlier hegemonies, with the conduct of human affairs being dictated to the globe by the enforcement of naked military or economic power, as in the days of Pax Romana or Pax Brittanica. Rather it was still the power of the American example. Americans expected that the very success they had experienced at home would be attractive to all the world, that nations all around the world, freed from traditional bonds by the sheer chaos of World War II, would now want to adopt the American model for themselves.

This was to be the American Century, in that the world found happiness for itself, from China to Europe to Africa, by doing things as Americans had done them, as Americans had found happiness for themselves.

HAVE AMERICANS BEEN IDEOLOGICAL?

It may well be that most Americans would not have been capable of articulating such assumptions, but this hardly proves that they were not operational over all the years from 1776 to 1967. Rather the lack of articulation may simply prove how strong they were as the heart of American foreign policy consensus.

De Tocqueville[6] and Louis Hartz have not been the only observers to note how the axiomatic and unchallenged propositions of agreement in American life sometimes have had the deepest hold on the people because they grip subliminally, because we are not even aware of the alternative propositions that would bring the tenets held into relief. One of the best statements of the case here is still to be found in Hartz's *The Liberal Tradition in America.*[7] Hartz notes how physical remoteness from Europe and the special nature of American frontier society produced a political system and political culture almost totally dominated by Lockean ideas, so much that they perhaps never need to be explicated, but are implicitly so widely accepted as almost to implant a straitjacket on American thought. Not having to struggle against the remnants of aristocratic privilege, Americans in effect took for granted their own political system, with which they were largely satisfied.

Being used to being content with their own political status quo, Americans then developed the habit of seeing themselves as the model for the outside world, but did not get any practice at being revolutionary with regard to their own society. In effect they missed the internal turmoil and disagreement about the proper ends of society that could bring their ideas to the surface, which would have prepared them for the possibility that other societies would pass by and reject the American example.

A theory that wins a wide following may thus become so strong that it does not need to be articulated. One might indeed discover that some of the strongest beliefs in a society are those which no one can bring to the surface. It is disagreement about issues that brings them into the open, as debate forces each side to be as articulate and openly persuasive as possible. When there is no disagreement and debate, when a society is largely united in endorsing a set of beliefs, the risk emerges that these beliefs will never be voiced openly, simply because they do not need to be.

Have we thus in effect been arguing that American foreign policy has been heavily ideological? In effect we have, although at least a few definitional questions would first have to be addressed. Some readers would reject a notion of "ideology" that referred simply to any deep feelings about right and wrong in the world, to any desire to try to increase happiness abroad. Rather they would save the label for the special character of the Fascist and Marxist states, in having a monolithic state-controlled treatment of the issues of political values, and also of descriptions of political possibilities. Such states artificially inculcate a catechism in young and old by tolerating no dissenting views, by applying the punishment of state reprisals against anyone who voices or prints a contrary statement of values or possibilities.[8]

By ideology, therefore, do we mean only a governmentally shaped consensus, or might we be referring to any consensus whatsoever, no matter how it is achieved and shaped? Does an ideology have to include a carefully theorized and structured set of values, or are we going to use the label to apply to any set of values?

If we were limiting the issue to government shaping of values, the comparison of the United States to the "ideological" Soviet Union would seem open and shut. One can illustrate this easily enough with a look at Soviet and American behavior at the unofficial "Pugwash" conferences that draw together delegations of disarmament experts from the USSR and the United States and other nations around the globe. It is typical at such conferences for members of the American delegation to disagree openly and vehemently among themselves, often assaulting the U.S. government, while the Soviet "unofficial" delegation will maintain a totally monolithic unity and calm about its statements of views, with never a criticism of the Soviet regime. If one wished to prove that the U.S. government somehow still had "control" over the American delegates here, the proof would be extremely difficult; only a theory of the most subtle and subliminal mind-control and brainwashing propaganda would suffice to support the idea that the U.S. government manages the shape of the ideas and values being expressed.

On the issue of the theoretical clarity and articulation of the national set of values, the contrast between the United States and the societies normally styled "ideological" is also stark. One knows where to find a specific statement of Soviet Marxist belief; by contrast, American efforts to encapsulate and articulate any statements of national purpose have typically come to be seen as an arid and useless exercise, settling into either the platitudinous or the controversial, in effect an "un-American" exercise.[9]

Yet it is not only state-managed, or well-articulated, sets of values that motivate men, that can steer them into foreign policies which are other than selfishly motivated by power-lust and economic need. And it is not only such artificially managed values that become inflexible, or develop a sense of shock and deep disturbance when challenged. A world view that wins as wide a following as that of the Lockean view in the United States may become so strong that it does not need to be articulated. If it is disagreement about an issue that brings it into the open, the basic consensus held in the United States was powerful precisely because no one ever thought that it needed to be articulated. Would Cuba or Burma or Bavaria be better off with contested elections? The American answer in 1880 or 1940 might have been automatic; but was it still so in 1980?

The United States is thus not ideological in the same sense as 1941 Nazi Germany, or 1981 Soviet Union or China, but there may be other meaningful senses in which it is indeed ideological, going back again to the high degree of consensus noted by Hartz, a consensus based heavily upon a shared experience that omitted many of the challenges to consensus.

When most individuals agree very totally on an issue (such as on the importance of free press even where it conflicts with economic equality), there may thereafter be sociological pressures at work making it extraordinarily difficult for any such individuals to suggest an opposite preference. Americans may therefore be unusually prone to groupthink in their schools, in their governmental decision-making processes, being conformist in a manner that involves little if any state manipulation and direction.

SOME TENSIONS FOR THE AMERICAN MODEL

How does one then want to summarize the American "ideology" here, the American outlook on world affairs? At the heart has been a stress on voluntarism, on "fair exchange is no robbery," on the social contract and the free exchange of agreements as presented in the Lockean model.

There is no denying that this world view is very well suited to capitalism. The major question may rather be which shapes which. The Lockean belief in free exchange historically of course predates the onset of capitalism in the United States and in the world, and it is more all-encompassing. Despite the Marxist view that all of this merely serves as rationalization and window dressing for capitalism as an economic system, it is likely that the American ideological world view is real here, with a life of its own.

Is there indeed such an inherent tension between political democracy and economic democracy—between free elections, freedom of speech, freedom of the press on one side—and an even sharing of wealth on the other? Much of the third world today would conclude that there is a tension, such that contested elections and freedom of the press have to be sacrificed in the pursuit of greater economic equality. "A free press is only a vehicle of the vested interests" would be one way that such a tension is often enough described, or "men cannot appreciate liberty unless they have enough to eat."[10]

The example of Sweden and the rest of Scandinavia would of course suggest the opposite, as democratic socialism amounts to an actual rather than theoretical synthesis, and free elections and continued freedom of debate coexist with a substantial sharing of material wealth. The recent concessions to liberal values voiced by West European Communist Parties in Eurocommunism suggest much the same thing. (Such concessions may simply be campaign propaganda, of course, to be ignored once the Communists won power in a free election. Yet they may instead reflect a genuine dismay with the human price paid in the USSR and Eastern Europe when free elections and free press and human rights in general were sacrificed as well as a concession to the success of the Scandinavian and West European experience.)

On the more pessimistic side of whether there is a tension here, Americans of a more right-wing persuasion sometimes come to conclusions similar to those voiced by more orthodox Communists and by many of the regimes of the third world that economic leveling cannot be compatible with individual liberties; in face of such need for choice, of course, such Americans endorse exactly this opposite priority from that of the Marxists. Friedrich Hayek may only have been stating such beliefs more starkly in *The Road to Serfdom*,[11] but some Americans indeed believe that a "free market of ideas" necessarily requires, as a prerequisite, a free market in the economic sector as well. Government regulation of industry and government taxation for the purposes of income redistribution, in this view, thus enlarge the power of the state enough to set the stage for dictatorship.

Most Americans however would not share the pessimistic perceptions of Hayek or Goldwater (or Castro or Kim Il-sung). Remembering the New Deal and the welfare state as generally positive accomplishments, they might continue to nourish the hope for themselves that a substantial degree of economic sharing can indeed be achieved without requiring any compromises first in the political system of free elections. Such Americans would point to Scandinavia and India in the outside world as examples that such a synthesis can indeed be achieved (although the disquieting thought then obviously emerges that multiparty democracies are difficult to find among the developing countries of the world, once one has gone beyond India).[12]

The arguments pointing to inherent tensions between economic democracy and political democracy are of course at least somewhat correct. Political democracy requires that we limit the power of the state, lest state power in the end be used to corrupt the very processes of elections and free debate that are the ultimate check on that power. Economic democracy, by contrast, relies on state power to redistribute wealth from those who have much of it to those who need it more.

Americans, through their history, have not been antiequality, often indeed achieving far more economic and social equality than the European states with which the United States was most readily compared. Yet they have not been consciously or deliberately pro-equality either. Rather, they have put individual freedom first, hoping that the material results would then be good all around.

Political democracy in the American model has not implied a guarantee of success, but rather a guarantee of the right to compete. Full-fledged socialism intends to put a material floor under things so that no one need "fail." Competition implies failure, as wrong ideas fail to win adherents, as businesses that do not suit consumer preferences go bankrupt, as incumbents fail to win reelection.

By many yardsticks, the United States might then still claim to be among the freest nations in the world, in the freedom given its press to ferret secrets out of the government, in the absence of threats of military takeover, in its intuitive sense that any government must face the check of seeking reelection. The United States may also be the most capitalist nation in the world. The important questions throughout are: "which requires which?" and "which leads to which?" If capitalism and a tendency toward economic inequality did not have to precede political democracy chronologically, are they still somehow logically necessitated by it? Are we only free because we have chosen to be capitalist? Or are we importantly capitalist because we have chosen to be free?

Despite its lack of explicit commitment to equality, the United States, like Sweden (clearly unlike India and most of the developing countries), has generally been a very successful place in material terms, so that the spin-offs and by-products of an individualistic system have still perhaps not been too bleak for those who "failed." Even if the tension between fuller economic equality and political freedom were to become more stark, most Americans would still long continue to opt for the latter, at least for the United States; life would have to become far more materially bleak, the pain of economic inequality would have to become far greater, before compromises of the election system and of press freedom began to look appropriate.

Yet how much of such an American preference remains in effect with regard to the outside world? Americans might continue to assume that political democracy takes priority in Scandinavia and Germany and France and Great Britain, but will they maintain this feeling for the rest of the world? Will they write off much of the rest of the world now as suited more to putting economic democracy first, as materially or culturally unsuited to political democracy?

BOUNDARY DISPUTES: SOME
LIMITS TO GENEROSITY?

Americans thus until very recently did not distrust their own motives in foreign policy. Yet radicals and realpolitik analysts might unite in regarding this as hypocrisy and distortion of history. If altruism explains some of American interventionism, we cannot forget that the United States has often been accused of pursuing a very *selfish* interventionism. Surely we could not claim that all of American foreign policy has been designed with a view to the happiness of foreigners.

The image of the United States as just as power-minded and expansion-minded as any of the traditional European regimes might seemingly be supported by the constant interest through the nineteenth century in annexing and absorbing Canada. Already during the American Revolution, and then in the War of 1812, and then throughout the rest of the century, American congressmen and newspaper editors, and the public at large, seemed not at all reticent about the prospect of taking over the huge territories to the north.[13]

Yet there is still some difference here. A large fraction of such sentiment seems at all times to have been based on the assumption, implicit or often explicit, that Canadians would want such a merger, i.e., would want to be freed from what was viewed as the colonial rule of London. Much of this was of course superficial, as Americans were influenced too much here by the formalities of constitutional structure (even in 1980, of course, Canada still did not have a constitution of its own, but was obliged to go to the British Parliament to redraw what it had) and not enough by the realities. Periodic unrest within Canada, and periodic linkages to unrest in Ireland via the workings of the Fenian movement, served to convince more Americans that there might be human value in a liberation of Canada.

What is fascinating is that all of this receded fairly abruptly at precisely the moment when United States military power indeed suddenly blossomed. After 1898, the British "deterrent" of bringing the Royal Navy against the coastal cities of the United States would no longer be nearly as intimidating[14]; in the years when the United States suddenly looked quite imperialistic in the Caribbean and the Philippines, the demands for a takeover of Canada markedly abated.

Those indicting the United States of inexorable predilections toward expansion might thus simply argue that the Philippines diverted Americans from their hungers for the north. A more persuasive case, however, would be that events within Canada had by the turn of the century at last convincingly showed that Canadians themselves wanted things as they were. Canada, for example, now finally took over its own diplomatic relations with the United States, and then moved to take all the rest of its foreign affairs; matching these important surface symptoms, Canada in every other respect now became a plausibly self-governing political democracy on its own.

A considerably less altruistic model might have to be applied to American nineteenth-century dealings with Mexico, where large pieces of territory were indeed absorbed by the United States between 1845 and 1850, at no benefit to the neighbor to the south. Could anyone argue that American expansionism here was intended to achieve self-government for an oppressed population, to respond to the felt needs of persons desiring political democracy and liberation?[15]

In a sense the answer is no, and in another sense it might be yes. The lands taken in the Mexican War were extraordinarily thin in population, and most of this population consisted of American Indians, about whom more must be said below.

Given such a small population base, an issue of self-determination for people in place at the present might always be overshadowed by the character of the potential migration of new people moving in. One such migration of English-speaking Americans had occurred in Texas, and another was due for California as soon as gold was discovered.

The United States may thus indeed always be ready to defend by force the privileges and the self-determination of any large number of its own citizens who settle into relatively empty lands abroad. In a situation of open and empty frontier spaces, this made the United States not so very different from British attitudes toward the Boer republics, or Russian attitudes toward Siberia. Yet this "frontier," as Europe pushed out into empty spaces over a period of three centuries, was very much of a special case for all of mankind. After the

Gadsden Purchase of 1853, or at least after the acquisition of Alaska and Hawaii, the United States then basically ceased to be expansionist in this sense, i.e., ceased to be involved in territorial spaces within which self-determination might be ignored because there were too few people there at the start to provide a "self" to be determined.

Far less altruistic still would have to be the attitudes of the United States toward the native American Indians with which it had to deal, whose land it basically seized all across the continent. If anything can be styled as racist, the attitudes of whites toward these Indians surely can, treating them as inherently incapable of civilized political activity or membership in the diplomatic community of nations, considering their lands as open for conquest by anyone prepared to make more extensive use of them.

Yet how much did this have to bend out of shape the idealism and liberalism of the Americans who had won their independence from Britain?[16] While most of the pioneers would have shown how "zero-sum" the conflict was by suggesting that there were too many Indians, that the right answer was "the fewer the better," the simple geopolitical fact was there were *too few* Indians, too few to force Americans to see any glaring contradictions or gaps in their attitudes toward all mankind, too few to make Americans view the North American continent as anything but empty land. A larger Indian population north of the Rio Grande after 1776 would have forced the United States to treat them more seriously as a political entity, just as it was ultimately to treat Mexico. It would have made it unthinkable that the lands west of the Appalachians would simply be seen as empty, as unaffected by anyone's preexisting land title, as demanding cultivation and exploitation by some higher natural law, after having been wasted or never been put to use.

As an indicator of the strength of the basic liberal republicanism of the American population, one should not forget that the move into an explicit and visible imperialism in the 1890s was confronted with a strong and open opposition. The takeover of the Philippines in the Spanish-American War in particular produced the formation of an Anti-Imperialist League, mustering some very prominent and respectable names from American politics, and the 1900 presidential campaign then saw Democratic candidate William Jennings Bryan base much of his campaign on a broader opposition to such imperialism.[17]

The fact that Bryan lost to McKinley in 1900 does not prove that this campaign strategy was badly taken, but rather shows a wider voter distrust of Bryan stemming from his "free silver" stand in 1896. The antiimperialist argument was very straightforward and very well linked to American sentiments in general. Either the United States should absorb the Philippines fully into the domestic arena of the United States, or it should avoid exercising authority over them altogether. "Does the Constitution follow the flag" was one way in which the argument was put. Could it be that the United States would govern territories in which the guarantees of the Bill of Rights and of the Fourteenth Amendment and of "republican government" did not apply? If such a precedent were even established, would this not be the beginning of undermining the sanctity of these constitutional principles at home?

In effect this was a blend of altruistic and selfish arguments for isolation, or at least for a different form of intervention from what the country might now seem to be adopting. The United States should avoid extending its authority into faraway islands because this might undermine democracy at home; to have military governors ruling people, against their will, might give such governors similar appetites with regard to the process in Washington. Or one should at least guarantee self-government for Filipinos because it was necessary for their happiness and well-being. A final touch of racism was then to be added by suggesting that the constitutionally logical form of takeover of the Philippines would have to be ultimate statehood, with the obviously unacceptable prospect thereafter of having some 10 or 15 million ethnically alien people claiming their fair share of votes in the House of Representatives.

One can of course argue that this still shows an excessive fixation on the American side with the issues of political representation, with a concomitant insensitivity to economic issues. Americans opposing the takeover of the Philippines in 1900 were mostly afraid of a display of arrogant political power comparable to what the British had tried to inflict on the 13 colonies before 1776, what the British and all other Europeans now seemed inclined to impose on the peoples of Asia and the Pacific. What was to be defended as an alternative, in the view of the antiimperialists and probably of most Americans, was self-government, "no taxation without representation." Of far less concern to any Americans here was whether some sort of capitalist takeover of markets was going to happen in the wake of the Spanish-American War, whether the entry of American entrepreneurs into the Philippines (either under American rule or under local Filipino rule) was going to produce some kind of new exploitation of the Asians and disruption of their traditional life-styles.

If one concluded that economics comes ahead of politics here, that economic democracy was somehow more important than, or prior to, political democracy, he would then have to conclude that the 1900 American opponents to any power-oriented imperialism were just as blind to (and as menacing to) the happiness of the world as the proponents of such imperialism. We will come back to discuss this possibility at greater length. Yet we may not have to accept this premise now or then. Was not political self-government and political democracy a great deal of what the issue has been about all along in life, or at least for very much of the time until the present? Would not the Vietnamese in 1900 have very much liked to be allowed to choose their own governors and policemen, rather than having them chosen simply in Paris?

The Americans who favored the takeover in the Philippines thus accompanied this with a promise that political self-government would be the ultimate goal, a promise that in 1899 had no equivalent in British statements about India, or French statements about Africa and Indochina, or German statements about Tanganyika. One can always question the sincerity of statements of this kind, but in the American case the promise to the Philippines was kept. The promise was not designed to gull Filipinos into accepting American rule, for indeed they did not accept it until defeated in a guerrilla war. Rather, more importantly, the promise was needed because *Americans* would not have sanctioned their country's takeover of the Philippines without it.

Frenchmen in 1900 did not ask their government for reassurance that their stay in the Congo was to be limited to a finite period of time; quite the contrary. But Americans in 1899 demanded that the conquest of the Philippines be defined as temporary from the start, and McKinley might not have defeated Bryan in 1900 if such a promise had not been given.

This is hardly to claim that the United States has not taken land in its history in a desire for permanent possession. California and Alaska and Hawaii were acquired to be held forever. The crucial variable here, as in the Philippines, was whether sovereignty could be extended without compromising republican government, without endangering political democracy at home, without denying it to someone abroad.

The process by which the United States filled out its contemporary borders may thus not at all disprove the claim that altruistic interventionism has been a dominant theme in American foreign policy. No one would claim that Americans are totally generous, putting the happiness of others ahead of their own at every moment of choice. Rather the claim would be that Americans have been unusually generous as a people, unusually concerned for the happiness of others, convinced that self-government and political democracy are crucial to such happiness, reluctant to expand in terms of political sovereignty where it would compromise such self-government.

And what is left today of the issues of the territorial extent of U.S. sovereignty? Very little, although the few cases that might arise could easily attract enough attention to produce a very misleading interpretation of American foreign policy as a whole. The territorial extent of the United States is basically a "domestic" question, after all, as well as a "foreign policy" question, and domestic issues have always, by their very nature, tended to capture more attention than issues of foreign policy.

Readers contemplating the amazing degree of American upset, after 1976, with the prospect of returning the Panama Canal Zone to Panama might thus wonder whether the altruistic picture of American foreign policy interests is all that plausible.[18] Yet the Panama Canal Zone question may be impressive precisely because it was enormously atypical of all the rest of foreign policy issues.

Whatever one would claim about American economic or social or political imperialism after 1890, the taking of political possession of the Canal Zone amounted to something different, something more, in that the United States felt a physical need to control the zone, and virtually to make it a part of the country. One does not have to get into complicated theories of economic imperialism at all here. The military explanation is obvious; who could conceive of a more strategically significant naval base than the banks of an interoceanic canal?

Yet the result was that the Canal Zone came to be seen as almost as much a part of the United States as San Diego or El Paso (not quite, because the euphemism was adopted of a "lease in perpetuity," with separate postage stamps, and so forth). The dramatic contrast between the spic-and-span U.S. atmosphere of the zone and the more typically Latin atmosphere of Panama itself was indeed altogether too reminiscent of the contrast between San Diego and Tijuana, or El Paso and Juárez.

If an orderly return of the Canal Zone to Panama had not been achieved, this would have amounted to a made-to-order issue for the most anti-American point of view in Latin America. As will be discussed further below, all the other sorts of American imperialism may be so subtle and debatable that an indictment of the United States is always less clear than it could be. Where the United States in this special case, for special reasons, however, chose to explicate its expansionism, to make it obvious with flags and demarcated boundaries, the picture was made all too clear.

Yet the very facts that make the Panama issue unusually useful

power of the segments of that country, making it easier for American producers to sell their wares.

Again, the naive American view about what is good for men and women in general takes some precedence over a selfish American view. Americans regard it as foolish and wrong and unnatural that anyone should string a customs barrier along the Quebec-Ontario frontier, just as they would probably think it foolish and wrong today if Germany and France should reerect customs barriers against each other. Free trade among Canadians helps all Canadians, so the logic would run; to intrigue to erect barriers against such trade is altogether against the American character.

THE UNITED STATES IN COMPARISON WITH EUROPE

We might come back at least one more time to cross-examine whether the United States has indeed been so *unusually* generous.[20] Could not other nations also claim to have been generous when they went out into the world? Could the assumption of American uniqueness here be an enormous delusion on the part of this author, and of most Americans?

The "white man's burden" was stated by Europeans (with not a few Americans agreeing) as a sort of noblesse oblige, whereby Africans and Asians incapable of governing themselves were uplifted by having a civilizing European regime imposed upon them. The French spoke of the "mission civilisatrice," and most countries sent out missionaries just as the United States did. Protestant denominations in the United States and Great Britain indeed went so far as to partition the world in terms of where each would concentrate its efforts, with the bulk of American Protestant missionary work going to China, while the bulk of the British went to India, with obvious implications for where future streams of identification would flow.[21]

It would be futile to deny that much or most of the European missionary effort was basically altruistic in nature, even if some of it also turned out to be venal.

Beyond the field of religious work, moreover, Frenchmen similarly felt that they had some genuinely beneficial work in converting black Africans into duplicate Frenchmen. To this day, the view in Paris is that one has truly accomplished something uplifting (and happiness-producing) when a Vietnamese or Senegalese or Tahitian has become fluent in the French language. One could thus try to portray French attitudes about culture as being exactly parallel to

American attitudes about political democracy. "If free elections work in Minnesota, why shouldn't they work to make people happier anywhere else" would have been the American attitude. "If the French language leads to the highest levels of precision of thought in Paris, why shouldn't it do the same everywhere else?" might have been the equivalent attitude in France. If this is all that the exercise of overseas influence had consisted of, we might seem to have an unresolvable debate as to whether either side was less generous than the other.

Each side could indeed be accused of simply making life more pleasant for itself by creating more travel space in which it can move with all the comforts of home. Americans might care about freedom of the press in India, just so that they can more easily keep up with the news while they are visiting there, or so that Indian friends will be less fearful of meeting with them. Frenchmen will care about the survival of the language in Gabon or Vietnam so that there will be more people to talk to, and so forth.

It is time then to state an American case why United States foreign policy indeed deserves to be remembered as more generous than the colonial policies of Europe. The American stress on political democracy, instead of ethnic culture, makes for other differences which in the end will probably justify this conclusion.

By assuming a cultural standard and the "white man's burden," European imperialism, even when honestly altruistic, seized a totality of political power, indeed with no long-term intention of ever surrendering it. Such power without the consent of the governed might to many eyes be an atrocity in its own right, but it was moreover to be coupled with periods of economic seizure no better than the American institution of slavery. By contrast, the general American stress was on hoping for the self-governance of overseas areas, with American economic investment being allowed under a rubric of free exchange.

Trading on a voluntary basis might strike anthropologists as just as disruptive in retrospect as the institutions of forced labor imposed when Europeans had assumed total sovereignty. Marxist and other critics of capitalism would similarly contend that Ecuador was no different from the Congo, in the degree to which foreign presence had produced economic exploitation.

Yet memories can mislead here, and ideological analysis can mislead even more. The difference between being forced to work on a railroad and being economically seduced into that work by the prospect of earning cash to buy the goods brought in by Yankee traders is not as trivial as contemporary accounts would have it. It was not trivial psychologically and politically, and it was not trivial in terms of the minimum conditions of material and physical well-being that could be won by the worker.

It is easy to demonstrate that the European colonies did not really amount to the safety-valve dumping grounds of excessive capitalist production the Marxist analysis often describes. The bulk of German trade before World War I did not go to German colonies, but to places like Great Britain and the United States. If World War I was in part the outgrowth of a competition for colonies, it was not really because the advanced capitalist economies of Europe and North America had been driven into some sort of zero-sum competition for markets, but rather because the ethnic nationalism of states on the European continent had become very attached to "places in the sun."

One can also demonstrate that most of the colonies did not even render a straightforward profit. Such "profit" would have nothing to do with capitalism and unemployment and an alleged need for markets, but rather would be a reflection of old-fashioned greed, the kind of thing that had—long before capitalism—pulled Spaniards out in search of gold and Portuguese in search of spices.

Yet a few of the European colonies did make a profit, and (an important point) most of them were expected to. Herein lies an important difference. The United States, in staying away from an assumption of sovereignty over Venezuela or Samoa or Shantung, would allow its traders to seek profits on a laissez-faire basis where they could find them. If no profits were to be had in the process of voluntary trade and exchange, the Yankee ships would simply have to sail elsewhere. The Germans or British or French, in assuming sovereignty over an area, would instead feel saddled with the costs of governing the area, and would be naturally tempted then to extract a profit, by the force of state power if necessary. If the native population was not disposed to work voluntarily at the projects needed to pay the bills of the civilizing regime, they could be forced to do so by compulsory labor.[22]

In the long run, the more civilized instincts of European opinion at home might catch up with such practices. Such opinion clearly went to work in the British and German colonial experiences earlier than in the Portuguese. Yet one should not exaggerate the numbers of Frenchmen or British or Germans or Italians who truly cared about the well-being of the populations they were subduing; and one should especially not exaggerate the quality of the policy they produced.

Simple nostalgia, which makes things in the past look better than they really were, may today prompt some "old-timers" in former colonies to speak fondly of the days of British or French or Japanese rule, or even of distant days of German or Spanish rule. In actual fact, such colonies were characterized by alternating waves of cruel exploitation and reactive reform, periods in which the native population was treated very badly in terms of health and education and compulsory labor, followed by periods of profound shock and guilt, and genuine improvement.

To assume that the U.S. economic impact on Latin America was just the same ("just as bad") as the Portuguese or French or Belgian impact on their segments of Africa may thus be as misleading as the analyses contending that the wage laborer of the northern states in 1860 was no better off than the slave in the South.

While some European colonial regimes were more willing to train the indigenous population in the techniques of government and public administration, others stayed as far as they could from this, the notable examples being the Belgians in the Congo, the French in Indochina, and the Dutch in Indonesia. The Afro-Asian world may be tired of hearing Americans pat themselves on the back for the way the Philippines were treated,[23] and recent developments in the Philippines provide a powerful argument for those who are becoming disillusioned about the advantages of political democracy for countries outside the West. Yet the Philippines clearly were handled very differently from Indonesia; and Cuba and Latin America and Liberia, for all the American failings, were handled still more differently.

A gap between the European colonial experience and the American remains. It is the kind of gap that Americans, by their own ideology, Lockean ideology, tend to make a great deal of. It is the kind of gap that some Europeans would see as overstated in importance, and that a Marxist would pass off as having no significance at all. At its widest point, however, the gap is as wide as the difference between coercion and negotiation, between "slavery" and "labor."

THE GLOBAL PERSPECTIVE

Leaving aside the more narrow comparisons of American and European attitudes toward the assumption of colonial sovereignty, toward the projection of ethnic or political culture abroad, what about the broader interpretations of the American experience by foreign observers over the years since 1776? How much do they confirm or disprove the complimentary assessments we might make of the American world role?

For some eighteenth- and nineteenth-century Europeans, the United States was the ideal model, free of castles and hereditary nobility, a land of political equality and of concomitant economic opportunity, indeed (without any particular effort to be so) a land of greater equality in economic accomplishment. At times based on direct observation, at other times based on naive and uninformed idealistic abstraction, such a European picture of the United States as the model for the future conforms very nicely with our general picture of the United States as a political democracy confronting tradition-bound Europe as a revolutionary alternative.[24]

Other Europeans, however, rather found America to be an ugly place of bad manners and shallow pursuit of material gain, a place lacking culture, and tradition and perspective.

Not surprisingly, those who migrated to the United States tended to be more positive, while those who never considered such migration tended to be more critical. Analysts of a more idealistic or theoretical bent in Europe might be more prone to admire the American model as they saw it, while those who were more pragmatic (more contented with the status quo and more skeptical of moves to make major changes in it) were more inclined to dislike the United States.

Turning to foreign policy, many European observers surely saw the United States precisely as Morgenthau and the realists look at it, as having all along been just as power-oriented and greedy and self-serving as any other state. Americans were seen as tiresome for their preaching and posturing (much as Americans might see Indians or Canadians or Swedes today), pretending to be more moral, fooling themselves in a hypocritical way.

Yet again, some other observers saw U.S. foreign policy indeed as something different and special, less imperialistic, more inclined to help the underdog, less inclined to military expenditures and military adventures. The European statesmen and newspaper editors who rooted for Spain in the Spanish-American War, insisting that the United States was acting from motives no more noble than those of any other power, were typically people very much identified with the European status quo. To be satisfied with Europe was naturally to brush off suggestions that the United States was succeeding at being something different. It was perhaps necessary to be less complacent and more critical of Europe, if one wished to have a fairer and more open-minded interpretation of the United States.

Interpretations of the U.S. Civil War provide some examples here. Many European editors and statesmen and military officers tended to regard the Union and Confederate armies as two incompetent rabbles, offering no lessons to be applied to the future battlefields of

Europe. Relatively fewer, more objective, European military officers saw things differently, saw two of the world's most modern military forces grappling with each other, with lessons about future applications of battlefield firepower that would have to be relearned on the Marne and in Flanders 50 years later.

"Democracy" is almost a universal term of praise today, with the two major contenders for world power debating which has the better claim on title, the Marxists with their "economic democracy" or the West with its "political democracy." It is easy to forget how much this was a term of criticism and derision in the nineteenth century, with Europeans often condemning the United States for its excessive democracy, its lack of respect for rank and title and merit, its desire to lower all decisions to the common sense of the common man.

Time has thus surely come out on the side of the United States on this fundamental question of language, for the European criticism that the United States is "too democratic" has very much been overtaken by events. Even if East German spokesmen might still stuffily criticize Americans for a lack of manners (along with a lack of effective health insurance), the German Democratic Republic would never today phrase this criticism of the United States as having "too much democracy."

Yet there would be pitfalls in having Americans rejoice too much about their vindication by history here. If the European ciriticisms of the nineteenth century in effect demonstrate that the United States was as progressive and forward-looking as it would like to remember itself, such a record of past rectitude can lead to a resting on laurels, and it can easily enough then lead to the United States being charged with being wrong for the present and in the future.

The world today would no longer blame the Americans of 1810 or 1870 for scoffing at heredity as a standard for assigning posts in society. It might however have decided that "liberal" or "bourgeois" democracy is the wrong form to settle into, in the move away from hereditary ascriptive political systems; perhaps the United States, in having freed itself of the grasp of such hereditary systems earlier, had lost the momentum for going further.

Some Americans could of course respond with some feeling that liberal political democracy was indeed the right form to settle into, that the "further momentum" being advocated is a momentum back into systems that would again repress the individual.

A most significant question about the evolution of American foreign policy will thus emerge from the ways in which foreign countries have treated the American model through history, and the ways in which Americans have interpreted such foreign treatment. Has the

"American way" of free elections and republican government been accepted or rejected as other countries had a choice to make? Have any of the rejections through history come in a form that would upset and undermine American self-confidence?

The French Revolution of 1789 followed close enough to the American achievement of independence to conjure up an obvious analogy for observers on either side of the Atlantic; the United States ambassador in Paris was indeed the only diplomat not voicing disapproval of the termination of the monarchy.[25] Yet the French Revolution then soon shifted away from the liberal democracy of the United States to a regime which (already in the eighteenth century, a precursor of tensions to arise two centuries later) placed more stress on economic equality and less on political liberty.

If such a "revolutionary trend" was likely to cast Americans into doubt about the validity of their own political model, tensions were eased soon enough when French dictatorship became more obvious; with the ultimate succession of Napoleon to power, the French political system for American eyes ceased to look markedly different from the more "legitimate" regimes to which it was opposed, becoming an empire like other empires, even at the end seeking legitimacy in Napoleon's second marriage to an Austrian princess.

The final defeat of Napoleon, by European powers fearing his political subversion of the ancient regime, or his military penchant for continental hegemony, thus came well past the point at which Americans might have seen him as following the American example, or as somehow being revolutionary enough in his own right to constitute an alternative to the American way. Napoleon's defeat, just as a Napoleonic victory if it had occurred, thus amounted in American eyes to a victory of the resilient forces of the past, of governors independent of the consent of those they governed, of simple military force and raw national power. The American model was thus passed by for France and the rest of Europe, but Americans could easily enough reconstruct the history here so that this did not suggest any popular rejection of the American model; rather it was an overriding once again of the popular will by stronger political interests (of which even Napoleon was one, just as was the czar and Metternich and the other members of the coalition that had defeated Bonaparte).

The second revolution plausibly matching the American experience came then in 1804 in Haiti, at one time perhaps the most profitable of all the European colonies, as former slaves defeated the army of occupation that had been dispatched by Napoleon. Yet any American analogizing here, and any possibility of disillusionment with the subsequent chaos and tyranny that became endemic after Haitian independence, was easily muffled and complicated by American attitudes on slavery.[26] Americans who rationalized their tolerance of slavery, by concluding that blacks were inherently not suited for political self-government, could thus see Haiti as bearing this out, the special case of a special race, an example that could not have much to say about the relevance of the American model for Europe or for much of the rest of the globe.

The subsequent declarations of independence by Spanish possessions in Central or South America of course brought a very different response, as the Monroe Doctrine enunciated strong American support for the idea that such countries should not again be subjected to European rule. Even if preventing any European return to such countries fit a more "realistic" American (or more importantly, British) concept of balance of power, it for Americans was also accompanied by the expectation that similar achievements of political democracy might now be accomplished from Argentina to Mexico.

Disappointments followed here also, of a sort which in retrospect might have appropriately shaken American confidence in the validity of the model. While many of the Latin American countries seemed to go through the motions of trying to match the United States accomplishment, virtually all of them then experienced a series of military coups and dictatorships and overturnings of election results that the United States has completely escaped. Close analysts of the achievement of Latin American independence could have noted that independence from Spain had not been as much of a liberal cause as had been North American independence from Britain; some of it had indeed come as a conservative reaction to the liberalization that Napoleon's conquest had brought to the Spanish motherland.[27] Again, the delays and failures here could in the end have been fairly ascribed to the lingering powers of the past, as the Spanish colonial tradition had never been so parallel to the New England experience, so inclined to republican government or Lockean limitation of state power. Where liberal constitutions were overturned by juntas, citizens of the United States could simply conclude that political democracy had not yet been given a chance in Latin America, had not yet really been tried, surely had not been found to be inconsistent with the happiness or preferences of the people at large. The greater bulk of Americans would not yet have written off Latin America at all, but simply presumed that the smooth functioning of free elections and balanced legislatures and independent judiciaries would take a little more time before they would become effective and well established.

As noted, the European regimes of the nineteenth century had felt compelled to make at least a partial accommodation with the masses, rather than continuing, as Metternich had advocated, to reject all moves toward ethnic nationalism as well as toward political liberalism. How would Americans thus have viewed the new wave of political style in Europe after 1865 that seemed to place so much stress on language and culture and attached less significance to any full submission to elected government? An American interpreter of Bismarck or Napoleon III was again hardly required to see some new "wave of the future" here, proving wrong the wave projected from the American experience. Rather these European moves toward nationalism could be interpreted again as the dead hand of the past, staving off a while longer the natural urge of the people to have control over the government under which they lived.

While some Americans perhaps felt a desire to emulate the Europeans now in their stress on national dignity, the bulk of American opinion still could retain confidence in the appropriateness of the American model for application to Bavaria or Indochina or Samoa. The difference between the American annexation of the Philippines and the British takeover of Kenya was not trivial, as noted above.

And what of American interpretations of self-government in Asia? Where self-government could be maintained, in China or in Japan, the United States tended to favor it. If such self-government did not then fulfill our standards by including popular elections or freedom of expression, Americans could be forgiven for seeing this again simply as the workings of the past; centuries of Asian tradition could not be expected to be erased and eliminated overnight. The relatively rapid progress of the Japanese government toward a Western-style modernization, even for a time including movements toward a liberal political constitution, thus amounted to supporting evidence for the American hopes and expectations here. Hope that a similar modernizing movement would take hold in China were central not only to the efforts of American missionaries, but to the American public at large.[28] Until 1949, therefore, most Americans would not have concluded that the failures to adopt an American-style Lockean political system in China had stemmed from anything but the weight of the past. The future was still on the side of what we were supporting.

Even the emergence of Naziism and fascism between the two world wars could be interpreted this way, with its suppression of political freedoms, with its renewal (with even greater vehemence) of the ethnic grievances of the pre–World War I world. While some Americans and other commentators could worriedly see fascism as "the wave of the future," as a major new alternative to liberalism, it was easy for many others to see it simply as traditional rule in a new guise. Hitler was thus sometimes simply painted as the tool of the Junkers, as the territories he was demanding were certainly the same that the Prussians had sought in the past. Hitler, after all, spoke of the Third Reich. The failure of Japanese liberalism then led Japan to join in the Axis with Italy and Germany, but Tokyo's stress on imperial rule as the basis for loyalty to an expansionist foreign policy allowed Americans again to feel that they were hardly out of step with the times by being drawn into World War II.[29]

It is thus not really until the years after World War II, perhaps not until the Vietnam War, that Americans are suddenly confronted with the awful possibility that their system is being rejected by the future, rather than by the past. In Africa and Asia in general, and also now in larger portions of Latin America as well, one sees American ideas of political freedom being rejected because of grander and more modernistic visions of economic sharing, rather than because of older notions of tradition and hereditary privilege and genetic or cultural superiority.

The United States had found it easy to shrug off the rejections of its model from 1776 to 1967. Indeed, it could feel buffered by the "acceptances" of its model in Canada and Australia and New Zealand, and Scandinavia and Western Europe. The rejections culminating around 1967 were however of a new form, indeed shaking American confidence in the heart of its foreign policy.

NOTES

1. For examples of such interpretations from the years when they were subjected to much less question, see Samuel Flag Bemis, *A Short History of American Foreign Policy and Diplomacy* (New York: Holt, Rinehart and Winston, 1959), and William G. Carleton, *The Revolution in American Foreign Policy: Its Global Range* (New York: Random House, 1963).

2. See Jean-Baptiste Duroselle, *France and the United States* (Chicago: University of Chicago Press, 1976), pp. 33-41.

3. See Gordon Craig, "The United States and the European Balance," *Foreign Affairs* 55, no. 1 (October 1976): 187-98.

4. The general nature of the Progressive movement is analyzed in George Mowry, *Theodore Roosevelt and the Progressive Movement* (Madison: University of Wisconsin Press, 1946).

5. See Henry Luce, *The American Century* (New York: Farrar and Rinehart, 1941).

6. Alexis De Tocqueville, *Democracy in America* (New York: Harper & Row, 1966).

7. Louis Hartz, *The Liberal Tradition in America* (New York: Harvest Books, 1955).

8. A discussion of contending definitions of ideology can be found in Thomas Molnar, *The Two Faces of American Foreign Policy* (New York: Bobbs-Merrill, 1962).

9. As an example of a relatively unsuccessful effort, see President's Commission on National Goals, *Goals for Americans* (Englewood Cliffs: Prentice-Hall, 1960).

10. For a widely read example of what amounts to such a reversed statement of priority, see Frantz Fanon, *The Wretched of the Earth* (New York: Evergreen, 1968).

11. Friedrich Hayek, *The Road to Serfdom* (Chicago: University of Chicago Press, 1945).

12. A most widely read example can be found in W. W. Rostow, *The Stages of Economic Growth* (Cambridge: Cambridge University Press, 1960).

13. A history of American interest in absorbing Canada can be found in Edgar W. McInnis, *The Unguarded Frontier* (Garden City: Doubleday and Doran, 1942).

14. See Kenneth Bourne, *Britain and the Balance of Power in North America: 1815-1908* (Berkeley: University of California Press, 1967).

15. See Karl M. Schmitt, *Mexico and the United States, 1821-1973: Conflict and Coexistence* (New York: John Wiley, 1974), pp. 1-72 for a valuable discussion of the U.S.-Mexican territorial contest.

16. An overview of the significance of the native American Indian for the ideology of the United States as a republic is provided in Helen Hunt Jackson, *A Century of Dishonor* (Boston: Little, Brown, 1903).

17. E. Berkeley Tompkins, *Anti-Imperialism in the United States: The Great Debate 1890-1920* (Philadelphia: University of Pennsylvania Press, 1970).

18. The historical background for the issue of the return of the Panama Canal is presented in Walter LaFeber, *The Panama Canal: The Crisis in Historical Perspective* (New York: Oxford University Press, 1979).

19. The shortage of U.S. curiosity about Canada, as an issue irritating Canadians, is discussed in Livingston Merchant, ed., *Neighbors Taken for Granted* (New York: Praeger, 1966), especially pp. 148-55.

20. See Philip W. Quigg, *America The Dutiful* (New York: Simon and Schuster, 1971) for a somewhat parallel argument about the ties between American material success and generosity toward the outside world.

21. The division of missionary activity is outlined in Paul A. Varg, *Missionaries, Chinese and Diplomats* (Princeton: Princeton University Press, 1958).

22. For a survey of various periods of European imperialism, including its harsher aspects, see George H. Nadel and Perry Curtis, *Imperialism and Colonialism* (New York: Macmillan, 1964).

23. The record of American government of the Philippines is assessed in Salvador P. Lopez, "The Colonial Relationship," in *The United States and the Philippines*, ed. Frank H. Golay (Englewood Cliffs: Prentice-Hall, 1966), pp. 7-31.

24. See Halvdan Koht, *The American Spirit in Europe* (Philadelphia: University of Pennsylvania Press, 1949).

25. See Duroselle, *France and the United States*, p. 36.

26. American attitudes toward Haiti are analyzed in Ludwell Lee Montague, *Haiti and the United States* (Durham: Duke University Press, 1940).

27. The at times antiliberal nature of Latin American independence movements is described in J. Fred Rippy, *Latin America: A Modern History* (Ann Arbor: University of Michigan Press, 1958), pp. 178–81.

28. For the special American feelings on China and East Asia, see A. T. Steele, *The American People and China* (New York: McGraw-Hill, 1966), pp. 1–202.

29. The persistence through World War II of American self-confidence in being a force of the future, rather than of the past, is clearly illustrated in Thomas Cook and Malcolm Moos, *Power Through Purpose: The Realism of Idealism as a Basis for Foreign Policy* (Baltimore: Johns Hopkins University Press, 1954).

5

The United States Better than Other Countries, Continued: Some Ethnic Complications

The United States, secure on the North American continent, has attained an unusual degree of political and economic success, which would account for much of any generosity toward the outside world. Apart from such success, it has been distinctive also for being a "nation of immigrants," a nation owing its origins to other "mother" countries, origins which similarly would be reinforcing to sympathy and altruism. Yet here the pattern of generosity will become more complicated.

If Americans cared unusually much about the happiness and political freedom of foreign peoples, this might indeed suggest a great tribute to them as a people. Yet do they care equally about foreigners, or are there some about whom they care more, and others with whom they identify less? To be somewhat differentiated in the degree of altruism here would seem entirely human; but to be very much differentiated might lead soon enough to a charge of racism.

To care about free elections in which each man has a single vote is in many ways to endorse equality, even if this is more directly a desire for voluntarism, for government by the consent of the governed. But to be unevenly engaged in the support of such Minnesota-style government around the globe is to imply a *lack* of interest in equality. Why should free elections in Belgium be more important to Americans than free elections in the Congo? Is there some sort of an implication here that government by the consent of the governed is more important for white Europeans than for nonwhite Afro-Asians?

Could this even lead us to the travesty of subliminally regarding South Africa as a political democracy, because its elections remain untampered with, even when its votes are restricted only to the white minority? South African government interferences with press criticism, and repressions of critical statements even by white spokesmen, happily might serve to resolve the confusion for the American observer, as the regime would fail to pass muster as politically democratic by any definition. But the worrisome issue is whether Americans, but for such final transgressions, would have tended to see the Pretoria regime as republican, and as an electoral democracy.

How ethnically oriented or racist have Americans been through history? What has been the trend in such racism? How have the trends in American assignment of relative importance to ethnic factors compared with trends in Europe and elsewhere over the same periods of time? If Americans tell themselves that they have attached less significance to such factors over the years, that they adhered to a liberalism that rose above all this, has this been some sort of self-deluding hypocrisy, or is there something to it?

SLAVERY AND BLACK SELF-GOVERNMENT

It would be futile to argue that there have been no aspects of ethnic nationalism (or "racism," if you will) in American foreign policy. To the extent that the foreign policy of any country is guided by altruistic considerations, an important basis for this is the simple resemblance between one's self and the beneficiaries of one's help. An elementary finding of psychology is that one vicariously feels pain the most when seeing suffering in things that resemble one the most. Americans have a Society for the Prevention of Cruelty to Animals (SPCA) therefore, but none for vegetables, and the SPCA takes better care of mammals than of reptiles, and so forth.

Since the bulk of Americans have been of European origin, the identification with the long-term happiness of Europeans has thus understandably been great. Conversely, the mere fact that American society for its first 87 years included the institution of slavery would make it no surprise that the United States long did not particularly identify with the prospect of republican self-government for black Africa. It is ironic, however, that the United States eliminated this one most bizarre and peculiar commitment to ethnic nationalism—slavery—at just about the time that Europe was letting ethnic considerations become emphasized as a substitute for political democracy.

The institution of slavery in the southern United States is something that most Americans remember with shame, and about whose heritage they still worry. By making it possible for a black to be held in involuntary servitude, it established the possibility of legal differentiation on the basis of skin color in many other aspects of life. Can it be that Americans at the same moment tolerated slavery and expected that the American model could also apply to Africa, with governments being elected by the governed, with economic transactions being conducted on the indispensable basis of a voluntary consent by the two parties?

The complete answer here will have to be at least a little complicated. To begin, the United States had hardly been agreed on the legitimacy of slavery in its first 87 years. Slave states were paired off against states abolishing slavery and forbidding it. If one wants to make a great deal of the Lockean political tradition in the United States, it must be stressed that it comes through history least challenged and diluted in the Northeast and Middle West, while the South, as noted by Louis Hartz, by contrast produced the only serious American political theory of a very different sort.[1]

Americans were thus hardly united in support of slavery. The same abolitionist who wished to terminate slavery wished to endow black Americans with all the prerogatives of citizenship, and inferentially assumed that blacks anywhere on this globe could benefit from the same form of rule as had conduced to happiness for whites in North America. If someone was assuming that the state constitution of Minnesota could usefully be adopted in Bavaria (an assumption most Americans would subliminally have accepted in 1860), the abolitionists would have sensed the same to be true for any black state in Africa as well.[2] The Emancipation Proclamation in 1863 merely terminated slavery in a part of the United States, but the Thirteenth, Fourteenth, and Fifteenth Amendments were intended to erase any and all legal distinction based on race that had existed anywhere in the United States.

One would of course greatly distort reality by breaking Americans into the two camps of slavery supporters (who saw no value in self-government for blacks anywhere) and abolitionists (who might have favored self-government for Africans just as much as for Latin Americans or Europeans). While the majority of northerners opposed slavery, a great many probably also took its historical existence as plausible evidence that blacks were somehow lower in political and economic potential, so that whatever vicarious zeal could be shown for a revolution in Germany or France would not be as likely to appear for resistance to European encroachments in Africa.

The Americans who mattered in the North were of course of European stock, and were likely to project the relevance of the American model first and foremost to those who resembled themselves physically and culturally. By these standards, China and Samoa might thus merit concern well before any particular regime on the African continent would even be noticed.

Yet again some other factors intrude. What in the end made the United States so slow to take an interest in the decolonization of Africa? Was it a racism of Americans that led them to see blacks as less relevant to American standards; or was it the lateness of the African decolonization process (indeed the lateness of the colonization itself)?

Throughout its history the United States has looked forward to the achievement of republican self-government in other states. In some cases, this seemed to follow soon after the American experience, while in others it seemed to approach very slowly.

As noted, the United States government and people tended to adopt a posture of moderate encouragement for revolution rather than active political or military intervention where a traditional regime had not yet been toppled. The attitude of Americans and their government became altogether more vehement, however, once such a traditional regime had indeed been deposed, and a fragile new regime of political democracy installed. At this point, as with Latin America and the Monroe Doctrine, great tensions have then arisen on whether the old regime would seek to try to return to reimplace itself; at this point, the willingness of the United States to use political or military force has been all the more manifest.

It is thus perhaps easy to understand why Africa captured less American attention and involvement, quite apart from any of the racist considerations that one might deduce from the one-time existence of slavery. Latin America captured American attention in the nineteenth century. Asia similarly captured it in the middle of the twentieth century, as Japanese conquests displaced European regimes and as the Japanese defeat then raised the question of whether the old system was to be allowed to return. The attitudes of Americans toward the French in Indochina or the Dutch in Indonesia would however not be matched with regard to most African countries until a decade or two later, simply and straightforwardly because the Japanese army had not been able to play the same uncorking role for self-government in Africa as in Asia.

A major illustration of this American commitment to preserving independence and self-government—once it has been established—comes then in 1960 with American opposition to the maintenance of a Belgian puppet regime in Katanga, after the granting of independence to the former Belgian Congo. Altogether parallel to the Monroe Doctrine in Latin America and the post-1945 American attitude in Indochina and Indonesia, this intervention might thus suggest that the American attitude toward all continents and peoples has basically been the same, with any difference in timing only being caused by the slowness of self-government to ripen in the African case. (As we shall see, moreover, the Congo in 1960 may not have been the first application of this American Monroe Doctrine mentality to Africa, but the second; the first came with long-standing American attitudes on the protection of Liberia.)

To stand the question somewhat on its head, the liberation of Africa from European rule was in many ways delayed by the lateness of the imposition of European rule. Until France and Great Britain and the other European states had carved out territorial units, there were indeed no recognizable political entities behind whose independence American sentiment could be mustered.

There were several reasons why Africa was spared government by Europeans until relatively late in the game, long after the conquest and "civilization" of North and South America, substantially after the British conquest of India and Russian conquest of Siberia, well after the American Revolution and the proclamation of the Monroe Doctrine.

The relative disapproval displayed toward ethnic nationalism within Europe prior to 1848 and 1866 had served to delay European drives toward coloring in the map of Africa and molding black Africans into Frenchmen or Germans. When ethnic nationalism came to dominate the political climate of Europe after 1872, the national result was then that great pride would be taken in "expanding" into Africa.[3]

Another factor delaying the imposition of alien rule in Africa was the attitude of the British government and preponderance of the British navy, already cited as also central to the Monroe Doctrine for Latin America. The British theorists of free trade frowned on the tariff barriers that might follow an establishment of European sovereignties through much of Africa. Not needing coaling stations in the earlier period of naval predominance, the British could also abstain from setting the bad example of any seizures of territory themselves, and could discourage others. When the British monopoly ceased to be as effective after the introduction of steam power, when coaling stations became much more important for considerations of naval power, the race to partition Africa was however to be on. Finally, an important part of the reason for delay was simply the natural barrier of disease. Until some breakthroughs were made in the control of tropical diseases, Europeans would not be especially anxious to move in to colonize most of Africa.

It would thus be foolish to deny that there was a racism about the United States at the time of slavery, or that much of this persisted even after slavery was abolished. A country that wished to be a model of self-government for the world after 1776, but also wished to hold most of its black nationals in slavery, could only overcome the inconsistency here by a global racist formulation about who were the potential "free men" of the world.

Yet the long delay in getting the United States concerned about events in Africa in the twentieth century does not by itself prove that such racism survived in a very strong form after 1865; as suggested, there are other explanations of American attitudes here. What was true for Latin America or Asia was perhaps true for Africa as well. The Monroe Doctrine never committed the United States to oust European regimes from the governance of territories in the Western Hemisphere; it merely forbade their return after they had once been ousted, and forbade the swapping of territories among colonial powers. Over the years, this was perhaps the American attitude also for other continents.

We fortunately do not have to leave these possibilities entirely at such a hypothetical level, for we have the history of American foreign policy toward two republics populated by blacks, Haiti in the Caribbean and Liberia on the continent of Africa itself.

The two cases are remarkably parallel.[4] Prior to 1861, American normalization of relations with either republic was complicated by the American institution of slavery, and indeed clearly precluded by the adamant opposition of southern senators. Yet after 1861, and even before, the United States was consistent in defending the independence of both these states against British or French or other assumptions of colonial sovereignty.

The years before the Civil War thus had seen the British government repeatedly trying to clarify the legal status of Liberia, and the legal commitment of the United States to this country, without real success. The issues for the British were practical, for if competing officials of the black republic were to levy customs duties on British merchants entering its coastal region, London would at least want to tidy things up so that its merchants should be advised on whom to resist or to pay, so that taxation could be distinguished from piracy, so that the Royal Navy should be deployed or withheld.

Since the Liberian colony was chartered originally as private company out of the state of Maryland, it was analogous in some respects to the British domain in India, or to earlier British domains in North America. Had the United States been willing to cover this with its own assertion of sovereignty, the British government would not have objected, in part because London now wished to be on

good terms with Washington, in larger part because an American assertion of sovereignty would presumably bring adherence to international law and international standards, what one automatically in
those times expected of a European regime, but could not count on
from the Liberian.

The U.S. response was not helpful, however, being chary of extending American sovereignty, but at the same time warning the
British that the United States looked with favor and sympathy on
the Liberian self-government experiment. In part this was because
Liberia was a test of whether blacks could be made free men and
happily returned to the continent from which their forefathers had
originated; in another part it was simply because this was a republican regime, an attempt at political democracy, comparable to the
republics of Latin America. The original American popular support
for the establishment of Liberia can thus be traced to a wide variety
of motives, ranging from some American high confidence that blacks
could run as republican and Christian a country as New Englanders,
to other racist desires that all freed blacks be induced or forced to
leave North America, as directly as possible, lest they somehow corrupt its political processes.

Interestingly enough, it was only with the outbreak of the U.S.
Civil War that the United States government brought itself to accord
regular diplomatic recognition to either of the two black-populated
republican regimes of the nineteenth century, Liberia and Haiti.
President Lincoln's decision to take this step may now have come
simply because the departure of Southern congressmen from Washington eliminated what had been the principal source of opposition.
Yet Lincoln and his advisers were surely not just acting merely out of
spite, adopting any policy that the Southerners would have opposed.

The picture of Lincoln as being largely intent on preserving the
Union, quite ready to tolerate slavery, is basically correct. Yet the
logic of the American Civil War was indeed obvious now that slavery
and secession were linked. Even if Lincoln himself voiced basically
racist opinions about inherent differences between the races, there
were those within his party, and others totally outside the United
States, who would now see tight logical linkages between the Union
cause and the total abolition of slavery, and the accordance of
equal status to foreign republics populated by blacks.

The clear trend over the years from 1861 to 1869, when the
Fifteenth Amendment was passed, was thus to abolish not just
slavery, but all legal distinctions based on race. Whether or not
Lincoln would have moved fully with this trend, had he escaped
assassination, is unknowable. But his party, in important part, was

committed to antiracist domestic doctrines, doctrines with important foreign policy corollaries as well.

Even after Liberia had thus won U.S. and international formal recognition as a state, however, European powers such as France and Great Britain and Germany found American attitudes puzzling. Had the United States declared a formal protectorate, or otherwise assumed sovereignty over the region, such European states would again hardly have objected, indeed welcoming a North American assumption of the European "civilizing mission" here. But out of disinterest, or out of principle, the United States consistently refused to do this.

If it had been only disinterest, of course, the European states could have carved Liberia up themselves, and the anomaly would have been disposed of. But European moves in this direction then repeatedly activated signals of American displeasure, as notes were sent that the United States was somehow committed to Liberian independence and territorial integrity.

Until the discovery of Liberia's potential as a producer of rubber in the 1920s, the American motive here was hardly economic, as the bulk of Liberian trade went to Germany and to other European states.[5] When German trade was cut off in World War I, the Liberian regime indeed had to plead with the U.S. government to increase trade somehow, lest the Liberian economy sink into destitution. Rather the American motive was a straightforward commitment to self-government. The United States did not want to govern Liberia, but wanted to assure that Liberia got to maintain its own regime, an attitude it had espoused for Latin America and for Samoa and China as well.

United States diplomatic recognition of Haiti had also been withheld until 1862, in what, by contrast with the recognition accorded all the Latin American republics winning their independence after the Napoleonic Wars, very clearly amounted to racial discrimination. The issue certainly did not lack explication in the U.S. Congress; Southern senators openly stated an opposition to legitimizing any state governed by former slaves, while senators from New England twitted the southerners by continually demanding such recognition.

Analysis inclined to an economic-determinist explanation of American foreign policy might note that such New England sentiments were "of course" reinforced by a desire to trade with Haiti, for the black republic had retaliated against the American denial of recognition by imposing additional taxes on trade carried in American ships. Such theorists sometimes go further to explain the entire northern abolitionist desire to end U.S. slavery on primarily selfish economic grounds. Yet all of such arguments may amount to a slander of the genuine antislavery sentiment that gripped much of the North, a sentiment based on nothing more selfish than an identification with the misery of enslaved human beings.

Haiti was indeed the "second new nation," the first Western Hemisphere state, after the United States itself, to win independence from a European colonial power. The manner in which it had reached independence in the wake of the French Revolution was already again quite complicated, however; in ways it provided a preview of the confusions North Americans might have to feel later about the conservative or liberal tendencies of declarations of independence further south. Complicated alliances of whites and mulattoes and freedmen and slaves, together with Spanish and British foreign forces, led into an extremely bloody guerrilla war, and a racial massacre of whites at the end. Given the institution of slavery in the United States, with its inherent fears of slave revolt, it is hardly so surprising that the United States elected to treat Haiti differently from Venezuela or Argentina or Mexico.

Traces of more general American principle were there, of course, in that the geographic logic of the Monroe Doctrine was soon enough to apply to Haiti as much as to all the rest of Latin America. Yet Haiti long remained in a racially determined limbo, even with regard to the rest of the established powers of the world. France and Great Britain had abolished slavery well before the United States, but still accorded Haiti (like Liberia) only a very cautious diplomatic acceptance. French recognition of Haitian independence indeed came at length in 1838, but only at the price of Haitian agreement to a substantial indemnity to be paid for the French investments that had been confiscated or destroyed at the moment of independence. This saddled the black republic with a substantial external debt from the very outset of its legal independence, a debt that would be difficult to pay.[6]

The problem of servicing external debt was to plague the independent states of the Caribbean and Latin America increasingly at the end of the nineteenth century, presumably giving European creditor states a reason or excuse to intervene if the debts were not paid, perhaps even an excuse for military occupation and the assumption of sovereignty. While most of such debts were freely entered into by regimes seeking capital for investment programs, in the case of Haiti this was in fact a debt accepted as the very price of French recognition of statehood.

As noted, the United States diplomatic recognition of Haiti may have been accorded as part of a clearing of decks on American attitudes about the moral issues of the Civil War. More practically, the black republic also now allowed U.S. navy vessels to use Haitian ports to support the blockade of the Confederacy. The American recognition, while not the first, amounted to the major break in what had been a diplomatic isolation of the black republic, removing, as in the case of Liberia, much of the outside world's doubts about whether nonwhite independent states were ever to be given a legal status equal to that of the European powers.

As we shall see, however, doubts about the reality of such equal status were to persist long afterward. The favorite approach of powers such as Great Britain and France would indeed still have been for the United States itself to assume sovereignty over Haiti as well as Liberia, if it was so determined to prevent any other white regime from doing so. The phrase "international nuisance" appears frequently in the European commentaries on both these black republics in this period, together with a continuous puzzlement about why the United States insisted on precluding their takeover by any foreign power, while avoiding a takeover of its own.

Such an American takeover of the republics was indeed considered at various stages of U.S. foreign policy. In the case of Haiti, part of this was explained by the prospect of securing a naval base; while Presidents Andrew Johnson and U.S. Grant worked for the total absorption of Haiti, most of the subsequent projects entailed the cession merely of a naval base and a coastal strip, comparable to what the United States would ultimately acquire not far away in Guantanamo, Cuba. Such American desire for a naval base can of course itself reflect a great variety of motives, ranging from designs on the hinterland to fear of foreign navies, or at least desires to become independent of the British navy.

The earlier proposals for the outright annexation of all of Haiti also stemmed from a very different logic, very linked to thinking about Liberia. A significant stream of American thought before and after the Civil War had favored emancipation of black slaves, but had also feared that such freed blacks would not be compatible with normal political and social life as the United States had known it, such that the solution would have to include the moving of such freedmen to another location. Liberia was in effect founded on this premise; Haiti also looked promising because its government at times had even asked to have such freedmen come to the island. Given recurrent reports of the abuse or mismanagement of such movements of people, at least some Americans were then to conclude that the full implementation of this solution would require political control over the territories to which such freed slaves were being sent.[7]

While some of the advocates of this solution had drawn no particular inferences of white superiority (some important black leaders favored similar solutions), others had indeed drawn such inferences, concluding that the elimination of slavery did not really mean that the black was to be seen as politically equal to the white, such that this early form of deportation "apartheid" was needed. (A few such proposals, recognizing the logistical difficulties of moving large numbers of people back across an ocean, had advocated a separated black republic in the far west, but this over time might clearly have posed a military and strategic threat to the United States, and was probably just as logistically impracticable in any event.)

Important feelings of white superiority thus remained among even those who had opposed slavery, even while the Fourteenth and Fifteenth Amendments to the Constitution specifically were written to ban all forms of political discrimination based on such assumptions. Some of such thoroughgoing endorsement of racial equality had of course been based on Northern resentment of the Southern recalcitrance in 1865 at freeing the black in the first place. The sentiment of the entire country was then to back away from meaningful equality for a long time into the future, as the two white segments settled into a reconciliation after 1876; the "excesses" of Reconstruction were now somehow remembered as having accorded too much political equality to the black population, and blacks on a de facto basis were systematically denied the vote throughout the South.[8]

Yet, for the purpose of establishing the legal basis for an ultimate expunging of racial distinctions from American domestic and foreign policy, a major deed was, in fact, done in the Fourteenth and Fifteenth Amendments, a constitutional pledge to the future that must still be seen as remarkably sweeping. Similarly, the remarkable fact about American relations with Haiti is not that the Grant administration persuaded the Haitian regime to sign a treaty of annexation by which the United States would assume sovereignty, but rather that the treaty was rejected by the Senate. Because Americans generally felt opposed to assuming sovereignty over foreign self-governing states, and because some Republicans still felt strongly that blacks were as capable of governing themselves as whites, the treaty was converted into a humiliating defeat for President Grant.

The historical connections between American attitudes on racism and imperialism are thus surely too complicated for a one-to-one relationship. Some Americans of course shared the European attitude that Africans and Asians were inherently in need of being governed, that this was the "white man's burden" or the "mission civilisatrice," and would thus have taken over larger portions of the globe without moral compunction.

Differing from the normal attitudes in Europe, however, a large fraction of Americans were disquieted at the prospect of any such permanent deviation from self-government. Unless new territories could, after some reasonable period of time, be made into states like Massachusetts and Minnesota, an assumption of sovereignty over them would be inappropriate to their needs, and it would be corrupting and dangerous to the process of self-government back in Washington as well. The country in this view could not be both a republic and an empire; the Roman example, if nothing else, showed how governing others without their consent led to similar practices at home.

Yet such a high-minded commitment to government only by the consent of the governed could link soon enough with a racism as well, as opponents of imperialism concluded that Haiti or Puerto Rico or the Philippines might never be capable of becoming states of the United States; these territories might perhaps be as incapable of governing themselves as the European imperialists contended, or at best they would have to devise new kinds of republican systems of their own, without any federal link to Minnesota and Massachusetts.

The American aversion to a federal linkage could have been phrased on as simple a point as language, as Haiti's French and Puerto Rico's Spanish would be an obstacle of future standardization. Yet this language problem would hardly have been the core of the problem for someone like Carl Schurz, a prominent German-American spokesman for the antiimperialist position.[9] More reasonably, one could have based an argument perhaps on legal and political tradition, as two perfectly republican systems of self-government based on different histories might have trouble meshing, and might do better if they retained their autonomy of each other.

Finally, most basically, the argument often however became one of race, that a non-European population would have trouble federating with the rest of the United States.

SPECIAL RELATIONSHIPS

However generous or liberal, a person is likely to identify more with family connections abroad than with people of no personal relation. Most Americans have ancestries going back to Europe, and hence may care more about Europe. It would more specifically be no surprise if German-Americans tended to be particularly sympathetic to the happiness of Germans, and if Polish-Americans identified with their kin in Poland.

Aside from the special feelings everyone has for cousins, the mere history of choice of language must also bias any country's foreign policy. It would be all well and good for the United States to welcome a free market of ideas and cultures abroad, and to cherish a notion of a melting pot, by which the best of all the many cultures of the waves of immigration into the United States had been smoothly and voluntarily blended into an alloy. Yet the United States had had to choose a single language for itself; did this not give the English language and culture a special hold on foreign policy?[10]

The most plausible case of such influence probably comes with the American decision to enter World War I on the side of the British, amid discussions of a "special relationship" between the two English-speaking powers. Some of the Progressive leaders, Theodore Roosevelt being an important example, were indeed quite explicit about wanting to enter the war on the British side specifically because of supposed differences between English and German culture.[11] If such arguments were understandably unpopular in Milwaukee and Cincinnati, they were conversely of some significance in New England and in the rest of the country.

Yet the Wilsonian formulation of the grounds for American entry was still closer to the feelings of most Americans, that Great Britain somehow was more of a political democracy than the kaiser's Germany, that the American entry into the war was needed to put an end to war itself, rather than to advance one particular culture.[12]

Such considerations of a cultural relationship also played a role again in the American entry into World War II, but surely the dominating difference here was not that Hitler spoke German, and Churchill English, but that Hitler was a genocidal dictator, and Churchill the freely elected leader of a free people. Lest one assume that the English-speaking community is somehow culturally immune to producing a politically repressive regime, one might consider Ian Smith's Rhodesia. What if Germany had been governed in 1939 by the Weimar regime, while Britain was governed by Oswald Mosely? Cultural considerations would hardly have outweighed the differences in the commitment to political liberalism.

OTHER SPECIAL VIEWS

Do the American people at large have any more special loves or special relationships, besides the obvious ones inculcated by the shared vested interest in the English language, and the memories of the European heritage in general? It is often suggested that Americans have shown a peculiarly strong affection for the Chinese, while by contrast showing a general dislike for Indians and for Russians. How true or deep is this, and why should it be so?

Americans may at various times have convinced themselves of a great actual or potential resemblance in the Chinese, who with their hardworking manners seemed natural-born Yankee Protestants. Not a little part of the American commitment to the defense of China against Japanese attack in the 1930s thus stemmed from this feeling of similarity, such that a lack of happiness in China made Americans more morose than if it had been some other people (for example, South Asians) under attack.[13] The letters home from American missionaries in China had forged a bond of altruistic identification that cannot be ignored if one wants to explain American foreign policy (which indeed cannot be ignored if one wants to explain the surprising American public acceptance of Nixon's opening to Communist China after 1970).

A part of this contrast in American responses to China and India might stem from the simple partitioning of the world of the nineteenth and early twentieth centuries for Protestant missionary activity, whereby India was more or less assigned mainly to the English effort because of British political sovereignty, while China was left mainly to the American. The mail home from such American missionaries often stressed success at Christianizing the Chinese, and portrayed virtues that may have made the average American conclude that the Chinese were every bit as suited for self-government and economic advancement and Protestant stewardship as Americans.

The immediate aftermath of the opening of Communist China to American visits in 1970 with the Ping-Pong diplomacy of Kissinger and Nixon thus saw the more superficial portions of the American press going on at length about the obvious energy and vitality of life in China, the sort of hardworking Protestant ethic that Americans find attractive.

Could this energy have been ironically the product of the Marxist regime? The answer was likely to be no, since the same visible energy could be found on Taiwan and in Hong Kong and Singapore, while it was just as obviously missing in Moscow. If the signs of such energy were missing in India, a few analysts might have attributed the difference to climate, but many would rather have assigned it instead to deep aspects of culture.

Much of such analysis of culture is of course extraordinarily superficial. The stereotype image of Chinese in American films changed within a decade from the evil and criminal Fu Man Chu to the honest and energetic Charlie Chan, and the kinds of generalizations with which Americans indulge themselves about Indian or

Chinese or Russian or Muslim culture are often nothing more than the simplest projections of imagination. Yet what we are discussing here is not so much the reality of the world, as how Americans view and relate to this reality. If Americans have developed a pecking order over the years in how they identify with and evaluate foreign human beings, it might be very misleading to deny that the Chinese have been high on this pecking order.

About whose happiness abroad do Americans thus care about the most? The answer in the end depends on aspects of superficial similarity to Americans themselves, and also on accidents of history. To have defended a people for a time is to get to know them better in the process of defending them, and thus to develop some attachments that last. To send missionaries is to convince one's self that one has duplicated one's self. The crude order of priorities of the average American's identification might thus in the end run as follows: Europeans, Latin Americans, Chinese, Africans, South Asians. The answers can shift up and down as events move along, and surely vary from some Americans to others (the order above being suggested is obviously more plausible for the white majority of the United States than for the black minority).

Some of American identification with the Chinese thus stems also from a history of remembering Americans defending Chinese self-government. We earlier discussed the possibility of a general "ratchet effect" in identification with the self-government of others: until a nation achieves independence, Americans are not so ready to mobilize themselves to protect it. When such independence has once been established, however, with the nation entering into the community of independent states, then the instinct of Americans, as in the Monroe Doctrine, is to resist any terminations of such independence.

Soviet visitors to the United States comment bitterly that American experts on China tend to be extremely sympathetic to all things Chinese, while American experts on Russia tend to be very hostile to the Soviet regime. Americans on average gave a low opinion of all things Russian, but the reverse bizarrely seems not to be true, as the man on the street in the Soviet Union typically radiates a great feeling of friendship for Americans, and for all things American. The emigre source of some American analysis of the USSR may account for part of the asymmetry. Many American interpreters of Soviet and East European affairs have been refugees from Communist rule, while the bulk of American analysts of China are not alienated refugee Orientals, but rather children of the American missionaries who served in, and loved, the Orient.

Yet this asymmetry of Russian-American popular feelings may instead reflect something much more basic, indeed the theme of much of this book. The United States, despite all the indoctrination of Soviet propaganda, is seen by the average Russian as it was in the days of the czar, as a model of progress and success. The Soviet Union conversely is seen by the average American also as it was in the days of the czar, a backward society of repression and superstition, having never undergone the liberal experience that sooner or later reached most of the rest of Europe as Americans had hoped.[14]

As substantiation for a suspicion that there may again be a fair deal of superficiality about all of this, one could of course point to the great admiration accorded to the Russian people, and to things Russian in general, during World War II, as the alliance produced much of such feeling in the products of Hollywood and the American press.

But these were the years when Hitler's Naziism was seen quite realistically as the greatest world challenge to American liberal ideals; six years later, Stalin's communism was viewed, again not so unrealistically, as having assumed this obnoxious preeminence.

At all stages, therefore, Americans may have been responding more to perceptions of the Russian political regime than to any fondness or dislike for Russian culture. As possible evidence for a different strain of ethnic influence, again buffeted by superficial movie attributes, we could similarly note the ups and downs of feeling about the Japanese, viewed perhaps as another set of power- and empire-minded Europeans earlier in this century, then as sadistic Asian barbarians during World War II, and finally seen somehow as relatively pacifistic Europeans since 1950. Yet it was of course not just American images that changed between 1941 and 1961; Japan indeed changed, and it might have been altogether inappropriate for American images not to change along with it.

"Cutting much closer to the bone," one would expect Americans at large to have strong special feelings about their most immediate neighbors, Canada and Mexico. Would it not be expectable that Americans cared a great deal and got excited about the issues of English or French language in Quebec, or about the issues of population and land reform in Mexico? Yet the actual situation is very much the opposite, of course, as the most common Canadian (and even Mexican) complaint about the United States in the 1970s has been "lack of attention," "lack of interest."

The worst insult for Canadians, of course, is not quite to be ignored by Americans, but rather to be told that Americans see Canadians as "just like Americans." If Americans are much in the mood to project models of their own political democracy abroad, to suggest that every place would be governed most happily according to the pattern of Maine or Minnesota, Canada since the beginnings of this century has already surely been seen as a successful implementation of this advice and model.[15]

Americans are thus supremely satisfied with the way Canadians govern themselves, and they pay little or no further attention to the matter. If Canadians resent this, we thereby find American public opinion put almost into a no-win situation, "damned if we do" and "damned if we don't." Would Canadians prefer that Americans felt strong opinions and offered high-pressure advice about how Canada could more happily be governed? Americans may be capable of offering no higher compliment than that they see others as duplicates of themselves; this can easily strike a Canadian or any other foreigner as the extreme of myopia or of arrogance, but the American expression of such feelings may nonetheless be very generous and sincere.

Some Canadians would undoubtedly feel more pleased if Americans went about wistfully showing envy of Canadian progress, or talking about adopting the "Canadian model," just as Americans have been pleased in the past whenever Europeans showed admiration for the "American model." But, if this is not meant to be, would Canadians really prefer to have Americans continually going about telling their northern neighbors how "different" they were?

LATIN NEIGHBORS

Most of the North American memory of having opposed European colonialism stems quite specifically from the U.S. political record with regard to Latin America, as particularly developed through the Monroe Doctrine. Yet it is ironically true that Latin America is an area in which Americans are very much disliked, in which they are most often accused of having been economically and socially colonialist. Writers on American "imperialism" concentrate sometimes on the acquisition of the Philippines, but more often are pulled to alleged U.S. dollar diplomacy after the 1890s, and even before, in Central and South America.

It should come as no surprise that antagonism to the United States is deeper in Mexico, and further south, than in Canada. The Southern border, unlike the border with Canada, was shaped by American expansion at a neighbor's expense, as the territories from Texas to Colorado to California (although they were in truth largely empty of population at the time) were clearly under Mexican sovereignty from the moment of the achievement of independence from Spain. Mexico's bitter memories of the lands it lost are shared vicariously among Spanish-speaking peoples throughout the hemisphere, as the simple religious and cultural identifications that have played a role all around the globe since the nineteenth century inevitably produce a resentment that the future of so much land was changed from Spanish-speaking Roman Catholic to English-speaking predominantly Protestant. Memories of the territories lost in the middle of the nineteenth century have also been reinforced at various later points by suspicions that American appetites had not yet been satisfied, that the United States might like to extend its sovereignty still further.

Such historical resentments are all the more exacerbated, moreover, by the obvious discrepancy between economic conditions just north and south of today's international border. While the Canadian and American life-styles facing each other across the northern border are, as noted, remarkably similar, the gap at the Mexican border is irritatingly large. It is exacerbated even more by a flow of surplus population northward from the interior of Mexico, seeking the employment in the border region stimulated by the propinquity to the United States, or indeed preparing to cross the border illegally into the United States, hoping then to melt into the U.S. population and after a time to escape any risk of deportation.

We cannot really therefore tell whether a different history, or a different causal and moral background to the partitioning of North America, would have made Mexican resentments become any less. Great differences of well-being, no matter what the cause, breed resentment.

With regard to this nearest of the Latin American countries, the immediate neighbor to the south, the general American attitude is again less one of hostility and more of indifference, in a tendency not to pay a great deal of attention to events south of the border, on the assumption (perhaps greatly at variance with reality) that Mexico is also a political democracy, a self-governing society with free contested elections and freedom of the press.[16] Mexico has indeed seen far less threat of military intervention in politics since the 1930s than has been typical in the rest of Latin America. When Mexican resentment at the United States becomes particularly obvious, it thus typically comes as a shock to citizens of the United States, precisely because so little attention had been paid.

Yet how do citizens of the United States react to Latin Americans in general? Are there also special relationships here, special loves or hates?

We might begin by suggesting that citizens of the United States (even if only in a relatively superficial way) have wanted to identify with Latin Americans. As noted, most Americans probably identify the fullest with Europeans, but next with Latin Americans, then perhaps Chinese coming third on the list because of the years of missionary activity (with Africans and South Asians still remaining furthest removed from this American gut reaction of "they're people just like us"). The Latin American comparison has stemmed from the assumption of a common European heritage (only partially diminished by the obvious differences of religion and language), and by the common experience of having confronted a wild and hostile frontier, while then winning a "new beginning" and independence from tradition-bound Europe.

This feeling of shared liberation experience was (as suggested earlier) in many ways misleading, for a significant number of the Latin American pushes for independence stemmed more immediately from unhappiness with liberalizing tendencies back in Spain, hence leaving the issues of domestic political democracy and international self-government somewhat inversely related to each other, rather than more directly related as in the United States. Nonetheless, the Latin American states (with the earlier exception of the empire of Brazil) at least styled themselves republics; in sincere emulation, or just in a desire to win United States support, they often patterned their written constitutions very specifically after that of the United States.

Americans thus only very reluctantly face the fact that they are generally not liked or admired "south of the border," this being the response drawn not just in Mexico, but all the way to Chile and Argentina. Having remembered themselves as generously supporting Latin American independence from Spain and other European powers in the Monroe Doctrine, Americans are bothered that Latin Americans instead remember this history as a continuous tale of United States attempts at domination of the hemisphere. Having seen Latin American countries often copy the U.S. Constitution and form of government, citizens of the United States have similarly been perplexed to see many or most of such countries then fall prone to coups and "revolutions" and dictatorships by military juntas.

Various kinds of interpretative responses could thus emerge in the United States, in face of the disappointments and rebuffs of American relationships with Latin America.

The newer, more radical, schools of American foreign policy analysis would simply explain American disappointments, and the severity of Latin American resentments, as showing the fundamental

inapplicability of North American liberal notions of political democracy to countries that are poor. Just as Marxist regimes are thus sup-
posedly preferable to elected regimes in Cambodia or Angola, they
are projected to be appropriate for all the countries south of the Rio
Grande. The United States, in this view, should already have lost
faith in its own model more than a hundred years ago, in the face of
Latin American inability to adhere to their written constitutions and
to honor their international monetary debts.

Far more typical until recently, and more liberal, is the American
interpretation discussed in the previous chapter, that successful applications of the U.S. model will simply take more time in the rest of
the hemisphere, as the dead hand of the Spanish and Portuguese past
will take more time to lift. This, to repeat, is a view that sees the
Latin American experience as in no way disproving the validity of
the American model. Nicaragua and Cuba and Brazil would still benefit from being governed in the same way as Minnesota.

Yet it is unfortunately only a small move from regretting the
burden of a heritage less liberal than the English tradition in Latin
America to adopting a set of special attitudes about culture and religion; genetic prejudices have not played nearly as large a role here
as in our earlier treatment of Haiti or Liberia, but ethnic factors still
can loom large, as North Americans come to see Latin Americans
somewhat more as "people not like us." Latin Americans speak
Spanish rather than English, and they overwhelmingly tend to be
Roman Catholic rather than Protestant.

Aside from the list of ethnic considerations we have posited thus
far, have Americans thus also had more particular commitments than
they are willing to acknowledge on religion? Perhaps the answer is
yes, if one construes the very notions of free exchange and voluntary
association as being an outgrowth of various strains of Protestant
Christianity. Americans have prided themselves on maintaining a
rigid separation of church and state in domestic affairs, and on exploiting the many cross-cutting cleavages by which differing Protestant sects have checked each other, in interaction with Catholicism
and Judaism. The checks and balances, together with the ban on
state enforcement of religious belief, go hand in hand with the rest
of the stress on voluntarism, but could someone not object that this
very voluntarism is an application of Protestant Calvinist theology?[17]

It thus would not be surprising if citizens of the United States
had at times associated the Latin American failure to stand by their
constitutional or economic contracts with a religious or cultural
background that attached less significance to all contracts. Foreign
regimes governed by non-Protestants might simply be less likely to

embody Lockean principles, and the disappointments with Latin America after independence would, at least subliminally, tend to be blamed on the Spanish Catholic heritage.

One must never forget the economic side of U.S. disappointments and Latin American resentments, but the economic issue very much blends with the political issue here. The North Americans who had taken such pride in seeing Latin American states win their independence were continuously to be disappointed on both dimensions. The new countries did not keep their internal promises to honor their constitutions and the outcomes of their elections; they moreover, as European and American investment had increasingly flowed into the needy sections of Latin America, did not keep their external promises about the service and repayment of voluntarily incurred debt.

A typical citizen of the United States might have again interpreted such deviations from promises as the simple lack of long-range time horizons, resulting from differences of tradition and religion. Derogatory references to Latin Americans as "mañana people," never looking past the immediate moment, reflecting the image that now had emerged among "Anglo" North Americans about Spanish-speakers. (A more radical American analyst of such tendencies would of course have linked them instead to a basic poverty, and/or to a very unjust distribution of resources that left the countries of Spanish America with very different economic prospects from the United States.)

Putting this into historical perspective, one thus sees citizens of the United States continually disappointed in Latin America, with the disappointment growing from decade to decade as the range of issues to which the question of "adherence to contract" was broadening. Latin American defaults on loans from North America or Europe simply looked irresponsible, as irresponsible as military coups deposing elected presidents.

Europeans had also invested substantially in the United States in the nineteenth century, and a temptation to default on loans had appeared as well among American individuals and governmental agencies, but never in such quantity that Americans had to remember themselves as inherently irresponsible about property and legal title.[18] Just as the Lockean notion of contracts, carefully negotiated and faithfully adhered to, was a central part of the mythology of the U.S. Constitution and political system, it was similarly part of the mythology of the American economic system. Laissez-faire Americans may have believed in "anarchy plus a constable," but the constable was essential, for debts had to be repaid.

Whatever subtle anti-Catholic bias applied to Spanish-speakers here might have been extended also to French-speakers in Quebec, who prior to 1763, had not shown any drive toward self-government comparable to that of the English colonies along the seaboard, and who in the American Revolution after 1775 had turned down requests that they join in the rebellion against Britain.[19]

Yet the more common U.S. image of Quebec was in later years to be very comparable to that of English-speaking Canadians, namely that the Francophone sections of Quebec would be assimilated into a totally English-speaking North America. The impression from south of the Great Lakes therefore was that Quebec was simply part of the general "Canadian problem." When would the descendants of the Tory Loyalists to the crown at long last claim self-government for themselves? When would this remnant of European colonialism to the north at last be ended?

One can only speculate whether an "independent Quebec" after 1783 (or after 1983) would have drawn the same sense of U.S. disappointment as has emerged with the political style of Honduras or Venezuela.

By the fact that Islam and Hindu and Buddhist beliefs are even more remote than Catholicism from the American Protestant mainstream, we might have been led to predict that their political and social styles were even more likely to fail to pass muster by American projections of the appropriate path to happiness for mankind. Such a projection would go astray here and there, however, the most obvious example perhaps coming with the early and persistent identification of Americans with the potential of the individual Chinese.

LATIN AMERICA IN THE INTERNATIONAL ARENA

Some broad questions remain to be posed for the Latin American region. In what ways has Latin America been typical of American foreign policy, and in what ways very special? Has Latin America's international political style indeed even been at all typical of the international system as a whole? Courses on international politics stress the continual threats of war underpinning the exercise of the Machiavellian diplomacy with which we are all too familiar. Yet Latin America has seen extraordinarily few wars in the years since its republics won their independence from Europe, as its armies and navies are normally deprecated for being only "parade-ground" forces, or sources of domestic anticonstitutional despotism.

The questions are not unrelated. Because of some special U.S.

feelings about Latin America, the region has had a special experience with international politics. Latin Americans might today hate to consider the possibility that their escape from wars is due to American political and military influence, just as they would earlier have hated to admit that it was due to the influence of the British navy. Yet the connections are there.

A great number of U.S. feelings about Latin America are still to be explained in terms of the political principles outlined in the last chapter, rather than the ethnic complications being discussed in this one. Latin America is special for the United States in terms of geography, but even more because it won its independence early. We have noted the ratchet effect whereby Americans have become particularly attached to supporting independence and self-government abroad, but only once it has been established. Whereas Americans could remain relaxed about the lack of such self-government where it had not yet been accomplished, as for most of Africa in the nineteenth century, they would rather be quite tense about threats of an overthrow of republican government after it had been accomplished in the Western Hemisphere.

The history of U.S. feelings about Latin America could thus fairly be described as one of continual tension, a tension producing interventions and threats of intervention, producing substantial annoyance among Latin Americans, but also very possibly sparing Latin America from any substantial involvement in great power politics and wars.[20]

The original United States motive for welcoming the departure of the European powers from Latin America was in part realistic and selfish, for Latin American independence helped to reinsure American independence, but was also largely idealistic and altruistic, very similar to the reasons for hoping that the Turks would leave Greece. The subsequent fears of a European return reflected a similar mixture of "realistic" and idealistic motives.

The fears were at first that a Spanish regime might attempt to recover its lost imperial domain. They then shifted to England, with its monopoly of naval power. While British use of such naval power indeed became a useful underpinning for American goals here, not every American was always so ready to trust British intentions in Argentina or Guyana or Central America, or anywhere else.

When neither Spain nor Great Britain seemed to threaten a seizure of territorial control over New World lands, the next clear menace came with Napoleon III's 1861 incursion into Mexico, while the United States was distracted and incapacitated by its own Civil War, as French troops were deployed to impose a traditional regime headed by the Austrian Prince Maximilian. The American support here for Benito Juárez might well be remembered today by radical analysts who contend that American foreign policy has always favored reaction in Latin America. Juárez was not only clearly the candidate drawing more indigenous support, but he was also the candidate of the liberalizing faction, seeking to terminate the prerogatives of the church and other traditional interests. American political recognition for Juárez was rendered early, but the deployment of substantial Union army forces to the Mexican border came only after the Confederate defeat in 1865, conveying a threat of war that clearly caused Louis Napoleon to abandon Maximilian and withdraw his French troops from Mexico.[21]

As the French threat receded, the American fear in later decades shifted to Germany, which after its national unification in 1871 seemed to show interest in colonial enterprises all around the globe. In the decades before World War I, the fear sometimes was focused on pockets of German immigration, for example in Rio Grande do Sul in the south of Brazil, but it was also focused on the general drive to acquire naval bases that now gripped many nations, as the British naval monopoly came under challenge in the shift from sail power to steam. Rather than seeing the Caribbean and Latin America pockmarked with naval bases just as the coast of China, American political leaders now girded themselves for what might be a continual challenge to the Monroe Doctrine, and formulated a Roosevelt corollary that Latin Americans simply despise.

It is of course true that some of this German presence in Latin America now came in the person of astute and able German businessmen, which would lead some commentators to contend again that all of the American vigilance here stemmed simply from a capitalist competition for markets, in the fear of German business skill. Yet the actual course of events often supports a reverse conclusion. Where the German government's presence was limited merely to the normal support of German business endeavors, little American resentment was aroused. Where German businessmen were conversely seen as agents of the German government, a German government perhaps bent on seizing sovereignty over naval bases and larger territorial enclaves, then Washington's anxiety was increased.

The German activities in Mexico during the first years of World War I, widely (and probably correctly) viewed as intended to inveigle Mexico into a war with the United States (so as to keep the United States from joining the Entente Powers in Europe), are thus symptomatic of what Americans feared. It was not the commercial activities of the German consulates that rankled as much as their political activities.[22]

In the aftermath of World War I, the fear of German penetration remained, now less with regard to possible German naval bases and more to the very visible German role in the opening of new airlines around South America. Such airline routes were again hardly being jealously coveted for their contribution to profits, for Pan American Airways had to be substantially subsidized by the United States government to be able to compete with the various affiliates of Lufthansa, and would have been uninterested in getting into the Latin American market if such subsidies had not been available. Rather the fear, especially after the Nazi rise to power in Germany in 1933, was that the pilots for Lufthansa or Scadta or Varig were actually reserve officers of the new Luftwaffe, training for future bomber raids on the Panama Canal, or on the south of the United States itself.[23]

The American fear of a German threat in Latin America after 1933 indeed had an ideological component; yet (as with the later Communist threat), Americans mainly saw themselves as reacting against a hostile and totalitarian ideology here, rather than so much conforming to the dictates of an ideology of their own. The ideology they saw themselves resisting here was, moreover, again one more from the Right, that of fascism.

As in the present, there may have been a tendency for Americans (and others) to exaggerate the Fascist or "anti-Fascist" character of the various political trends and factions in Brazil and Argentina and Chile and Mexico. The "domino effect" possibilities of one country's being used as a base for subversion and aggression against another may similarly have been exaggerated, as was the power, and loyalty to Berlin or Rome, of the German and Italian immigrant communities in the various Latin American countries. Many Latin American rulers, ranging from dictatorial to popularly elected, may have shared an ethnic desire to show some dislike for the United States. In the 1930s an easy way to display this was to adopt some Fascist terminology here and there, as outsiders speculated about a "wave of the future." The same movements (Juan Perón's in Argentina perhaps being a prime example) might in the 1960s and 1970s have instead adopted some Marxist terminology, again with the straightforward intention of showing some hostility to the American predominance in the Western Hemisphere, amid the result that such statements are often taken more seriously abroad than at home.

The irony of examining the German-American competition in Latin America after the fact is that each side saw itself as losing, that each side attributed to the other elaborate offensive plans for taking over the hemisphere. While American embassies reported back to Washington on hegemonic German plans for taking over country after country by means of local German populations and Fascist movements, Berlin's ambassadors reported on a concerted American effort to align the continent against Germany, on a sustained effort to put all the German-affiliated airline companies out of business, to be replaced by companies affiliated with Pan American.[24] One in many ways thus finds a suggestion of mirror-image conflict here, as each side puts more effort into the conflict simply because of its perceptions of the other side's input, as the conflict becomes a self-nourishing and self-confirming imbroglio. Just as with the post-1945 cold war, the confrontation here can be viewed in part as illustrating the prisoners' dilemma, a situation where each side feels driven to move into first strikes and first hostile moves, simply because the power distributions and payoffs reward such moves no matter what each side does.

All of these components of U.S. interest in Latin America thus set the stage for the projection of the cold war into the Western Hemisphere, in a series of preemptive moves by which each side to the confrontation finds itself attributing aggressive opportunities and aggressive intentions to the other. Whether the confrontation correctly is to be seen between Washington and Moscow, or between Washington and more radical forces indigenous to the Latin American scene, becomes less important than some interpreters would suggest, for one of the early moves of the local radical force in each case is to identify itself at least somewhat with Moscow, with the conflict exacerbated almost immediately thereafter.

The American fear of a return of foreign domination to Latin America is thus a continuum from 1823 to the present, a fear based on noble motives as much as on selfish, based on principle more than on ethnicity, a fear exacerbated whenever the intricacies of power politics have made the Latin American regimes look vulnerable to foreign takeover. What the Holy Alliance had intended to inflict on Latin America after the defeat of Napoleon very much resembled what Hitler imposed on Czechoslovakia, and what the Soviet Union imposed on Eastern Europe after the defeat of Hitler.

And how central was the role of economics in all this? It is indeed true that the United States intervened more actively and visibly in Latin America after 1890 than before, but American influence was not missing in earlier years; the expansion of American activity in the 1890s moreover may have had as much to do with a new decline of British naval power as with the dictates of American capitalism. In the earlier years, the United States did less, not because it cared less, but because the free ride of British naval power made the risk of a European takeover of territories in the hemisphere less worrisome. The British for their own reasons were reluctant to seize territory on shore for themselves; had they not been so reluctant, the United States might indeed have bestirred itself to begin building a navy earlier to challenge the British monopoly.

ETHNIC MINORITIES WITHIN THE UNITED STATES

In a pluralistic society, one hardly would exhaust the impact of ethnic issues by sticking merely to national majority feelings, for there will be very strong particular sentiments of specific subgroups within the electorate to be taken into account. If a minority feels very strongly about an issue related to the welfare of its ethnic kinsmen abroad, while the majority feels more lukewarm or indifferent about such an issue, the minority will quite fairly tend to get its way, in the political process of logrolling and consensus-building in the Congress, and in the political arena as a whole.

We might begin with a most obvious example in American foreign policy toward Israel, which surely is related to the fact that a portion of Americans are Jewish in religion. While endorsements for military or financial support for Israel often fall below 50 percent for the entire population of the United States, the support among Jewish Americans must exceed 95 percent. One finds among Americans, of course, virtually no sign of desire for active support of the Arab cause in the Middle East, but a great number of such voters endorsing a policy of "hands off."[25]

Some of the American support for Israel can be traced to the broader considerations that have been advanced earlier as explanations of American foreign policy. Israel is clearly a political democracy, while its opponents in the Arab world are not, being either very traditional monarchies or very modern and "revolutionary" regimes that (like most of the developing world) have explicitly placed economic equality ahead of the political pluralism of contested elections and free press. The fact that the Soviet Union after 1955 elected to support such Arab regimes against Israel confirmed this impression in the minds of at least some of the non-Jewish Americans that matter.

Yet much of the American support for Israel must also be traced to ethnic ties. Jewish Americans probably would support the existence of Israel even if Jordan and Syria and Egypt were models of the free election process. Many other Americans thus go along, just because their Jewish neighbors felt strongly about the subject.

It is interesting to note how the tone of some of the non-Jewish support for Israel has changed over the years from 1948 to 1978. At its founding, Zionism seemed to be an ideology that was very Socialist in nature, with a commitment to economic equality perhaps just as strong as its commitment to political freedom. Stalin's Russia found much to praise in Israel before 1949, and the American Left also tended to identify with it, as perhaps the model of a more egalitarian society. Thirty years later, the egalitarian or proletarian nature of Israel has become less visible to Americans and other outsiders, while its position beleaguered by states aided by the USSR has made it look quite different. As more of Israel's strength has come to depend on periodic displays of an impressive military prowess, as more of Israel's enemies have come to style themselves as Marxists rather than traditionalists, some of the background support for Israel in the United States has shifted to emerge from the Right rather than the Left.

And what of other ethnic minorities in the American political picture? Comparisons have been made between the supporters of Israel and the role of Polish Americans, with their obvious sympathies for the political or economic well-being of Poland. While such political clout was obviously strong in the 1940s, with Democrats and Republicans having to bid for Polish-American votes in Buffalo and Detroit just as assiduously as they courted Jewish votes in New York City, such Polish-American commitments to the specific foreign policy question have become less fervent over time. Why has this been so, when Poland obviously today remains in the grip of a regime dominated by Moscow, a regime for which the great majority of Poles in Poland (or in the United States) would never vote if they were given any alternative choice?

The easing of feelings about the imposition of a Communist government in Poland in part shows a resignation to the inevitable, but in another part shows that ethnic feelings have a dimension going beyond any ideological principles about the manner in which men are governed. As the 1940s passed to the 1950s and 1960s, life became a little more normal in Poland, even when major decisions still required the approval of Moscow. Frontiers were secure, the speaking of the Polish language was secure, a measure of home rule emerged after 1956, economic prospects, while never very promising, had improved. Above all, the Roman Catholic church was after a time allowed a certain freedom to continue to offer its services, as the explicitly atheistic Communist regime decided that the religious faith of the majority of Poles made compromise necessary. Rather than waxing indignant about Russian imperialism, Polish Americans over time thus came to resign themselves to what there was of Polish national life in the home country, accepting the opportunity to visit the country as tourists, in some cases even to return to it for retirement. The half-a-loaf of ethnic nationalism is thus still being indulged back in Europe, just as it was indulged in Germany or France after 1848.

The contrast with the Israeli case is thus obvious. What American supporters of Israel fear is a pushing of Israel "into the sea," as the Jewish religion and Hebrew language would lose its special status in the territory that now is Israel. If a similar fate threatened Poland, Polish Americans would be vehemently disposed to cast their votes against any American foreign policy that tolerated this. But the threat to Polish national life has been whittled down, as language and religion are not threatened for the moment, with political freedom being the only loss. An American without any particular ethnic attachment to the cultures of Europe might feel that the last was the greatest loss of all. Yet the point here, of course, is that many Americans have more particular attachments, comparable to the particular attachments of Europeans in the past that have been labeled "nationalism."

Another speculative comparison sometimes is made with Irish Americans and the issues dividing Northern Ireland under British sovereignty today. It is clear that Irish Americans were a powerful lobby for Irish independence in the years before 1922, and therefore worked against American entry into World War I on the British side. Most of the financial support for today's Irish Republican Army (IRA) still also comes from Boston and New York, from people who see the conflict in Northern Ireland simply as an extension of the original struggle for national independence. Yet, with a few particular exceptions, Irish Americans have deployed remarkably little of their political clout in Congress or in the general American political process on the issue of Ulster, and one again would want to ask why this is so.[26] When compared with Jewish Americans or Polish Americans, or Greek Americans on the Cyprus issue, it surely has not been that the Irish lacked votes in important districts, or that they have shown any lack of political skills.

The explanation might rather be a little more complicated. Thoughtful Irish Americans will see a difference between the original struggle through the whole of Ireland, where the overwhelming majority wanted an end to British rule, and the current struggle in Ulster, being waged by terrorist means by the IRA. While there is undoubtedly an underprivileged Roman Catholic minority, the majority of people in the six northern countries are Protestant in religion, most certainly reluctant to be governed as part of a unified Ireland. The fact that the great majority of non–Irish Americans are themselves Protestant in religion would moreover inhibit supporters of the IRA from raising such issues too boldly in the United States. (Consider the problems a Zionist would have in the United States if most Americans were Muslims.) Finally, the continuing attachment to Great Britain, through shared language, shared political traditions, and current alliance against the Soviet Union, further makes it difficult for Irish Americans to devote any great effort to trying to steer American foreign policy on the Ulster question.

As a most impressive recent demonstration of the possibilities of ethnic politics in the determination of American foreign policy, one might then look simply to the deployment of political clout by Greek Americans on the issue of Cyprus, leading to a suspension of American military assistance to Turkey after the 1974 invasion and partition of the island, a suspension of assistance that imposed a real price on the U.S. strategic and political position when Turkey imposed various forms of retaliation.[27]

The ability of the Greek minority to exercise such influence may have been enhanced by the particular mood of the country at the end of Nixon's stay in office, as the Congress and public had become annoyed with secrecy in government (and thus were difficult to persuade by the entreaties of Secretary of State Kissinger), and indignation at possible Turkish sources of American narcotic supplies had added a domestic issue to reduce any feelings of friendship for the Turks. Yet the issue also again shows how a determined minority can get some of its way in any democratic political process, as long as it channels its votes and influence and demands to the one set of issues about which it cares the most.

We turn then to a last major ethnic group about whose impact on American foreign policy we are seeing increasing speculation, black Americans. A fair number of commentators have now drawn the picture of blacks caring about black Africa in the same way that Jews have cared about Israel, or Poles about Poland; noting the increasing political power of black Americans, they have then predicted that this would impose some new guidance and new constraints on American foreign policy. While the bulk of black political influence is undoubtedly still likely to be channeled to domestic issues, given the large inequities left in American domestic political and economic arrangements, a certain amount of the influence and energy here may be channeled to external issues, just as has been the case with other American minority groups.[28]

There are, of course, some major gaps in the analogies as drawn. Very few American blacks, as a result of the length of the time

118 American Foreign Policy

elapsed since the arrival of this group in the United States, and more particularly of the brutal and involuntary selection processes of slavery, can trace a kinship to living persons in Africa. The ties of letter writing to cousins are thus missing, and so are most of the cultural links, since very few black Americans adhere to anything like an African religious belief, or speak an African language. The effort to instill some of such feeling among black Americans by learning Swahili is somewhat ironic, since Swahili is a language of East Africa, while the majority of slaves brought to America necessarily originated in West Africa.

Because of the eroded direct links between black Americans and black Africans, the special interest of black-American voters here may thus have to be more symbolic, more tied to issues of U.S. domestic policy. Given the historical memories of slavery and political discrimination against persons of black color, any overseas vestige of such political arrangements is likely to draw opposition, and the white regime in South Africa is blatantly the most obvious target here. The Portuguese regimes that tried to hang on in Angola and Mozambique previously drew a similar attack, as did the last vestiges of a white regime in Rhodesia.

Some of the other complications and issues of American policy toward Africa will be quite unwelcome to black Americans, if only because of the way such issues can be used by traditional forces. For example, the mere prospect of seeing black regimes fighting each other, as between Uganda and Tanzania, or Ethiopia and Somali, or between the factions in Angola, can be exploited by supporters of the "white man's burden" to justify traditional colonial regimes here, as the implication will be drawn that Africans are somehow not capable of governing themselves in a peaceful and stable way. Similarly, if the American government and other Americans show signs of concern about the spread of Marxist regimes, and the concomitant suppression of any possibility of political democracy, a certain number of American blacks will share such feelings, but many will be wary of seeing the issues phrased in such terms, lest this again be used then as an excuse for continued support for the white regime in South Africa.

The American effort to support an anti-Russian faction in Angola in 1975 (an effort in which, interestingly enough, the Communist Chinese also participated) thus clearly illustrates the fears of many black Americans, as South African participation on the same side was tolerated and encouraged by Secretary of State Kissinger, in what could have been a move toward a de facto alliance against Russian influence, an alliance from which the white regime in Pretoria would have drawn its own benefits.

Looking far down the road, one might thus venture the prediction that the American black community will not be so permanently mobilized into concern about Africa, but may indeed detach itself, once the remnants and prospects of white domination of black majorities are at last erased. Until this is accomplished, however, blacks will have to be engaged, simply because the symbolic and psychological implications of a tolerance of regimes such as the South African regime are unbearable. Until this happens, black Americans will correspondingly often seem at odds with many of their white fellow Americans about the importance of resisting Soviet influence in Africa.

This hardly suggests that the white American interest in preserving the possibility of a pluralistic or liberal system of political democracy for Africa is insincere, or that black Americans have somehow come to share the perspective of American radicals, by which economic equality must always come ahead of free elections and freedom of the press. There is little evidence that American blacks differ significantly from whites on their choice between political and economic democracy in the abstract. Both groups probably share much the same values, while confronted by the same new doubts about the compatibility of these two kinds of goals.

Rather, in the case of American black voters, there is the added input of the derogatory implications about race, implications that were taken for granted by most of the whites of the world in the nineteenth century, and only very slowly are being erased and overcome. For a black American to accept a slur on black culture or genetic potential is just as obnoxious as for a German American or an Irish American to accept such slurs about origin.

Ethnic factors thus do not necessarily outvalue considerations of principle and ideology here, but they clearly play a role in altering and limiting American commitments to them. As noted, the connections one feels on such ethnic matters vary however from group to group, such that the Irish link is different from the Jewish link, which in turn is different from the black link.

CULTURAL IMPERIALISM

When baited too much by foreign critics since 1945 (critics denouncing the alleged hypocrisy and imperfections of the U.S. political system, or the alleged depredations of the U.S. economic system), Americans have understandably been tempted to snap back and ask how many people are lined up waiting for permanent entry visas

to other countries. As the tragic plight of the "boat people" trying to escape Cuba or Vietnam since the Communist takeover illustrates, those who "vote with their feet" vote for the West, i.e., vote
precisely for what Americans once felt such self-confidence in
defending.

Americans believe in free choice. They believe in existential
decisions, decisions by which human beings decide their own fate,
by which they commit themselves to the futures in which they must
live. The world should be offered choices, this has been the American
belief. When they thus choose *to be able to choose* in the future, this
all the more warms the hearts of the Americans of a Lockean persuasion. "Voting with their feet" thus fits all too well into a general
pattern, together with "voting with their movie tickets" or "voting
by the twisting of their radio or television dials."

Before Americans become too gleeful and content with this endorsement of their way of life at all the movie box offices of this
globe, however, we must entertain at least one counterview presented
by Marxists and other radicals, and indeed by many nonradicals,
around the world.

If American cultural appeal is to any extent simply the fruits of
the advantage of speaking English, this would merely be a historical
fluke, a result of the strength of numbers, complimenting the American way of life no more than the metric system should be seen as
particularly a praise of France, or the use of Arabic numbers as a
praise of Arabian life-style.

If American cultural appeal is more than the economies of scale
of a worldwide swing to English, moreover, it may reflect the particular talents of Hollywood; but is this any more relevant to the free
exchange of ideas than would be a Turkish pride in the growth of
heroin addiction? Many Americans would indeed share the disdain
of cultured Swedes or Russians or Frenchmen or Canadians for
American "pop culture," for the manner in which Hollywood products and American mass-television seem directed to the less stimu-
lating and creative and thought-provoking levels of entertainment,
for the way American products marketed by Madison Avenue techniques come close to addicting the customer to want what he buys.

A Marxist view here, consistently translating phenomena into
material terms, would see cultural power simply as a function of, and
form of, economic power. Russians indeed have spoken of the
"Coca-colonization of the world," endorsing the unhappiness of
many of the elders around the world who must watch their children
slavishly and modishly switching to drink Coke or Pepsi, or to wear
American-style jeans, or to listen to American jazz music, or to
watch American movies and television.

Even in the more serious arenas of academic interchange, one can offer the argument that what seems to be the free flow of ideas and free choices actually reflects basic material and economic power. The reference here emerges then to something called "cultural imperialism." How many Americans can afford to study India or Indonesia or Tanzania, becoming experts on these foreign countries, hiring researchers to help them, giving advice on the future development of these areas? How many Indians or Indonesians or Tanzanians, by contrast, can afford or find the opportunity to study the United States? It is not that such scholars would not be very welcome, for many an American university might indeed like to hire the Afro-Asian scholar who had made a career of studying American politics or American history. Rather it is that, by the force of university endowments and economic environments, virtually no Africans or Asians are presented with an opportunity for developing such careers.

If we let the natural economic forces of the academic market work themselves out, one side then gets overwhelmed by the other. It would be foolish to conclude, the critics would argue, that such an imbalance occurs only because Africa needs American advice more than the United States needs African advice; at the very least it would be impossibly insulting to settle on such a conclusion. Rather the imbalance occurs because American universities simply are richer in physical assets, in the money to pay for airplane tickets, than the universities in the developing countries.

A similar kind of problem shows up at a point between the sheer entertainment of pop culture movies and the serious university business of comparative political development analysis, specifically in the circulation possibilities of mass circulation periodicals. Turning again very close to home, we have seen continuous Canadian concern about the widespread Canadian readership of U.S. magazines, along with the tendency of Canadians to watch American television programs wherever they can be received along the border.[29] If great numbers of Canadian children grow up answering "George Washington," when asked the test question of "Who is the father of our country?," Canadian educational leaders may be justified in feeling some concern. (Given the realities of history, of course, "George Washington" might in a roundabout way be the correct answer, if we concluded that the only difference between English-speakers on the two sides of the border shows up in how they felt about the institution of the British monarchy.)

The Swedish government, in its management of television broadcasting, has similarly shown a great concern to ration and limit the amount of programming from sources in the United States, even when such programs are almost invariably the most popular items

on the week's schedule. The decision to restrict what would otherwise have been the natural result of straightforward consumer
demand stems from at least two concerns. First, the government
concluded that American programming is habit-forming and of se-
ductively low quality in its entertainment, rather than being enlight-
ening in the process of being enjoyable; second, it also feels that
excessive reliance on a foreign form of cultural expression would be
bad per se for the cultural life of Sweden, by analogy would be a
form of cultural dependency and imperialism.

Is there indeed any way to resolve this debate, to decide whether
Americans are proving merit about their own political and cultural
system by having their films and magazines so much in demand, or
instead are producing a kind of a drug that actually reflects rather
demeaningly on their own society? Almost surely there is no easy
way.

Americans will continue to take pride in the appeal of their own
life-style, whether this be evidenced in the popularity of their movies
or jazz or American-style blue jeans. When thinking hard about the
vagaries of fashion, Americans will at times cross-examine and somewhat discount this appeal, but most are not ready to conclude that
they are simply peddlers of a cultural narcotic, that they are somehow brainwashing the world into liking things that are American.

Above all, Americans have many reasons today to distrust the
Marxist argument that cultural preferences (preferences about what
to read and what to listen to) are simply reflections of basic material
and economic arrangements. Such arguments are all too often used
by regimes as an excuse to restrict freedom of the press, to prohibit
the kinds of criticism essential to political democracy, the criticisms
that force regimes either to satisfy their electorate or step down.

As part of all that has been said about American Lockean assumptions and their links to foreign policy, a generalization might be
offered here that freedom of sale of literature is probably the most
sensitive issue on which the United States confronts the domestic regimes of foreign countries, far more sensitive than restrictions on sales
of other products. For the Japanese to be obstinate about discour-
aging the sale of American automobiles or foodstuffs is irritating, but
acceptable in the end. For the Japanese government to restrict import of the *New York Times* would in ideological terms amount to
the declaration of a change in world alliance. The *New York Times*
and the rest of the American press would of course denounce such a
move out of self-interest, as would the American academic community by and large. But much more than the special interests of the
"information industry" would be involved, for such an imposition of
state controls involves the crossing of some very important lines in

political philosophy. Canadian efforts to restrict the sale of American periodicals have thus raised some issues that go far deeper than any other disputes along the border, far more profound than arguments about who is most at fault for polluting Lake Erie. The fear is not just that American publishers will lose customers, but that an opening wedge on the denial of freedom will have been entered.

The dilemma remains. Without political controls, one assuredly gets a fair amount of unpleasant academic imperialism. With government controls, however, one can lose all ability to know and judge what one is getting.

It is clearly a fact that Americans go very far at home in freedom of the press, and in constricting the ability of government to withhold information from the press. There are Americans who for good reason worry for the continued freedom of the press, and who think that the U.S. government is too free to keep secrets (especially to keep secrets in the area of foreign policy, where the particular excuse of "the enemy may be listening" can be used to cover many sins).[30] Yet it is difficult for such persons to find any foreign country to point to, anywhere, as a model of better protection of the press; even such thoroughly civilized places as Great Britain and Sweden feel much more disposed to tolerate government control and obstruction of press inquiries.

Americans are a people of curiosity, Perhaps this is the result of years of so-called "isolation," when they could indeed speculate with interest about other nations at a detached and militarily safe distance. Perhaps it is instead primarily because freedom of information is necessary to free elections, and to government by the consent of the government.

At any rate, this very much colors American views of the outside world. Despite the contrary skepticism of radical critics, the issue of freedom of information will probably continue to loom larger in American dispositions on foreign events than the backs and forths of capitalism versus socialism, and it probably will count for more than the protection of American investments abroad. Has it been the American instinct to leap more quickly to the defense of the United Fruit Company or to the defense of United Press International? In truth, it has probably been the latter.

NOTES

1. Louis Hartz, *The Liberal Tradition in America* (New York: Harvest Books, 1955), pp. 145–202.

2. The atttitudes of American abolitionists on international questions are noted in James McPherson, *The Struggle for Equality* (Princeton: Princeton University Press, 1964), pp. 140–43.

3. See William Langer, "Farewell to Empire," *Foreign Affairs* 41, no. 1 (October 1962): 115-30 for a good discussion of the nature of the European drive toward imperialism in Africa.

4. American foreign policy toward Haiti is discussed in Ludwell Lee Montague, *Haiti and the United States* (Durham: Duke University Press, 1940); and policy toward Liberia in Edward W. Chester, *Clash of Titans* (Maryknoll: Orbis Books, 1974) and in Charles Morrow Wilson, *Liberia* (New York: Harper & Row, 1971).

5. See Chester, *Clash of Titans*, pp. 169-73, 190-95.

6. The burdensome nature of the indemnity Haiti had agreed to, in exchange for a French recognition of independence, is described in Robert Debs Heinl and Nancy Gordon Heinl, *Written in Blood* (Boston: Houghton Mifflin, 1978), pp. 170-72.

7. Projects for settling freed American slaves in Haiti are noted in Montague, *Haiti and the United States*, pp. 66-80.

8. The end of reconstruction, and the shift away from full equality for blacks in the United States is analyzed in C. V. Woodward, *Reunion and Reaction* (Garden City: Doubleday, 1951).

9. A useful picture of Schurz and his views is provided in Claude Fuess, *Carl Schurz: Reformer* (New York: Dodd, Mead, 1932).

10. For a discussion of the significance of American linguistic and ethnic characteristics on foreign policy, see John Higham, *Strangers in the Land* (New Brunswick: Rutgers University Press, 1955).

11. Roosevelt's arguments for entering World War I are outlined in Robert E. Osgood, *Ideals and Self-Interest in American Politics* (Chicago: University of Chicago Press, 1953), pp. 135-53.

12. Wilson's substantially different rationale for entering the world war is well presented in Edward H. Buehrig, *Woodrow Wilson and the Balance of Power* (Bloomington: Indiana University Press, 1955).

13. See Harold R. Isaacs, *Scratches on Our Minds* (New York: John Day, 1958) for a very revealing picture of American attitudes toward Chinese as compared with other Asians.

14. The imbalance of respect between Americans and Russians is discussed in Max Laserson, *The American Impact on Russia* (New York: Macmillan, 1950). See also Nikolai V. Sivachev and Nikolai N. Yakovlev, *Russia and the United States* (Chicago: University of Chicago Press, 1979).

15. American confidence in Canadian governmental institutions since the turn of the century is discussed in Edgar W. McInnis, *The Unguarded Frontier* (Garden City: Doubleday and Doran, 1942), pp. 330-70.

16. U.S. feelings about contemporary Mexico are analyzed in Daniel James, *Mexico and the Americans* (New York: Praeger, 1963), especially pp. 394-439.

17. The links between Protestant religion and Lockean American values are developed in Seymour Martin Lipset, *The First New Nation* (New York: Basic Books, 1963), chap. 4.

18. The extent of U.S. defaults on debts owed abroad is described in Lance E. Davis, Jonathan R. T. Hughes, and Duncan M. McDougall, *American Economic History* (Homewood: Richard D. Irwin, 1965), p. 253.

19. For Quebec's opposition to the American Revolution, see Sir Reginald Coupland, *The Quebec Act* (Oxford: The Clarendon Press, 1925), pp. 123-86.

20. The continual U.S. tension about any European reentry into Latin America is made clear in Dexter Perkins, *Hands Off* (Boston: Little, Brown, 1941).

21. For Louis Napoleon's French venture into Mexico, see James, *Mexico and the Americans*, pp. 72-106.

22. For an interesting account, see Barbara Tuchman, *The Zimmerman Telegram* (London: Constable, 1959).

23. The U.S. concern to have German-affiliated airlines in Latin America replaced with affiliates of Pan Am is described in Hubert Herring, *A History of Latin America* (New York: Alfred A. Knopf, 1955), p. 553.

24. The confrontations of American hopes and fears for Latin America with German hopes and fears are described in the memoirs of Spruille Braden, *Diplomats and Demagogues* (New Rochelle: Arlington House, 1971).

25. A typical poll on American support for the sides in the Middle East is presented in *Current Opinion* 3, issue 6 (June 1975): 56.

26. Irish-American commitments to the issues of Northern Ireland are discussed in Kevin M. Cahill, "America and Ulster: Healing Hands," *Foreign Policy*, no. 37 (Winter 1978-79), pp. 87-101.

27. See Laurence Stern, "Bitter Lessons: How We Failed in Cyprus," *Foreign Policy*, no. 19 (Summer 1975), pp. 34-78 for an account of the mobilization of Greek Americans on the Cyprus issue.

28. The possibilities of Black-American identification with events in Africa are discussed in Martin Weil, "Can the Blacks Do for Africa What the Jews Did for Israel," *Foreign Policy*, no. 15 (Summer 1974), pp. 109-30.

29. Canadian concerns about the influence of American television and American periodicals are discussed in Ian Lumsden, ed., *Close the 49th Parallel, etc.* (Toronto: University of Toronto Press, 1970).

30. See Morton H. Halperin and Daniel Hoffman, *Freedom vs. National Security* (New York: Chelsea House, 1979).

6
The United States Becomes a World Power: 1890–1945

The chapters thus far have shown the variety of ways in which the beginnings of the twentieth century can support one explanation or another for American foreign policy. This chapter now will attempt to fill in some of the pieces, from the first onset of a more active American world role to the outbreak of the cold war, in each case again asking whether one theory is supported more than another, whether American foreign policy has been best explained by the pursuit of power, or of markets, or of liberty and human happiness abroad.

For the sake of argument, the analysis has thus far largely gone along with the historical generalization that 1891 was a more significant "turning outward" than others. Skeptics may cite historical detail to question the special importance of this particular shift, noting the earlier turnings outward listed by Klingberg and American involvement in Samoa already in the 1880s. Yet it will still be the events since 1890 that inevitably most grip us here.

Radicals, to repeat, make a great deal out of this 1890 turning outward as showing a change in American motivation, reflecting new pressures from the imperfections of capitalism; by contrast, the liberal and power politics views both might argue that the change came mainly in new American opportunities. Liberals would contend that the United States had always striven to do good in the world, simply not being able to do as much before 1890 as after; realpolitik analysts would contend that the United States had always striven for power position, being less able to grab it before 1890 than after.

WORLD WAR I

Yet the liberal and power politics positions are hardly destined to remain conjoined as we explore the subsequent events in American foreign policy. Continuing the challenge to the particular significance of the 1890s, one could wonder what to make of an even more momentous American decision to turn outward and "intervene" toward the end of Klingberg's 1891-1919 period, namely the 1917 U.S. entry into World War I. Compared to the costs of the Spanish-American War and the moves that accompanied it, this was a far more profound step.[1] It was indeed accompanied by an American decision after 1916 to build a navy second to none,[2] i.e., challenging the British fleet in a manner that few had ever dared. When Germany had moved in the same direction earlier, it had alienated Great Britain in ways that set the stage for the outbreak of World War I.

The United States had indeed shifted policy with some vehemence as World War I evolved. Prior to 1914, Americans shared with Europeans a general optimism that this was the best of all ages for man, that war in the future would not work to blight this, but at most would amount to some short bursts of military activity, lasting weeks or months, rather than years.

When the war broke out, the predominant American concern for the first year or two was for the maintenance of neutrality, i.e., how best to remain isolated from, rather than involved in, the conflict. After 1916, the United States then moved more to enter the war, producing great intensity of feeling and great intolerance of dissent within the United States itself.

Was this U.S. entry into the war simply a reflection of power-oriented realpolitik? At times it has been explained that way, as the United States presumably intervened to keep Germany from conquering all of Europe, and thus to keep a German fleet from menacing the shores of the United States in the future. Yet the prospect of a total German victory had receded, instead of grown, as the war became stalemated after the Germans were stopped short of Paris in 1914; a total defeat of the Allies, with Germany emerging as a menace to the whole world, was not yet such a real prospect.

From a power position, the United States might thus have indeed seen this prolonged stalemated war as a great opportunity, for it simply pitted one European regime against another, weakening all of them so as to make less likely any new ventures in the Western Hemisphere or the Far East. It was the growth of the German navy and the prospect of a European war that had at last forced the

British to withdraw their fleet from the Caribbean, a move that most American naval officers, and most Americans in general, welcomed.

British dominance of the seas had indeed served as a very useful accessory to the Monroe Doctrine, as British interests coincided with American commitments to the maintenance of self-government in Latin America. Yet relatively few Americans were in the mood to admit this or dwell on it. The British fleet in these waters was clearly preferable, as a known commodity, to a German fleet that might replace it, but the U.S. first choice would most certainly have been to have no European navies at all in these waters. Why should it not thus have been to the interest of the United States to allow the European war to drag on, while the American fleet continued to expand? The elementary tenets of balance-of-power logic would have suggested that it was to the national interest to let potential rivals continue their stalemated war, draining each other of military and economic potential for the future.

A second kind of argument might be focused again on the alleged economic dictates of capitalism. Yet advocates of such explanations of American foreign policy tend to make much more out of the Spanish-American War than out of American entry into World War I, and the reason is not hard to find. The links to capitalism simply do not amount to a strong and central explanation of the U.S. 1917 decision, anymore than they explain the studied American neutrality of the first two years of that war.

Did the United States grab for control over new markets at the 1919 Versailles Peace Conference? When offered a mandate over Turkey, or a possible share of the German colonies, the United States under President Wilson waived all such options aside. Or did the United States (as discussed elsewhere) enter the war because a small portion of its industry had sold munitions to the Allies on credit, and feared that it would not be able to collect its bills from the British and the French unless they defeated Germany? The influence of this special interest is generally discounted by historians today.

U.S. trade was being interfered with in the war by the British blockade and by German submarine warfare, and the United States displayed a major sensitivity about such interference, just as it had made an issue of principle about the "freedom of the seas" in 1790 and 1812. If the historical parallels of a century earlier are significant, however, the workings of an "advanced stage of capitalism" do not then seem so central.

Turning away from explanations in terms of military power or economic capitalism, a small part of the American entry into the war might be attributed to a straightforward ethnic nationalism patterned here on the European model. Russia had come to the defense of Serbia because the Serbs spoke a Slavic language related to Russian. France was ready for a war with Germany because there were speakers of French in Alsace and Lorraine, forced to live under German-speaking rule. As the United States had itself gone through a stress on the speaking of English and the showing of respect for the national flag in the Progressive movement, this had led some Americans, especially in the Republican Party, to feel that the United States should behave internationally as other nations, standing up for its culture and national rights, and so forth. Such feelings would then naturally have been exploitable in favor of an alliance with Great Britain, and a fair amount of the prowar propaganda along the American eastern seaboard stressed the importance of the cultural tie.

Yet the most important explanation of the 1917 American entry into World War I, it will be argued here, stems not from lust for military power or for economic markets, or from any kind of culturally oriented nationalism, but rather again as a reflection of American values or "American idealism," a reflection of the altruistic strain of American foreign policy that has been at work all along.

In smaller part the American entry into the war now occurred because the Germans had after a time come to be seen to be more inhumane, more indifferent to the happiness of human beings in general. The "militaristic, antidemocratic Prussians" had been painted in Allied propaganda as inflicting atrocities on Belgians. The German reliance on submarines for their form of blockade not only disrupted commerce, as the British blockade similarly disrupted it, but took a regular toll of noncombatant lives because of the inability to provide warning of attack.[3] When a revolution in Russia deposed the czar, the most visibly obnoxious and antidemocratic regime on the Allied side faded from view, so that the United States could find it morally easier to identify a better, and worse, side in the war.

Yet even more important than such moral comparisons of the Allies and the Germans, the United States under the leadership of President Wilson now saw a need and opportunity here to intervene in pursuit of traditional American principles, to intervene to cease such bloodshed once and for all, to intervene to reform the political system of the world once and for all.

The American motive was thus very different from what a "let them fight" balance-of-power logic would have suggested. It was rather to "stop the fighting." The war in Europe was hurting the American economy, to be sure. Yet, far more important, it was, to American eyes, dragging down all of European culture and European prospect for full human development. The United States thus intervened to tip the balance, so as to push at least one side through to victory, in a way that might hopefully then abolish all of traditional power politics and diplomacy and war, and, with it, politically unrepresentative government. The unrestricted German submarine warfare campaign is normally seen as tipping the scales in American deliberations, but the horror of Europe's stalemated war supplied the bulk of the motivation.

If the naval technology of the years after 1890 had thus lifted American opportunities (and fears) to a new level, the outbreak and prolongation of World War I lifted them once more. Opponents of tendencies toward American entry into the war were inclined to picture it as a total departure from all of past American tradition. President Wilson was to respond by an analysis very parallel to that presented here, namely that a new role had been thrust upon the United States in terms of the values it had cherished all along.[4]

The "war to make the world safe for democracy" was a phrase that would afterward have a very hollow and hypocritical ring, for the German regime of 1914 was far more democratic than the one that was to follow in 1933. Yet the intention of Americans at large was not badly stated in this phrase. The intention was to change the diplomatic system of the world so that war above all would be prevented. Linked to this, it was to foster political democracy in place of traditional unrepresentative regimes around the globe.

Woodrow Wilson is regarded as a failure historically because the United States Senate rejected the League of Nations, and his health was destroyed in the process of campaigning for the league. With the election of 1920 seemingly putting its cachet on this rejection, he is retrospectively often portrayed as having been out of touch with the American public, as having idiosyncratically or neurotically pursued his own high moral standards for a system of world order, in a manner that had far outrun his consituency.

Yet this may be a very misleading picture of how little Wilson's world view had been shared by Americans at large. Public opinion polling had not yet been developed in the years before the 1930s, but indirect evidence suggests that a majority of Americans in 1919 indeed may have favored the League of Nations.[5]

When Wilson led the United States into World War I in 1917 as an "associated" rather than "allied" power, this was specifically to indicate that American goals would be different from those of a Britain or a France (as well as from the goals of a Germany or an Austria). While others had begun the war seeking territory or power or colonies, the United States had entered the war to end war, and hopefully to end the world system that had made wars like this happen in the first place. Closely linked to this goal of maintaining peace (and closely linked to American foreign policy attitudes all along), the United States also came into the war committed to fostering self-determination and self-government, i.e., republican government and political democracy. As embodied very clearly in Wilson's Fourteen Points and his design for the League of Nations, this proposed self-determination for many of the troubled areas of Europe; it similarly proposed a temporary "mandatory," rather than permanent colonial, status for the European government of what had been German possessions around the globe.[6]

The Republican opposition to Wilson had criticized this formula for American entry into the war, suggesting that the United States should become as self-interested and power-oriented as other states. Yet the public, only in part because Wilson was the incumbent president, accepted his view of "associate" status much more than the alternative of "allied" power politics.

An illustration of Wilsonian attitudes, and of generally altruistic American attitudes, on entry into World War I shows up in the responses to the two 1917 revolutions in Russia, first deposing the czar and then deposing Kerenski.[7] It is generally held to be nontrivial that American entry into the war was eased by the overthrow of the czar, thus eliminating a blatant example of nondemocracy from the Allied side. Lenin, to be sure, did not institute political democracy after ousting Kerenski from power, and the United States was to wait many years before recording diplomatic recognition to the Bolshevik government. Yet the attitude of the United States during the ensuing Russian Civil War was indeed the most sympathetic of any of the Allied and Associated powers toward the new Russian regime, and the most suspicious of the selfish motives of the other powers supporting the White Russian forces in that war.

The European powers with whom the United States thus "associated" itself in 1917 were not so prone to accept American moral wisdom as proven here, as remedying all the mistakes made by the old world. While American entry into the war was assuredly welcome, the inclination of the British and French was nonetheless to try to win the war in 1917 if possible, before American intervention became crucial, thus perhaps to avoid whatever conditions Wilson and his country threatened to impose. If the offensives of 1917 did not succeed (indeed they did not), the American reinforcements would then guarantee against defeat in 1918, and probably would afford a victory.

Why should the entente states thus have been so apprehensive about the prospect of becoming dependent on American intervention to defeat the Central Powers? The first "realist" interpretation is that experienced European statesmen like Clemenceau and Lloyd George saw Wilson and his fellow Americans to be quite mad, impossibly idealistic, and naive about the realities of the international system. What Americans thought high-minded would thus be condemned as foolish by the regimes of the old world. Clemenceau at the Versailles Conference was to lament his relationship to Woodrow Wilson as follows: "How can you negotiate with someone who thinks he's Jesus Christ?"

The second realist interpretation of European apprehension would not have accused the Americans of naivete here, but of hypocrisy, assuming that the United States was just as power-minded as any other state, just as interested in its own national welfare, but pretending to be naive and high-minded and altruistic. This had after all been the general European interpretation for all of the emergence of American activist foreign policy since the 1880s. Germans and Britishers and Frenchmen did not view American activities in Samoa or China, or the Spanish-American War, or the extensions of the Monroe Doctrine via the Roosevelt Corollary, as anything more noble than their own behavior, but saw it rather as simple power politics, and resented any American claim that it was better than that.

Leaving aside such resentments of style, the European apprehension about emerging American influence here might thus simply have amounted to another round in the workings of the old-fashioned balance of power. The Americans were going to intervene to keep the Allies from defeating the Central Powers too badly, by this logic, just as any bystanders in the old balance system would have so intervened. If the Allies could not get the war over with in any other fashion, this was better than a prolonged stalemate. But if the British and French could defeat the Germans and Austrians on their own in 1917, without running up any moral debt to the Americans for their assistance, the cashing in on the victory could have been more total, the territorial and other gains that had been negotiated in the secret treaties could have been claimed to the fullest.

Yet this second European interpretation of the American intervention as selfish may have been wrong (and so may the first). The Wilsonian policy (despite Republican suggestions that it should be more nationalistic—more like what the Europeans expected it to be) was not limited to narrow American material interests, was not designed to intervene just as a traditional balancer of power would have intervened, but was rather intended to reform the system once and for all. Europeans had been claiming ever since the 1880s that Americans were no more altruistic or high-minded in their foreign policy than other nations, but this may have been factually wrong, a simple psychological defense against the elementary guilt that the United States example could engender in European governments. Just as in ordinary life, real generosity is rare, and much of such apparent generosity is feigned. Yet those of us who are not very generous will tend to charge all of it with being feigned, at the least serving as a shield so that we will not need to reconsider our position.

The concrete details of American performance indeed suggest serious differences in foreign policy performance, just as the concrete political culture and domestic political system of the United States was quite different from that of any European state. The Marxist attack on American foreign policy at many points accuses the United States of being more imperialist than other powers, because it was more capitalist than other powers. The realpolitik attack rather contends that the United States has been just as imperialist as other powers, because this is inherent in the nature of being a "power"; because Americans insist on refusing to admit this to themselves (this attack would then contend), they at times become more erratic and destructive in the playing out of their roles.[8]

Both these critiques of American foreign policy will thus often have difficulty in accepting any evidence or argument that the United States has been genuinely altruistic in some portions of its foreign policy behavior. Yet there is evidence and there are arguments here that indeed need to be addressed.

If Wilson's concern for the well-being of the world, not just of the United States, was thus genuine, we still have the first rebuttal from Paris or London, that it was naive and foolish and psychologically aberrant. Again, while this is a charge very much echoed by theorists of realpolitik in the United States, it also might not be so well-taken.

THE RETREAT TO ISOLATION: 1919

Some of the erosion of American commitment to the League of Nations might thus be traced to the simple accident that Wilson was personally impolitic in his dealings with the U.S. Senate, rather than to any gap between his moral feelings and the feelings of Americans at large. Yet the ensuing period of explicit and self-conscious U.S. isolationism after World War I will probably require more explanation than this.[9]

One kind of explanation, perhaps here for a time coming into closer agreement with the Klingberg "cyclical" picture, might simply be that the sheer human cost of the participation in World War I had come as a shock to Americans, just as battlefield gore always has an immediate negative effect (followed after some decades by positive nostalgia and heroic sagas). Americans had not been involved in any such carnage since their own Civil War, and had not been expecting it when they had gotten into it, and would now be shy of it.

As a slightly different interpretation, did Americans in the Harding and Coolidge years simply revert to a totally selfish isolationism, caring nothing about the outside world, as long as that world could not hurt them? One slice of the electorate was of course of this opinion, just as it had been all along, but could this slice by itself explain the totality of the swing in American policy? Was the 1920 "return to normalcy" somehow an open espousal of the crass and the anti-moral in life? Were the 1920s primarily an example of the United States losing interest in the well-being of peoples anywhere else?

The era of Prohibition is often painted this way, as a time of Babbittry at home, and of conscious and deliberate isolation abroad. Yet the disrespect for law in the years of Prohibition can lead to exaggerated conclusions about the decline of American concern for what was good or generous otherwise. The American withdrawal from the world after 1920 is not yet really an example of American callousness toward the outside world, but rather a disillusionment about the sincerity and motives of the other nations and regimes in it.

A substantially different (noncyclical) theory would thus suggest that the altruistically interventionist sentiment in the United States remained as strong as before, but now had, in the processes of Versailles, passed through a seeming "moment of truth," namely that one could not trust foreign regimes anywhere to share American values. Upon entering World War I, Americans had manifested some such distrust, by their Associated rather than Allied status, but had nonetheless let themselves believe that there might be a real qualitative difference between the war intentions of Great Britain and France and Italy on one hand, and Germany and Austria on the other.

The petty territorial squabbles of Versailles,[10] amid the disclosures of the earlier secret treaties among the Allies, now suggested to many Americans that they had exaggerated their leverage abroad, simply in misreading the like-mindedness of other powers. Americans could still believe that their model of political democracy would be ideal for Germany and for Poland, and for every other state, but they felt betrayed by foreign partners who had only pretended to believe this, while enlisting American support in the war. "Making the world safe for democracy" in retrospect looked like the reason Americans had fought, but was less the reason most other states had fought, and this at the very least occasioned a rethinking of American strategy.

If no one out there was as high-minded as the United States, this would not necessarily affect the commitment of the United States to such goals as the establishment of political democracy and an international system conducive to peace. But it had to alter our American perceptions of how much power and leverage we had. In the nineteenth century, Americans had also not been uninterested in the future of Europe, but had felt low in power to affect it. The events of World War I had seemed to offer great power and influence here, but if some of this was based on the assumption of there being like-minded states, such power and influence now had to be seen as overrated.

Wars might now break out in Europe, or they might not. If such wars did occur, the American suspicion, after a bitter experience, was that there would not be any clearly "right" side. If such wars occurred, it might be wiser for the United States now to do the best it could to ensure itself against material damage, rather than putting any great effort into reforming the system overall, into trying to help the Europeans to peace.

It is interesting to note the intensity with which this new yearning for isolation emerged. In part this was simple nostalgia, as efforts to go back to the past always become more deliberate than the past itself had been. Where isolation previously was more of an unself-conscious adaptation to the opportunities of geography and strategy, the new "isolation" was a deliberate search for a predetermined style of foreign policy.[11] Americans now sensed that they had made a *mistake* in entering World War I, and this was indeed the first widespread conclusion about such an error of foreign policy to grip the American people in its history. Rather than just forgetting about foreign power politics, the isolationism of the 1930s thus amounted to a deliberate looking away, a fear of being engrossed once again. It was less a change of the American instinct, and more a distrust of the ways Americans had been misled into believing that others shared this instinct.

The new and deliberate aversion to foreign entanglements thus shows up in the neutrality laws passed in 1935 requiring that in the future any foreign purchasers of war material would have to adhere to a policy of "cash and carry."[12] Weapons presumably would not be sold on credit anymore, avoiding the risk of distorting American preferences about winners. Only foreign-flag ships could be used to carry materials to countries at war, avoiding American indignation at the sinking of ships in the blockades and counterblockades. The United States was thus ready here to relinquish some of its classical concern for "freedom of the seas" to avoid being pulled into a war.

Public opinion polls first emerge in the middle of the 1930s, and one of the questions posed quite often now concerned American's willingness to use military force to defend remote locations against attack. At all points, the responses for the 1930s are startlingly low, with even such American possessions as Hawaii and the Philippines drawing thin support here.[13]

It was hardly clear that the United States would therefore have been drawn into any repeat of World War I, for example if Weimar Germany had fought a war with France. At the very least, the initial years of such a war would have found the American public and government as neutral as they were in 1914, and probably more deliberately inclined to remain so. Ethnic sentiments of the English-speaking link, of "Lafayette, we are here," would now have encountered a serious skepticism.

How American opinion would have reacted to any prolonged and stalemated war may of course be an impossible question to answer. But the guess would have to be that more than three or four years of such a war would have had to elapse before Americans became inclined again to help terminate it—by entering it, before they became convinced again that there was a prospect of reforming the entire system through American influence.

The United States, as noted, could have sat back from 1917 to 1919, and allowed the European powers to wear each other down. Despite the retrospective analyses claiming that Americans only intervened to head off a German colossus that would soon be threatening their very shores, this was not the real reason for intervention. The U.S. entry into World War I had come because the American government saw an opportunity to accomplish something more.

In a 1927-to-1929 situation, Americans "would not have made the same mistake"; they would have let the Europeans simply wear each other down until they became too exhausted to persist with such folly.

The isolationist period of 1919 to 1939 was thus again less a change in American values, and more a reassessment of foreign threats and opportunities. Germany having been defeated, the threat of a hegemony over Europe had receded for the time. As the British and French had been shown to be disingenuous, the opportunities for concerted efforts on behalf of human happiness had also seemingly receded.

U.S. self-confidence in the values to be exported remained as high as before, but the impression of opportunity had receded; it did not recede in the 1920s to the level of 1880, perhaps, but to that of 1910. In terms of self-description and self-consciousness, the 1920s and 1930s saw the United States much more actively *trying* to be introverted, and Americans therefore perhaps misleadingly concluded that the reality could approximate 1875; but it did not.

THE END OF ISOLATION: 1939-41

What then accounts for the termination of this isolationism, for the failure of these new attitudes of the 1920s and 1930s to stick? Two major kinds of changes explain why the United States was to shift again into an interventionist style of foreign policy after 1940.[14]

The first was simply the surprising and enormous military threat that the Nazi regime in Germany now seemed to pose to all of the world. It is trite and somewhat misleading to note how Lindbergh's trans-Atlantic flight had signaled the impracticability of physical isolation in these years, for Americans after 1927 had grown even more determined to stay removed from European quarrels. Yet the military power of Hitler's Germany grew over the same years as air transportation grew, and in many ways grew more rapidly.

When Hitler had seized power in 1933, Germany had still been substantially disarmed, with no forces on or west of the Rhine. In six short years Hitler's Germany then put together a war machine to outclass that of Britain and France, the victors at Versailles. And in another year, Hitler's armies had conquered Poland and France, coming into political and military domination of all Europe to the borders of the Soviet Union. The German entry into Paris was thus the unignorable march of a colossus greater than what had threatened in 1917. The sheer speed and momentum of the Nazi growth in power, when projected ahead into the future, now suggested awesome prospects indeed for the outside world.

Second, perhaps of just as much importance in terminating American isolation, we must note the obviously evil character of the Nazi regime under Hitler in Germany. Americans had concluded in 1920 that all foreign regimes were selfish, that none could be counted upon to be saintly, or even to be particularly altruistic or generous about the political well-being and peace of the outside world. Yet the new German regime was far worse than this, "totalitarian," perhaps totally evil. The treatment of the Jews and other minorities at home, the stamping out of dissent, the persecution of all dissidents, presented a model that to American eyes had to be the worst of steps backward in a European society.[15]

We have already noted how Japan's behavior in China had similarly caused Americans to stop seeing the Japanese as "fellow Westerners" bringing law and order to China, and rather as barbarians inflicting the worst of atrocities on innocent civilians. Contrary to the radical views that see the United States supporting Nationalist China simply in a competitiveness about markets, the major American concern here was clearly the happiness and well-being of the Chinese people. Japan became the enemy after the mid-1930s not because it looked so much like a rival, like a duplicate of the United States, but because it looked so antithetical now to what American society stood for, so much like a duplicate of Nazi Germany.

Two "lessons" thus emerged, lessons that Americans would carry forward into the postwar world. Totalitarianism was seen to be especially evil, not just a run-of-the-mill postponement of political democracy, but the most intense antithesis one could imagine of it. And such totalitarianism unfortunately had a capacity for expansion outward, not by means of popular appeal, but by raw military power and brute force.

Naziism with its concentration camps was the extreme, but its similarities to Italian fascism now brought a reexamination of Mussolini's regime, and of any others that professed similarities in philosophy, thus compounding the alarm. If totalitarian fascism was an aberration, it was nonetheless breeding emulation and submission in domino fashion through Eastern Europe, Spain and Portugal, Latin America, and in Japan.

The "totalitarianism" of Stalin's Russia was also to undergo closer scrutiny, at least prior to Hitler's invasion in 1941, and then after 1945, for the combination of purges and secret police, and slave labor camps and ideological catechism, showed up there too. Americans, with only a few exceptions, did not regard the totalitarian model as a legitimate "wave of the future," as something natural and appropriate to the needs of human beings. But they did regard it as a major threat, not just something to be lamented and avoided, but something against which one had to intervene.

The two American discoveries at the end of the 1930s, that a totalitarian regime was especially powerful and that it was especially evil, were moreover to be remembered now as being very much linked. A regime that was particularly repressive of domestic freedom, far more repressive than had been the regimes of Louis XVI or Metternich, or Bismarck or Kaiser Wilhelm, was also threatening the freedom of people in neighboring states, and ultimately threatening to the physical security and freedom of the United States of America itself.

Such a linkage should hardly have been inherently necessary. One can easily imagine situations in which the domestic suppression of individual liberties will produce a loss of the power to expand militarily, with less of a threat to the military security of a country like the United States. The Great Cultural Revolution in China would be seen that way by many American observers.

Yet the linkage seemingly applied very well to Nazi Germany. (The same assumption of such a linkage was then to be carried forward into the reexamination of Stalin's Russia after World War II; the combination of forced-draft investment in military potential, suppression of domestic dissent, and subversion and ideological "fifth columns" abroad seemed to characterize the Communist monolith very much as it had Nazi Germany.) Such a linkage is bad news indeed, combining several evils into a single package. Yet such "overall bad news" also has the redeeming feature of letting different motives collect behind the same policy. Was the U.S. entry into World War II, or the U.S. concern to contain Communist expansion after that war, based on fears of a possible military threat to the North American continent itself, or was it based on genuine altruistic identification with the welfare of the Poles and people like the Poles? In these cases, it can be both.[16]

The United States entered World War II for motives that testify both to real power threats from abroad and to real altruistic feelings toward the outside world. Were Americans stimulated to play an active role in the world again only by the sufferings of Poles and Jews and Belgians? Of course not, for Hitler looked like a threat to the whole world.

But, if Hitler had seemed to be confining his tyranny entirely to the continent of Europe, with no interest whatsoever in pushing further, would Americans then have sat back, content with the security of the hemisphere? Again, the answer is most probably not, for Nazi rule contradicted the principles of American government in a manner unmatched within Europe since 1776. A similar degree of tyranny and barbarity and genocide might have been more easily written off for Mongolia, perhaps, from which very few Americans could have traced their origins. But Europe, after all, was the "mother continent."

The latest extroverted phase in American foreign policy can thus be traced to the rapid and abrupt appearance of the menace of Nazi Germany, conjoined with Japanese strength in the Far East. Once again the American sense of threat, and opportunity, rose above

1913 levels; this time it could be argued that threat ran ahead of opportunity, where in 1917 it had been the opposite. The United States had played the role in World War I of the crucial tipper of the balance, but in World War II it counted for much more, being the central source of material for defeating Germany and Japan. The war was costly, but in some ways less dramatically costly for Americans than World War I had been; it was correspondingly more decisive in its outcome.

American hopes for great benign influence after 1918 had been premised in large part on the existence of similar attitudes in France and Great Britain, thus setting a stage for some disappointment. Such hopes were premised much more in 1945 on the possibilities of American power and influence all by itself.

The serious process of surveying opinion data in the United States began in the mid-1930s, leaving no such data to turn to for the earlier shifts in American foreign policy preferences, but giving a good view of the turning outward, as the United States found itself forced to come into World War II.

The turning outward is illustrated most dramatically in a question posed regularly about the wisdom of U.S. participation in World War I, as shown in Poll 1.

A great deal of doubt seems to have been erased by the 1941 Japanese attack on Pearl Harbor (a little ironic, since Japan, after all, had been on the U.S. side in World War I).

POLL 1

GALLUP: Do you think it was a mistake for the United States to enter the last war (World War I)?

	Yes, Mistake	No	No Opinion
1937: January 18	64%	28%	8%
1939: February 2	48	37	15
October 18	59	28	13
1940: November 19	39	42	19
1941: January 22	40	44	16
March 12	39	43	18
April 8	39	48	13
October 22	35	47	18
December 10	21	61	18

Source: Helen Gaudet Erskine, "The Polls: Is War A Mistake?," *Public Opinion Quarterly* 34, no. 1 (Spring 1970): 136.

REVISIONISM ON WORLD WAR II?

American scholars have an admirable tendency to cross-examine any previous decade's foreign policy positions. Because this serves the cause of truth, and/or because it advances academic careers, it has generated wave after wave of "revisionism." The Spanish-American War was hardly over before academic critics were attacking the rightness of the American position in that war. By the 1930s, American academics had substantially switched sides on whether it had been the Germans who were at fault for World War I, or whether it was instead our wartime partners, the British and French. Much of contemporary revisionism on the outbreak of the cold war amounts to a radical analysis, as noted, whereby it was more the fault of the capitalist world led by the United States than of the Soviet Union that genuine peace and harmony did not follow the defeat of Hitler.

Because the cold war erupted so soon after the defeat of the Axis powers, however, Americans by and large missed the normal wave of revisionism that would have reinterpreted Hitler and Mussolini and Tojo. Yet, as the Vietnam War brought to the surface the debate about the real intent of American foreign policy, a few analysts did the service of skeptically reexamining even the alleged American need to enter World War II. Some of the younger dissidents on Vietnam, who saw the American intervention in Southeast Asia as a foolish venture linked to the capitalist system, now offered the same explanation for the earlier decision to fight Hitler. If they thus felt a need to be consistent here, they nonetheless shocked their elders who had lived through the Nazi experience and could not see how anyone could interpret opposition to Hitler as a simple machination of capitalism. (Not surprisingly, the greatest shock often emerged here when the young radicals, and surprised elders, were Jewish.)

Bruce M. Russett presented an interesting and extended version of this argument in the book *No Clear and Present Danger*, basically arguing that the power accumulated by Nazi Germany by 1940, or even as it could have been projected to 1945 or 1950, really had not produced enough of a geopolitical and military threat to North America to justify U.S. entry into the war.[17] The U.S. entry into World War II, in this view, was simply an illustration of domestically inspired addiction to intervention, a part of a capitalist need for war production, or an attachment to markets in China, producing conflict with Japan, producing Pearl Harbor, and in the end producing war with the European Axis as well.

How valid, or relevant, is Russett's criticism, or any revisionist criticism of the American entry into World War II? Many Americans, having watched the momentum of Nazi power outlined above, were indeed now inclined to project a trend that would soon enough cross the Atlantic. This might perhaps be criticized as reflecting a lack of expertise, as the man on the street did not see all those weaknesses in Hitler's position that made any early invasion of North America very unlikely. Yet, among the knowledgeable few, there was a longer-range fear that would indeed give pause, namely that Hitler's Germany might be the first to develop weapons using nuclear fission. Even if its forces were otherwise incapable of crossing the Atlantic, the prospect of a Nazi Germany threatening the nuclear destruction of Washington and New York would have been enough to convince even the most selfishly power-minded American that an intervention was needed to put an end to the Nazi menace.

Yet such concern for the physical well-being and political security of the United States can not really explain the depth of the American commitment to the war, either in the president's decision-making councils or with the man on the street. If Russett is correct that North America as yet faced no danger, this may simply again show how generous and morally concerned Americans have been.

The U.S. thus did not, as in 1917, enter a world war simply to end it. Unlike World War I, it now rather entered in part because of genuine fear of its own safety—after the fall of Paris, but in larger part to end a particularly vicious totalitarian regime. Naziism and war may have been closely linked. Yet the United States had mainly entered into World War I to end war, and now mainly entered World War II to end Naziism.

UNCONDITIONAL SURRENDER

If the U.S. entry into World War II is thus not so much of a paradox, what about the way chosen to fight it, demanding "unconditional surrender," pursuing total victory, even where lesser victory might have spared American lives, and might have better served some other considerations Americans hold dear? If the United States had been intent on preserving national military power and physical security, would it not have been wiser to stop short of eliminating Germany (and Japan) as independent military powers, after they had been trimmed back in power, leaving them in place to be played off against the Russians and the British?

The drive to "unconditional surrender" can of course be tied in small parts to a hardheaded power consideration, in the fear of a

German atomic bomb. Those few Americans familiar with the possibility of nuclear weapons, including the president of course (but not Vice-President Truman, until he actually succeeded Roosevelt in office) might have thought it impossible to negotiate a peace with any German regime in 1945, given the prospect that such a regime would then acquire its own nuclear weapons in 1947 or 1949.[18]

By the spring of 1945, however, very few Americans still had any knowledge whatsoever of the possibility of nuclear weapons. The larger bulk of the American population, and the larger bulk of the American drive for prosecuting the war all the way to total victory, thus must be tied to motives other than a maximizing of American power. Naziism was seen to be inherently evil, bad for the neighbors of Germany, inherently more likely to produce wars in the future, bad even for the Germans themselves. As such, the United States felt that it would be serving good purposes, assisting the happiness of peoples everywhere, by pursuing unconditional surrender, by deploying armies in conjunction with its allies until all of Germany was occupied, until all German military forces had been disarmed.

The United States thus did not lose track of the balance of power in 1945, as the accusation is sometimes made, but rather it overrode such considerations in the pursuit of peace and human happiness. It did not make the mistake of failing to notice that the USSR would grow enormously in power with the elimination of Germany and Japan as military powers. Rather it made a different mistake in underestimating how much political democracy would be found missing also in the Stalinist regime in the USSR, and missing in the governments Stalin would impose on neighboring states.

Some of this was simply wartime enthusiasm, of the kind noticed already in 1917. In World War I the United States somewhat convinced itself that France was just as prepared to put considerations of peacekeeping ahead of considerations of territory. In World War II, Americans now convinced themselves that Stalin's Communist rule was not really totalitarian like Hitler's, but rather in some roundabout fashion more tied to a genuine endorsement by those governed.

American opinion has thus tended to swing between extremes in wartime situations, converting U.S. wars into spasms of action and reaction and overreaction, as one set of enemies replaces another, as "lessons" are replaced by new "lessons" in rapid succession.[19] However much authors may disagree about U.S. motives, it is easy to indict American perceptiveness on this count, an indictment implicit already in the Klingberg notion of cycles introduced at the outset.

The American self-delusion about the extent of political democracy and freedom in the USSR thus accounts in important part for the national enthusiasm in seeing the Russians enter Berlin. It at the same time amounted to an important time bomb for the future of Soviet-American relations, for the reaction was to be severe once Americans discovered that political liberties were to be no greater in Warsaw or Dresden now than they had been under Hitler's rule, i.e., that the United States had overriden considerations of power balances on a false premise.

To be disappointed in the Russians (as one had been disappointed in the French in 1919) was bad enough. Simple disappointment might only have led to another withdrawal into the domestic arena. But to discover that the object of one's disappointment might now become the very Eurasian power colossus always feared was more like a prescription for the cold war.

NOTES

1. Among the important discussions of the American decision to enter World War I are Ernest R. May, *The World War and American Isolation, 1914–1917* (Cambridge, Mass.: Harvard University Press, 1959) and Charles C. Tansill, *America Goes to War* (Boston: Little, Brown, 1938).

2. See George T. Davis, *A Navy Second to None* (New York: Harcourt Brace, 1940) for a valuable discussion of U.S. decisions to build a fleet equal to that of Great Britain.

3. American sensitivity to the costliness of submarine warfare is discussed in Patrick Devlin, *Too Proud to Fight* (New York: Oxford University Press, 1975).

4. For an interpretation quite favorable to Wilson, see Charles Seymour, *American Diplomacy During the World War* (Baltimore: Johns Hopkins University Press, 1934).

5. Strong support for entry into the League of Nations, based on the evidence such as newspaper editorials, is reported in the *Literary Digest* 61 (April 15, 1919): 13 ff.

6. The Fourteen Points, and the philosophy behind them, are discussed in John M. Blum, *Woodrow Wilson and the Politics of Morality* (Boston: Little, Brown, 1956).

7. For a profound analysis of American attitudes toward the Russian revolution, see George F. Kennan, *Russia Leaves the War* (Princeton: Princeton University Press, 1956) and *The Decision to Intervene* (Princeton: Princeton University Press, 1958).

8. For the specific accusation of hypocrisy and self-delusion as directed at the Wilsonians, see Hans Morgenthau, *The Purpose of American Politics* (New York: Alfred A. Knopf, 1960), pp. 104–10.

9. Longer analyses of the American decision to pursue isolationism once again are to be found in Thomas A. Bailey, *Woodrow Wilson and the Lost Peace* (New York: Macmillan, 1944).

10. The less noble aspects of postwar bickering at Versailles are described in Harold Nicolson, *Peacemaking 1919* (New York: Grosset and Dunlap, 1939).

11. See Selig Adler, *The Isolationist Impulse* (New York: Abelard-Schuman, 1957).

12. The details of the Neutrality Laws and the reasoning behind them can be found in Robert A. Divine, *The Illusion of Neutrality* (Chicago: University of Chicago Press, 1962).

13. Poll data on American opinion here can be found in Hadley Cantril, *Public Opinion 1935-46* (Princeton: Princeton University Press, 1951), pp. 780-81.

14. Good discussions of the American move back away from isolationism after 1939 are to be found in John Wiltz, *From Isolationism to War* (Arlington Heights: AHM, 1968) and Manfred Jonas, *Isolationism in America* (Ithaca: Cornell University Press, 1966).

15. The uniquely evil character, in American eyes, of Nazi Germany is demonstrated in Saul Friedlander, *Prelude to Downfall: Hitler and the United States 1939-41* (New York: Knopf, 1967). See also James V. Compton, *The Swastika and the Eagle* (Boston: Houghton Mifflin, 1967).

16. For an influential interpretation, very neatly blending the two kinds of motives, see W. W. Rostow, *The United States in the World Arena* (New York: Harper, 1960), app. A, pp. 543-50.

17. Bruce M. Russett, *No Clear and Present Danger* (New York: Harper & Row, 1972).

18. The reasoning prevalent among the few Americans privy to the secret of nuclear weapons development is described in Robert Jungk, *Brighter Than a Thousand Suns* (New York: Harcourt Brace, 1958).

19. The general indictment that American opinion is too prone to swings back and forth between extremes has been voiced many times. Some examples are Dexter Perkins, *The American Approach to Foreign Policy* (Cambridge, Mass.: Harvard University Press, 1952), chap. 7, and Kenneth Keniston, *The Uncommitted* (New York: Harcourt Brace, 1965).

7
The Cold War

As we now survey the years since World War II, we might easily enough agree that the period from the 1940s to the 1960s was burdened with tension and conflict, amply meriting the label of "cold war." Whether the "detente" that followed was so deep and genuine, and what actually underlies the changes in the 1960s, will be discussed in the next chapter. What this chapter shall do is to attempt once again to relate our three basic perspectives on American foreign policy to the years of the cold war, the years in which a great deal of hostility loomed between the United States and the Soviet Union, dashing the hopes of cooperation that had arisen during the common effort against Nazi Germany in World War II.[1]

How are we indeed best to explain the cold war? We shall begin once again with the power politics view, a view that sees all nations as basically alike in seeking after power, and places the "blame" for conflict rather on the objective situation. Radical or liberal analysts will try to prove something about the capitalistic—or instead the freedom-loving—character of U.S. foreign policy by references to the chronology of changes as they occur in such policy. Yet might the changes as they occurred not be more explainable simply by shifts in the international power environment, so that the United States would have behaved the same way with either of the sets of goals argued above? Was the United States altruistic or treacherous in 1945? Was the USSR altruistic or treacherous? Could either of the powers have been *both* altruistic and treacherous? Could there be something about the international arena that makes it difficult or impossible now to tell who was the less cooperative, and that indeed made it impossible to tell at the time?

The issues of chronology and the dictates of the international system thus have an impact for the cold war case somewhat different from that of 1890s imperialism. In the earlier instance, the coincidence of the closing of the frontier and U.S. investment in a fleet seemed to support the radical case, until one brought in the international changes in naval technology—which supplied another explanation for the U.S. fleet, and might have left the ties to frontier closing and capitalist maturation entirely coincidental. The introduction of a power politics analysis for the 1890s case thus contributes in the net to the liberal interpretation of American foreign policy— if only in that it undercuts the radical argument.

With regard to the 1945 emergence of the cold war, the application of a power politics model is a little more neutral in impact. Liberals will wish to claim that the Russians struck first. Radicals will claim that the Americans struck first. Analysts of power politics may deliver learned analyses of why it is impossible to tell who struck first.

The second approach, the radical view (often also styled as "revisionist") would instead place blame largely on the United States, seeing the Soviet Union as defending itself against the onslaughts of a capitalist expansionism and a peaking sense of American power in 1945. While this second view was endorsed by hardly any American scholars in the 1940s and 1950s, it won a much wider hearing in the 1960s as part of the general public and academic disenchantment with the American foreign policy that had led us into Vietnam.[2] Such an analysis tended thus to project backward the impressions of Vietnam to find fault with most or all of the major American policy choices made after 1945, to see the Russians as basically the injured party, reacting in self-defense against pressures imposed by the United States.

Even if the bulk of the revisionist interpretation is not accepted, many Americans have tended, perhaps subconsciously, to accept at least a part of it. When looking back on the cold war period, such Americans are thus prone to apologize today for the style and logic of their country's approach, seeing the straightforward antagonism of the late 1940s toward the Soviet Union and its allies as mindless, as foolishly or misleadingly ideological.

As noted earlier, Americans indeed unquestioningly used to accept a central presumption that now is no longer a matter of agreement, that political democracy should be supported and encouraged wherever possible around the globe; the lack of dispute about this question induced a corresponding lack of articulate discussion, so that one easily enough can inherit an impression of a mindlessness about U.S. values in the cold war years. If Americans thus gave too little thought to what the United States was pursuing in these years, might they thus have also been guilty of a second mindlessness, as they (without meaning to be) were more aggressive than their adversaries? Perhaps the domestic way of seeing problems made Americans focus too much on the straightforward risks of violence and military aggression, without sensing how the system tended to expand on its own through economic or sociological power, through nonviolent forms of political strength.

The third view will of course be the interpretation defended throughout this book, that of the American liberal, by which American goals have been unusually noble and generous.[3] This would be an interpretation of the cold war by which the United States was basically cooperative and guiltless, thus placing the "blame" for the cold war squarely on Soviet aggressiveness and failure to adhere to promises.

INHERENTLY IMPOSSIBLE TO TELL?

Why do the radical critics of American foreign policy, as well as its defenders, both make such a big issue of the origins of the cold war, insisting on arguing the perhaps unanswerable question of "who struck first"?

The explanation is easy enough. Marxists and other supporters of economic democracy like to believe that such social justice would tend to produce a peaceful foreign policy. American liberals similarly like to believe that political democracy is not only good in its own right, but also consistent with, and conducive to, international peace. To have the Russians blamed for the return of armed confrontations after the end of World War II would thus seem to undermine the Marxist view that "socialism leads to peace." To have the United States again blamed for this confrontation would similarly tend to undermine the liberal view, as a free-election system becomes linked with militarism and treachery and aggressiveness.

The power politics perspective deprecates the importance of the question of guilt, of "who struck first," in part because it regards these as moral issues of no real merit for anyone's foreign policy, but in part also because it is very used to international interactions in which all the evidence on sequence and guilt gets blurred by the pace of events.

Someone familiar only with the existence of four or five great powers, and totally unacquainted with their comparative ideologies or world outlooks, might still have expected the alliance of any two of them to break apart as soon as the common enemy has been defeated.[4]

The series of situations ripe for conflict thus began in 1945 at the very termination of the German resistance. While the principle of unconditional surrender called for a simultaneous German surrender to all the Allies, what if individual German commanders on the Western Front offered to surrender to British or American commanders immediately, as happened in Italy and the Netherlands, sparing the local populations further suffering, even while their compatriots continued to resist the Russian advance to the east? Related to this was the custody into which German soldiers, as individuals or in groups, would surrender themselves. If the Germans were allowed to choose, they would, for a host of reasons, opt for surrender to the Western armies. If the Allies stuck together in refusing to give the Wehrmacht such a choice, would it not simply prolong the fighting?

The 1945 "unconditional surrender" of the Germans was thus adulterated in practice to allow the Germans to win some conditions, as millions of German soldiers and civilians managed to escape coming under Russian control. Very few Americans favored such adjustments for their own sake at the time, it should be noted, for the predominant American view was still to identify with the Russians as allies and as potential social democrats, while viewing the Germans as Nazis. It is startling how much American perceptions have changed in the years that have passed. If anyone today were to propose a maneuver by which 10 million Germans or others could escape Communist rule, he would win instant governmental support for the scheme. The West German government currently pays some $20,000 a head for emigration visas for persons from behind the Iron Curtain, which would make the 10 million who slipped out in the confusion of the Nazi surrender (the very confusion that may explain the beginning of the cold war) worth some $200 billion. At the time, however, this concession to German preferences was instead viewed as a way of terminating the fighting more rapidly, of winning a quicker Nazi surrender.

Hitler himself might have counted on the balance of power mechanism to do much more than this, indeed to bail him out of any total defeat. Elementary logic of power considerations suggested that the United States and Great Britain would have to turn against Moscow before the Russians reached Berlin, before the German state had been erased totally as a power factor. What the Nazis underestimated was the extent to which the American people and government, along with other peoples and governments, had put considerations of value and ideology ahead of power, had come to see Nazi Germany as a saliently different threat to the happiness of people in Europe and beyond. But once Naziism was defeated, the balance of power model might indeed have seemed to go into operation.

Still more serious issues were now to emerge on which side got to liberate territory from the occupation of the Germans, since this would obviously tend to influence the political future of the territories involved. As British troops were advancing across Northern Germany, rumors came in of Russian paratroopers landing in Denmark (they in truth were landing only on the Danish island of Bornholm, far to the east out in the Baltic). General Montgomery's response was to order the immediate dispatch of British forces into Denmark, to be sure that the country was liberated by Western rather than Soviet forces. Perhaps it was the behavior of the Russians in Poland that had made the British so concerned to beat them to Copenhagen; yet such a rush forward of Western forces could then only be viewed by Moscow as showing distrust and potential hostility as well.

As the mirror reverse of this, American troops, pursuing the defeated Germans, crossed the border into Czechoslovakia, advancing as far as Pilsen. This produced a strong demand from Moscow that the Russians be allowed to liberate all of Czechoslovakia, and that the American troops be withdrawn, a demand to which the United States acceded. Perhaps the Russian concern here reflected having seen the Communist Party shouldered out of influence in Italy and elsewhere in Western Europe. Yet the Russian intensity about who would liberate the Czechs similarly produced suspicion in the West.

Each side in 1945 thus could see the other's hurry as evidence to support its own suspicions, and then let its own suspicions produce greater hurry, in the kind of self-sustaining cycle that underpins "prisoners' dilemma," which explains the pernicious impact international relations sometimes can have on the raw motives of the powers entering into it.

There is thus a certain degree of plausibility, as always, to a power politics interpretation of the origins of the cold war. Just as czarist Russia and England were to become less close after Napoleon was defeated, so the United States and the Soviet Union were destined to have a falling out after Hitler's demise.

Yet something more than this is probably needed to produce the intensity of conflict and counterproductive energies seen in the cold war. Great Britain and the United States also began a minor naval arms race in 1919 after the defeat of Kaiser Wilhelm's Germany, but it was settled and ended quickly enough in the Washington Naval Conference. For a level of arms race and political and military conflict as great as that seen since 1945, many Americans would want to blame the schemes and motives of one of the principle powers, rather than simply a power vacuum allegedly generated by mother nature.

THE UNITED STATES AS AGGRESSOR?

We shall now shift to trying to explain cold war origins by assigning the bulk of the fault to the United States. While ordinary Americans are inclined to blame Stalin's dictatorship for most of what went wrong after 1945, the radical interpretation is instead inclined to argue that it was the United States which was expansionist after 1945, while the Russians were simply defending themselves. Stalin was not a power-mad threat to the peace and security of the world in this picture, but rather a moderate, still intent on "socialism in one country."

It was Stalin who thus persuaded Tito to cease supporting the Communist guerrillas in Greece, rather than the reverse, as one would often imagine it. Stalin in 1945 and 1946 had apparently urged restraint and patience similarly on the Communist Parties of France and Italy, when they were in effect being eased out a chance for power by the United States and its allies, and he also was not very encouraging to Mao's Communists in China in their dreams of winning a total victory over Chiang Kai-shek's Nationalists.

Yet such evidence of Soviet restraints under Stalin might not be so very conclusive for shifting the indictment to Washington, for it might simply illustrate the limits of opportunity. Would Stalin not have told the Italian and French and Greek and Chinese Communist Parties to move for total power, as they did in Czechoslovakia and the rest of Eastern Europe, if he had thought these parties had a chance of winning?

The argument for indicting the United States thus typically turns to more positive evidence of American expansionism and power lust here, allegedly proving the United States aggressive even if we cannot prove the Russians to have been nonaggressive, perhaps thus showing that any Russian toughness here would merely have been a reasonable response to American provocation. In what ways did the United States now show its hostility to the USSR, in effect "firing the first shot"?

We could of course begin by reintroducing all the economic arguments discussed earlier about the alleged capitalist pathologies of the American system.[5] Revisionist attacks on postwar American foreign policy can indeed find occasional passages of speech or testimony to support such an argument, although these are rare, as noted, and are surrounded by a very much more political context. Perhaps the economic drives will always explain American foreign policy at a psychological or subliminal level, in a way which one can never admit to himself, in a way which therefore can never be proven.

Turning to the more open and deliberate noneconomic lines of argument, we can find some very explicit references in 1945 to the desirability of the extension and expansion of American power. Henry Luce's American Century phrase often is cited as an example here.[6] A little more subtly and subliminally again, the very phrase of "containment" may, as noted earlier, have served as a cover for American expansionism. By focusing on drawing a fence around the Russian sphere of influence, the phrase could have been keeping Americans from noticing how much their own power and sphere of influence were growing. Our attention was riveted on the state of the fence around the Soviet bloc, and on what was presumably happening inside that fence, as George Kennan's formulation indeed hopefully predicted that boxing in Stalin's system would after some time destabilize the Soviet system, and force a relaxation of ideology and dictatorial control.[7] What escaped our attention, however, according to this second view of the cold war, was the change on our side of the fence, as American influence in the defense of the free world replaced that of Great Britain or France or Japan, and so forth.

Turning to the more concrete actions that a reasonable jury might find hostile, the United States at the cessation of hostilities with Japan abruptly canceled the lend-lease shipment of materials and weapons to the USSR, without allowing for any orderly transition to let the Russians adjust to the cutoff, without even planning for an orderly use of the materials in the pipeline.

While the United States had earlier talked with the Russians about granting a major loan of perhaps some $6 billion for postwar recovery, this loan was now to be denied, unless the Russians accepted some important conditions about opening Eastern Europe (and perhaps the USSR itself) to international trade, the kind of trade that some would view as an entering wedge of political leverage and capitalist influence.[8] The USSR had indeed suffered much during World War II, losing perhaps 25 million of its people and a great deal of its industrial productive capacity. Such losses had been suffered in what was a common war against a common menace, Hitler's Germany. Looking back on this by the standards of the 1980s, we might indeed wonder why any rich outside nation would not have felt an obligation to help in the recovery from such a disaster. Yet American assistance here was not to be forthcoming, and Russian demands for $10 billion in reparations from Germany were also to be denied.

Turning totally away from economics, the revisionist argument about the origins of the cold war often points to the American decision to use the atomic bomb against Japan, when Japanese surrender in retrospect seemed very likely.[9] Was the bomb thus used in a hurried effort to defeat the Japanese before the Russians could enter the war to share the spoils and influence (analogous to Allied efforts in 1917 to defeat Germany before Wilson's America could join the fighting)? Stalin indeed had to accelerate his schedule for Russian entry into the war against Japan when the bomb was dropped on Hiroshima, so as to become party to the Pacific half of World War II before it ended.

Or was the bomb dropped on Hiroshima and Nagasaki to frighten the Russians for the years ahead, to establish the precedent that the United States would have no compunctions about using such a horrible weapon in any future war? If the bomb had never been used against Japanese cities, with the ensuing photographs of badly burned bodies and radioactive rubble, the power of nuclear weapons might always have been a little more abstract and hypothetical, rather than the real and frightening menace that we have known since 1945.

The use of the atomic bomb was followed quickly enough by the Japanese surrender, and a decision to keep the Russians from having any serious share in the occupation of Japan. That military occupation became largely an American monopoly, with no "Russian zone" comparable to what emerged in East Germany. The use of the bomb was also directly followed by President Truman's announcement that the United States would retain the secrets of this form of weapons technology. The United States had shared most other forms of military technology fairly freely with its allies during World War II, by the shipments of lend-lease, and so forth, and this announcement of a different policy on nuclear weapons thus had to amount to a signal of some new guardedness or hostility, to a punctuation mark of the cold war. (President Truman's announcement of American unwillingness to share nuclear weapons had to be most immediately disturbing to the British, however, who had been promised a share of such weaponry by President Roosevelt during World War II; the British took the rebuff in stride, however.)[10]

Moving along the trail of military or political actions that the USSR might fairly have viewed as hostile or provocative, we could turn then to the Western decisions to prevent a Communist government in Greece, beginning already with the British intervention in

Athens in 1944. The civil war in Greece was to continue on until 1948, when the aid from across the mountains in Bulgaria and Yugoslavia was at last to be terminated.

Communist participation in government might similarly have been appropriate enough in places like Italy and France and Belgium, on the basis of raw electoral strength, or the history of the anti-German partisan movements, but the Western pattern after 1945 was to ease such parties out of all sensitive positions, and ultimately out of government, just as the non-Communists were pushed out in Stalin's Eastern Europe.

The liberation of France, and especially the liberation of Paris, had at times in 1944 seemed a contest more between Gaullists and Communists than between Allies and Germans, with de Gaulle's Free French armed forces being rushed forward by the Americans to accept the surrender of Paris, lest the city go instead to French partisan forces of a different stripe. De Gaulle was indeed shot at as he walked through the city. While the official account blamed the shootings on Germans, or on French Quislings who had worked for the Germans, de Gaulle was apparently forever convinced that the shots had instead been fired by the Communists.[11]

THE USSR AS AGGRESSOR?

We shall then complete the trilogy with a view of the post-1945 years that blames the cold war primarily on the USSR, which in effect matches up fairly well with the American self-image of being the cooperative and generous and peace-loving party here.

One can begin by citing American public opinion at the time, as shown in Poll 2, which showed Americans quite disposed to trust the Russians during the war, but then becoming quite apprehensive, as Soviet behavior at the war's end seemingly began to cause problems.

If Americans cannot be trusted to be objective about the merits of a dispute between Washington and Moscow, one might be more impressed by the findings of some other observers. Consider, for example, Poll 3 of world opinion taken in 1948.

Of the nations listed in Poll 3, only Sweden unfortunately qualifies as neutral; yet its views are quite distrustful of the USSR. Consider also the 1946 Swedish opinion in Poll 4.

Skeptics might interrupt at this point to argue that the Swedes should be discounted as well, as also lacking in objectivity; unfortunately one does not have any great number of opinion polls from

POLL 2

Do you think Russia can be trusted to cooperate with us after the war is over?

American Opinion toward Russia, 1942-49	Yes	No	Undecided; No Opinion; Don't Know; No Answer
NORC Feb 14 '42	38%	37%	25%
OPOR Mar 26 '42	39	39	22
NORC May 6 '42[a]	45	25	30
OPOR June 17 '42	41	33	26
NORC July 1 '42[a]	45	26	29
OPOR July 15 '42	50	30	20
NORC July 18 '42[a]	43	27	30
NORC Aug 21 '42[a]	51	25	24
NORC Nov 19 '42[a]	51	24	25
NORC Nov 27 '42[a]	52	26	22
AIPO Jan 7 '43	46	29	25
AIPO Apr 6 '43	44	34	22
NORC June 18 '43[a]	48	27	25
AIPO Nov 10 '43	47	27	26
NORC Nov 15 '43[a]	48	20	32
AIPO Dec 15 '43	51	27	22
AIPO Jan 18 '44	40	37	23
NORC Apr 8 '44[a]	50	22	28
AIPO June 7 '44	47	36	17
AIPO Nov 15 '44[b]	47	35	18
AIPO Feb 20 '45[b]	55	31	14
AIPO May 15 '45[b]	45	38	17
AIPO Aug 8 '45[b]	54	30	16
AIPO Oct 17 '45 (first cross-section)[b]	38	45	17
AIPO Oct 17 '45 (second cross-section)[c]	44	40	16
AIPO Feb 27 '46[c]	35	52	13
AIPO Apr 10 '46[c]	45	38	17
AIPO Sept 25 '46[c]	32	53	15
AIPO Dec 11 '46[c]	43	40	17
AIPO June 26 '49[c]	20	62	18

Note: NORC = National Opinion Research Center; OPOR = Office of Public Opinion Research; AIPO = American Institute of Public Opinion.

[a] The question was: Do you think Russia can be depended upon to cooperate with us after the war?

[b] Do you think Russia can be trusted to cooperate with us after the war?

[c] Do you think Russia will cooperate with us in world affairs?

Sources: Hadley Cantril, *Public Opinion, 1935–46* (Princeton: Princeton University Press, 1951), pp. 370-71; "The Quarter's Polls," *Public Opinion Quarterly* 13 (Fall 1949): 550.

POLL 3

Do you think Russia (the United States) would start a war to get something she wanted (such as more territory or more resources)—or would she fight only if attacked?

Opinion in Eight Nations, February 1948	Would Start War	Defense Only	No Opinion
Russia:			
United States	73%	19%	8%
Canada	60	26	14
Holland	57	27	16
France	51	22	27
Italy	50	17	33
Brazil	43	16	41
Sweden	42	21	37
Norway	37	37	26
United States:			
Norway	23%	55%	24%
France	20	56	24
Holland	16	60	24
Italy	16	48	36
Canada	13	77	10
Sweden	13	54	33
Brazil	9	53	38
United States	5	92	3

Source: George H. Gallup, *The Gallup Polls* (New York: Random House, 1972), vol. 1, p. 709.

other neutral or "nonaligned" nations in these years. Sweden, according to a Russian analysis, is really a part of the capitalist world, as, in Khrushchev's words about United Nations Secretary General Dag Hammarskjöld, "there are no neutral men." Anyone who has studied the defense plans of the Swedish armed services since 1946 would indeed note that all such plans (despite Swedish official neutrality) are prepared for an attack from the East.

Yet the revisionists cannot have their cake here and eat it too. When Swedish opinion turned against American foreign policy during the Vietnam War, critics of such policy within the United States were quite happy to cite Swedish opinion as a somehow detached and relevant source of objective evaluation. If such later revisionists had been asked to guess how Swedes would have assigned the blame for the cold war in 1946 or 1948, they would most probably be surprised that the actual polls were so one-sidedly favorable to the United States.

POLL 4

Do you think that one or more of the great nations should limit their own claims for the sake of a more peaceful cooperation in the world?

Swedish Opinion, March 1946	Response
Russia	30%
United States	4
England	5
France	1
All nations	41
No nation	3
Don't know	23

Note: Percentages add to more than 100 because some respondents gave more than one answer.

Source: Hadley Cantril, *Public Opinion, 1935–46* (Princeton: Princeton University Press, 1951), p. 788.

A general theme of the analysis in this book is that it may be a mistake to project backward into the history of American foreign policy the patterns and lessons thought to have been uncovered in the Vietnam War. Or, if we are determined to learn from the Vietnam experience, we must be careful to identify the motives of American foreign policy as they actually were, rather than simply accepting a model that fits the academic or ideological trends of the moment.

Turning to the factual evidence itself, rather than viewing it through the perceptions of public opinion, how would one outline the case here that Soviet expansionism was the cause of postwar difficulties?

Early in 1945, one saw Soviet demands for a share of the former Italian colonies in Africa, colonies that were to be administered now for a time under a United Nations trusteeship. Such a Russian claim was not so bothersome yet on its surface, and might have been viewed simply as part of the normal postwar wrangling for a share of the spoils. The colonies had not been occupied by Russian forces, but by British and French, and would be administered by these governments' military authorities until independence was achieved in the 1950s; yet the Russian armed forces had fought hard and had made great sacrifices during World War II, sacrifices by which all the Allies had benefited, such that a redistribution of the territorial booty was not out of the question. The demand here was thus logically comparable to later Russian expressions of interest in an occupation zone in Japan, a request that was also denied. (In retrospect, it is interesting to speculate on what Libya or Somalia would be like today, if they had been required to go through a period of Soviet administration after the war. Would such places be more anti-Soviet, seeing the Russians as the last of a series of foreign colonialists? Or would they be more like North Korea, saddled under the firm control of a Communist Party dictatorship?)

Greater concern then arose about Soviet behavior and demands in Iran in 1945 and 1946. Iran had been occupied during World War II by Russian and British forces, when its government seemed to be leaning in the direction of the Axis.

The occupation ousted the Iranian monarch, carrying him into exile in South Africa, and installed his son in his place, the shah who reigned until 1979. Some of the shah's concerns for displaying Iranian power in the 1970s were thus alleged to reflect his humiliation and bitterness at the manner by which he was put on the throne.

Iran, in truth, was thus a defeated minor coalition partner of the Axis, as was also perhaps Iraq, which similarly had its government overthrown by British intervention in 1941 when the regime (and the population) displayed blatant sympathies for the Germans and Italians. Despite the clear lack of pro-Allied sympathies in either country, however, the Allies had not been in the mood after 1941 to acknowledge that Axis ideology had any wider appeal for the underdeveloped world, or that the Allies might have to override local desires in such areas, just as the Germans were overriding them in Yugoslavia, and the Japanese in China. A euphemism was thus adopted by which Iran was made into a partner in the resistance to Axis expansion, somehow by its own consent temporarily occupied by British, Russian (and then also American) forces. This euphemism would of course then play an important role four years later in how outsiders would view any Russian attempt to make the occupation permanent.

For the Russians now to be dilatory about evacuating in 1946, in the process supporting a separatist movement in Azerbaijan, thus struck the American public as unreasonable behavior, not something by the circumstances that could simply be viewed as a continuation of World War II and the anti-Axis effort. The United States government thus remonstrated quite strongly in 1946 about the Russian posture in Iran, and in May of that year the Kremlin backed down.

Going one notch up on the scale of provocation, the Soviet Union from 1945 to 1947 began to make demands also now on Turkey, a country that by no stretch of the imagination had been a "defeated Axis power," but rather had stayed neutral through most of the conflict, and then had declared war on the Axis at the end. Soviet demands for changes in the boundary, and for control of the Dardanelles, thus struck many observers as a straightforward return to the traditional imperial goals of the czar.

Most serious of all, for triggering American alarms about Russian behavior, were presumably the events in Poland during and after its Soviet liberation from the Germans. Poland was in no way an Axis power either, but, as the first victim of Hitler's armed attack, had indeed been an ally from the outset of World War II. Poland in effect was "what World War II was all about," for Great Britain, and then in turn for the United States. The Polish case was likely to receive a special hearing from Americans, moreover, because a substantial number of Americans were of Polish descent, with great electoral significance in places like Detroit and Buffalo. The independence of Poland at the end of World War I had served as the perfect example of what Woodrow Wilson regarded as natural in self-determination for the peoples of Europe.

While there had been a Polish government in exile sitting in London all through World War II, the Russians now proceeded to ignore it, establishing their own such "government" in Lublin. Each of these governments could be faulted somewhat as being less than fully representative of Polish democracy, as the London Poles tended to represent old aristocratic and landed interests; yet the odds were heavy that the London Poles would easily have beaten the Lublin Poles in any free election. The dubiousness of the representativeness of the pro-Russian Lublin government in exile was illustrated all too well in discussions about the future border between Poland and the USSR (which was to be shifted westward at the same time that the Polish border with Germany was moved westward to the Oder-Niesse line). Representatives of the London government in exile argued that the city of Lvov should remain in Poland, while the pro-Russian group would, with a straight face, state that "the people of Poland demanded" that Lvov be part of the USSR.[12]

Soviet behavior here came to seem more devious and worrisome now, as details emerged of various Russian actions during the war. Troublesome rumors had circulated that the large number of Polish officers massacred at Katyn in 1941 had not been killed by the advancing Germans, but by the forces of the Soviet Union, which had taken them into custody at the partition of Poland in 1939. Since such officers represented a class interest contrary to a Marxist future in Poland (as well as a bolstering for future Polish military strength), the motives were not lacking for Stalin to order such a massacre. The reports that the Russians had been the perpetrators had been dismissed for a time as German propaganda, but by 1945 these looked more and more like the truth.

Similarly, the Polish nationalist underground had launched a rebellion in Warsaw in 1944 during the Russian advance on the city; rather than assisting this insurrection, the Soviet forces mysteriously stopped to "regroup" on the opposite side of the Vistula, allowing the Germans to suppress the insurrection, once again thereby eroding what would have been postwar Polish forces hostile to a Communist dictatorship. Stalin indeed would not even allow the British and American planes flying aid to the Warsaw rebels to land and refuel in Soviet-occupied territory.

As the closeout of what thus looked like a pattern of Russian treachery, a coalition government of sorts had been negotiated, somehow blending representatives of the Lublin and London governments in exile. Representatives of the London group came to Warsaw to take part in the new government, but a number of them were to be arrested and imprisoned.

Poland, for reasons of historical associations, was clearly the most visible case for Americans, but a similarly bothersome pattern of Russian obstruction of political democracy now occurred throughout Eastern Europe. In several countries, this was again easier for the Russians to slide into place, since entire factions of the possible political process for the moment could be disqualified and immobilized as having worked on the side of the Axis during World War II. The punishment for such groups in Hungary, Rumania, and Bulgaria was thus understandable, just as the Germans themselves would first have to prove themselves ready for free elections and self-government. Yet such disqualifications were still not enough to give the Russians what they apparently felt they needed. Even with the far-right parties kept off the ballot, experiments with multiparty elections in such countries again and again gave very few votes to the Communist Party. In each country, therefore, more brutal measures were then applied, to ensure the end result of a Communist dictatorship, with midnight arrests of opposition political leaders, the suppressing of the independent press, and an intimidation of the democratic Left into joining with the Communists.

The one significant exception to this in Eastern Europe showed up through 1946 and 1947 in Czechoslovakia, another country which had embodied the 1919 Wilsonian dream and seemed to symbolize all of the need to resist Hitler. [13] Czechoslovakia had also of course escaped being enlisted as a pro-Axis state during the war, indeed had been the only functioning political democracy in the region all through the 1920s and 1930s, when Poland had seen military coups and other states into the Balkans and along the Baltic had become dictatorships of Fascist or other stripe.

For a time, the Czech Communist Party did not do so badly by the process of free elections, never coming close to winning a majority, but gaining as much as 20 percent of the vote, and participating in coalition governments in Prague. Its role in effect was comparable to that of the Communist Party in Iceland in the 1970s.

By 1948, however, the Communists seemed to be slipping in their electoral appeal, so that the party might not be included in the next coalition government. The result in February of 1948 was a Communist coup, the kind of coup that has generated nightmares around the world since, as violence and intimidation were applied to impose a regime every bit as Stalinist as those in Bulgaria or the USSR. The domestic specter of midnight arrests and sudden demonstrations by paramilitary "worker's militia" traumatically confirmed an impression of Soviet treachery that seemed to match an international policy of brute expansionism across the board. Stalin's Russians, like Hitler's Germans, did not keep their promises. They did not have any respect for the institution of free elections. They were growing rapidly in military power, and in geographic control of territory.

Rounding out the decline of American trust in the Soviets, one saw disclosures after 1946 of Soviet espionage rings in Canada and the United States seeking to learn how to make nuclear weapons. Russian public statements under Stalin feigned a disinterest in such weapons, arguing that such big bombs could not make any strategic difference, that the "permanent operating factors" would always assure victory, if a war were ever to come, to the side with the correct class outlook. These were the years in which Americans also discovered a substantial clandestine Communist Party penetration of their own society, when party members still were most slavishly loyal to the dictates from Stalin in Moscow. The extensive involvement of Communist Party members, many of whom had kept such membership a secret, in labor unions and academic organizations and the Hollywood film industry again suggested a pattern of conspiracy and treachery by the new Soviet adversary.

If Czechoslovakia, in 1948, was the first capstone for the American decision that the Russians had to be feared (because the overturning of representative government here was so blatant and unmistakable), the second such capstone then came in 1949 with the fall of China to the Communist Party led by Mao Tse-tung. Mao's announcement that China would henceforward "lean to one side" did not particularly startle Americans, for it merely seemed a repetition of what had become depressingly normal all across the globe (Tito in Yugoslavia now seeming the bizarre exception that proved the rule), that all Communists did exactly what the leadership in Moscow told them to do.

American references to the establishment here of a "Slavic Manchukuo" were thus not simple rhetoric, but expressed exactly the fears and attitudes that guided policy.[14] With the exception of a few China specialists within the State Department, most Americans in and out of government now concluded that Stalin's control over Mao would be just as tight as his control over the American Communist Party or the French party or the Czech party. Just as the Communist Poles put Stalin ahead of what their fellow Poles might desire, just as the puppet regime in Manchukuo had served the desires of Japan, the Chinese Communists would put Soviet interests ahead of those of the Chinese.

What was startling about the Communist takeover of China was thus not that Mao would "lean to one side"; this was to be expected. Rather the startling difference from the East European takeovers came in that some 600 million people were this time involved, more people than in the USSR, more than in the USSR plus all the territories Stalin had come to dominate since the German surrender.

"It was no accident," therefore, that full-fledged comparisons of Soviet Russia with Nazi Germany now began to come to mind. Each had a dictator. Each had a formalized ideology, providing no paper or ink or radio time for any contradictory point of view. Each had a secret police, with midnight arrests and torture and concentration camps. Each had private military forces at the control of the dominant political party, in part as a means to keeping its military under control.

Each of these monoliths moreover had seemed in the mood to test Western resolve, perhaps counting on the political democracies to be averse to the mobilizations required for armed combat, so that they would give up in crises, rather than fighting them out. Each seemed in the mood to expand wherever possible, and each had seemed to be expanding at a startlingly rapid rate. Nazi Germany had come up from a country still weakened in 1932 by the restrictions of Versailles and the economic impact of the depression, to a threat to conquer the world by 1941. Stalin's Russia had been in danger of military collapse in 1941, and by 1949 now seemed to control the bulk of the Eurasian land mass.

There are important gaps in the comparison, however. The British and French had declared war on Germany for the invasion of Poland in 1939; they had not declared war on the USSR for joining that invasion some 17 days later. The United States and the Allies had then deemed it necessary to keep fighting until the Nazi regime could be totally eliminated, until troops had actually fought their way into Berlin and into every German city; almost no one now proposed a drive for total war and total victory against the USSR.

BLENDING THE INTERPRETATIONS

Some of the blame for the cold war should certainly be directed to the suddenness of the change in the international system at the end of World War II, so that somewhat fewer negative aspersions need to be directed at the character of foreign policy of either the United States or the USSR. This would not be suggesting that either side was without fault or malicious intent; rather the world may simply be cursed with settings in which malicious intent is not really necessary to make conflicts happen, and hence cannot be so clearly proven.

With the best of intentions, either side might thus have now seemed to be threatening the other. The United States might, on quite purely Wilsonian principles, have felt strongly about democratic rule and self-determination for the nations of Eastern Europe. Rather than being economically oriented in a pathological concern for markets in such areas, or looking for powerful allies for future wars, Americans may simply have felt that Poland and Czechoslovakia should be allowed the free election processes that the World War II German occupation had so totally suppressed. Yet the historical and political reality of Eastern Europe was that many of the nations of this region (Czechoslovakia perhaps being an important exception) would have felt strong hostility to the Russians, and thus in an act of self-determination would have wanted to join in a military alliance with the United States.

What Americans wanted, for good reasons, could thus easily have become threatening to the USSR for other reasons. One must at least consider the possibility that the Soviet desire to control the foreign policy of the Eastern European states, and to control their domestic political development as well, sprang quite simply and naturally from the Russian experience in having been invaded twice since 1914.

As will be discussed later, when we turn to the alternative of disengagement, Finland and Austria are examples of countries successfully splitting the difference, achieving self-government for themselves on most issues, however tying their own hands on foreign policy so as to reassure the USSR; specifically the option of forming a military alliance with the United States is decisively foresworn.[15]

Even in the cases of Finland and Austria, however, the Soviet success at curbing these countries' natural anti-Russian leanings was achieved only by persistent toughness. For Rumania and Poland and Hungary, Moscow may well then have concluded that something more direct and brutal was required, the imposition of Communist governments, shielding the Soviet Union against attack by ideology as well as by treaty commitments.

Yet such trampling on the popular preferences of Eastern Europe, even if it was basically "defensive," constituted a precedent that would then inevitably worry Americans about Soviet behavior in the rest of Europe. Security for the Soviet Union now meant having Russian troops poised within a day's drive of the Rhine; as the Russians developed their reliable protective buffer in Poland and Hungary and East Germany, the road to Paris became a great deal shorter. The cycle of mutually precautionary responses to suspicion, inducing new suspicions, was again complete.

Much the same possibility of initially nonhostile intent emerges in the American decision to use the A-bomb against Japan, to which revisionist interpretations of the outbreak of the cold war often point in accusing the United States. Was the bomb dropped with a view to "impressing the Russians"? To be sure, one can find references to this kind of consideration in the American deliberations before the decision, although they are again much overshadowed in volume by straightforward discussions of the bomb's impact in "impressing" the Japanese, i.e., persuading them to surrender.

Even if impressing the Russians carried any importance here, this could take some very different forms, positive as well as negative. The most negative version, of course, is that the United States was paving the way for threats it would make in the future, as it hoped to intimidate and dominate the Soviet leadership by the example of the A-bomb's destructiveness. Yet references to the Russians in American discussions here lend themselves just as easily to a much more positive interpretation, by which the United States would be proving to them that it had indeed done its part during World War II in the joint effort against the Axis. The Soviet leadership had throughout the war often voiced the suspicion that the Western democracies, in particular the United States, were not doing enough to defeat Hitler, were not making enough economic and human sacrifices in this important cause.[16] The atomic bomb did not come along early enough to be used against the Germans (or else it surely would have been used), but its use against the Japanese could still be offered to the Kremlin as evidence that the United States had not been lazy nor unproductive during the years of the war, but had rather channeled some of its resources wisely to the production of the very most useful of weapons, a weapon that could have defeated Hitler if nothing else had sufficed.

Apart from "impressing the Russians," the other revisionist charge is that the nuclear bombings of Hiroshima and Nagasaki came because the United States wanted to keep the Soviet Union out of the war against Japan, wanted to win a quick Japanese surrender while the USSR still remained neutral, and thus could be cut out of any share of the spoils.

But all these accusations presume something that can only be argued in retrospect on the basis of inside evidence not available to American decision making at the time, that the Japanese were about to surrender very soon in any event. If the Japanese surrender was not imminent, but (as many Americans believed) would not come until 1947 or so, it was hardly in the selfish power interest of the United States to keep the USSR out of the war, and the United States had indeed been urging Moscow to join in the fighting against Japan as soon as possible. To have kept the USSR out of the war might simply have meant that more American boys were killed and fewer Russians, and (supposing that Washington was already so tuned in on the coming cold war, which is probably not the fact) that any future Japanese revanchist sentiments would be directed only at the United States, and not at the Russians as well.

Those who argue that the Japanese were about to surrender in a month or two, even without any nuclear attacks, are making a certainty out of something that even by hindsight cannot have been certain, but at best is only more likely than the opposite.[17] Even here the revisionists' criticism of the nuclear attacks begs the question, as it argues that the use of such A-bombs was uniquely immoral, thus a double blot on American behavior here. What, if anything, was making the Japanese government become so ready to surrender in any event? It was an indispensable condition here that the United States Army Air Force was already making life miserable in Japanese cities by conventional bombing, having burned Tokyo to the ground by such means, in a single night, with a considerably greater loss of life than occurred at either Hiroshima or Nagasaki. One is hard-pressed to find the moral difference between the nuclear bombings here and the conventional bombing of Tokyo (or earlier of Hamburg and Dresden in Germany). Yet, if all such terror bombings had been stopped, the Japanese might indeed have been content to sit and wait into the 1950s without surrendering.

The conventional bombing of Dresden incidentally faces some of the same complications of interpretation as the nuclear attacks on Japan.[18] In a bombing that again probably took more lives than either of the A-bomb attacks, was the American intent to accelerate the German surrender, or to assist the advance of the Russian ground forces closing in, or to "impress the Russians" (negatively or positively)? A close study of the decision process in this raid illustrates the bureaucratic momentum that often governs political decision processes in many places around the globe. As the raid was planned over a period of months, its background rationale changed repeatedly; as the defeat of Nazi Germany approached, the project seemingly had a life of its own, so that in the end it was executed for one reason just as much as for another.

All of the reasons are thus *partially* valid here. Perhaps the planners of the U.S. and British air forces wanted to show Stalin that they had a weapon that could not be ignored. Perhaps they just as much wanted to show him that the English-speaking powers had done all they could to defeat Germany, with the rubble of a devastated Dresden thus inspiring some gratitude and alliance sympathy among the advancing Russians. The Russians in the later years of the cold war would pretend to be militarily unimpressed by the destruction of the city, and morally appalled by it; but the pretenses of those years cannot be taken as measures of true feelings, or of the intentions of the Western decision makers on their side.

The issue of where to find malicious intent here becomes even more complicated when we turn to the more general complications introduced by the U.S. possession of nuclear weapons and the overall military strengths of the two sides. The United States has often concentrated on the question of what has held the Russians back from sending armored columns toward Paris, after the rapid demobilization of Western conventional military forces at the end of World War II. Presumably the threat of American nuclear attack sufficed as the counterdeterrent here, as Winston Churchill and others surmised.[19] Yet what was it that in turn kept the United States from brandishing its nuclear monopoly against the Russians in the years before 1949 (perhaps a question discussed much more often on the Soviet side)? Presumably the threat of a Soviet move against Paris was precisely the counterdeterrent that sufficed here. In neither case do we know that there was anything to deter. Yet a reasonable man asking for reassurance on either side might have found himself grasping, for insurance, at precisely what the other side had to see as a threat.

The Soviet suppression of Polish freedom was perhaps not just necessary to keep Poland from becoming a base for another ground attack against the Russian interior, but also to maintain a sufficient threat against Paris, to keep the Strategic Air Command (SAC) from being brandished or used against the USSR. This must explain the inconsistency of suppressing all political democracy in Poland, while tolerating some in Finland; Warsaw is on the "road to Paris," while Helsinki is not.

In reviewing the years after 1945, any observer thus faces some enormous problems of "how do you tell?" Would Stalin have declined to take Paris, if Paris had been left available, if the power of the United States Air Force had not stood in the way? As noted, some forms of retrospective analysis contend that he would not have done so, because his intentions were always peaceful and defensive or perhaps because he at least would not have trusted his ability to control the Communist empire once it had expanded to including all of Western Europe. Stalin, fortunately or unfortunately, was never given a chance to pass such a test. An elementary distrust had led the United States to take steps to eliminate any chances of Stalin taking Paris.

Conversely, would the United States have failed to pressure the USSR itself if Eastern Europe had been left free to hold democratic elections, very likely producing governments in Poland or Rumania desirous of political and economic and military alliances with the United States? The prevention of Russian domination of Eastern Europe might have blocked any Soviet ground force threat to Paris, and might thus have emboldened the United States to brandish its nuclear monopoly much more, perhaps even then beginning a "human rights" campaign about Stalin's rule in the Soviet Union itself.

The United States was also therefore not given a chance to prove how it would have behaved if the USSR had possessed no effective counterlevers to the A-bomb. The U.S. nuclear arsenal or U.S. defenses for Western Europe were never really strong enough to tempt the United States with hegemony, with the option of imposing the U.S. picture of world peace and proper domestic order on the USSR. Many Americans today believe that the United States had the power to dominate the world after Nagasaki, but deliberately abdicated it; this would seem like a powerful confirmation of the beneficent and modest intentions of Americans toward the outside world, but the facts of the matter may indeed spoil the purity of this test.

Each of the three views brought to bear thus has something useful to say about the origins of the cold war. One must decide which has the *most* to contribute.

The power politics perspective is correct in counseling one toward a certain degree of agnosticism about procedural morality and "blame" in international dealings, in warning against becoming excessively mired in a search for the historical "facts" of who did what

Berliners as friends and potential participants in democracy, rather than as former Nazis. Similarly the defenses of Turkey or Greece or Korea would after a time raise the degree to which Americans saw these as friendly and progressive.

Looking back on the enunciation of the containment doctrine, from the time of the Vietnam War some 20 years later, Kennan himself was to express some substantial discomfort with what the policy had come to mean.[21] Kennan's criticism could come in various forms. He suggested that too much emphasis had been placed on the military side of containment, and not enough on the economic and political, although his own original article had indeed placed substantial stress on the military.

Kennan could most certainly have been bothered by the way containment was announced so loudly and explicitly, and he had perhaps favored a more subtle implementation of it as policy. To make a policy explicit is sometimes necessary to getting it put into practice. Yet Americans sometimes have a tendency (U.S. policy on preventing nuclear weapons proliferation may be another example) to insist on very loud and graphic explications, with the risk that subtlety and flexibility are lost, so that the policy itself loses effectiveness.

Kennan's criticisms of the way containment was implemented are on record already from the end of the 1940s.[22] Yet such criticisms are not the same as the radical critique of American cold war policy in general, as it was advanced during the Vietnam War, a critique with which Kennan might understandably have wanted to get into step. Kennan's disagreements with policy in the 1940s and 1950s were based simply on the argument that the United States was not properly affecting events *inside* the iron curtain, but not that the United States was somehow abusing or exploiting areas outside that curtain.

THE IMPLEMENTATION OF
CONTAINMENT: BERLIN

Was there indeed a need for containment in the years in which the concept was formulated, a need to establish such a forward line of defense in Europe, rather than sitting back and letting the classical tendencies toward balance take care of themselves? The Soviet threat of political takeovers here may not have been so very military at this time, since the USSR did not have any A-bombs until 1949, and since Soviet conventional armed forces had indeed been substantially disarmed after the German and Japanese surrenders, in response to the demands of the Soviet economic recovery effort. (The demobilization of such forces was however not nearly as drastic as those of the United States.)[23]

Yet the possibility still loomed of an economic and political, and paramilitary, threat, as 1946 passed into 1947 and 1948, due to a mixture of delayed-action impact from the destructiveness of World War II and outright bad luck. As these all came together in the unusually severe winter of 1947–48, sinking Western Europe into a combination of commodity shortage and unemployment, the possibility emerged of a social discontent that might set the stage for violent unrest, and the application of military force by whomever had such force to deploy. "The crisis of 1948" thus combined disasters of climate with the unpredicted damages leftover from the war, and with the prospect that the USSR, once it had its own recovery process under control, would be in the mood to advance to exploit this unhappiness.

The model of American fears was then in many ways supplied by the fall of the political democracy in Czechoslovakia to Communist dictatorship, a takeover that required no participation by the military forces of the USSR, but merely the supporting threat of such participation as they stood poised across the border, as "workers' militia" suddenly appeared to dominate the streets as a paramilitary force, in a style that could not be ruled out also for Communist-dominated labor federations further west. This combination of midnight arrests and intimidations by secret police, combined with the deployment of muscle by Communist labor groups, all backed by the distant power of the Red Army, was enough now to convince Americans that alliances might generally have to be confirmed, that a firmer line of containment might have to be drawn, at least for Europe, where the closest analogies to Czechoslovakia would have to emerge.

Marshal Tito's assertion of Yugoslav independence from Stalin, coming just a few months later in 1948, might in some ways have been viewed as balancing the loss of Czechoslovakia in geopolitical or power terms, but it surely was not a matching gain in terms of the extent of political freedom in the world. In the same months Communist movements, however, began to look increasingly strong in France and Italy, amid widespread strikes and sabotage that could have looked like the forerunners of later guerrilla war; the most peaceful prospect was that the Communist parties might win elections freely, but then (as in Czechoslovakia) prevent any new elections if the tide of voter feeling turned against them. These trends in France and Italy thus saw the United States government doing all it could to persuade voters to reject the Communist appeal, even urging Italian nationals who had established residence in the United States to be sure to cast absentee ballots in the Italian elections against the Communists. The United States Army, with its meager forces in West Germany, nonetheless found itself composing plans for the contingency of a violent Communist coup in Italy or France, with a view to doing something to prevent a repetition of the Czech outcome.[24]

Capping the 1948 crisis was then the continued sluggishness of the economic recovery process in West Germany, as Soviet vetoes of currency reform prevented anything like a maximum economic performance. The fearful prognosis was that the Soviets were deliberately exercising their prerogatives here with a view to prolonging discontent and food shortages and unemployment in the Western zones, so that the American and British and French administrations would catch the blame, so that the Communist Party would in the end reap the gains.

The Western response in the end was to ignore Soviet protests and introduce a currency reform in June of 1948; economically it was an instant success, producing what thereafter was to be remembered as the West German "economic miracle," but it also led the Russians to impose a blockade on West Berlin, the Western enclave deep inside East Germany. The Russians had now for the first time thus applied a military tool, in a position where the advantages of military pressure were inherently on their side.[25]

The option clearly must have been considered that the Western position in Berlin would now be renounced as inherently too difficult to defend, but the fear in Washington and elsewhere was obviously that this would amount to a very damaging precedent and example of resolve if the Berliners who had endangered their futures by speaking and voting against the Communists were abandoned. What would be the likely impact on the free elections of France and Italy and West Germany if those who had so staunchly resisted the forced merger of Socialist and Communist Parties into a "Socialist Unity Party" were abandoned to Russian and East German Communist retaliation?

The option of a purely military Western response, of trying to push through East Germany with a convoy down the Autobahn to West Berlin, was considered, but not tried, because the situation so inherently favored the military position of Russians trying to block such a convoy. The western response was rather to experiment with flying supplies across East Germany to Berlin in an "airlift" that the

Russians may well have tolerated at first only because they doubted that it could succeed. Yet the airlift succeeded handsomely in the end, as West Berlin's survival became so definitely assured that the ground blockade became an exercise in futility and embarrassment for the Russians, and the blockade was then lifted in the thaw or detente of 1949.

These events of 1948 thus impressed a series of seeming "lessons" on the American decision maker and the American public. It would apparently, as in the case of Berlin, now be important for the United States to declare its commitments, lest the Soviet Union try to expand simply on the expectation that no one would resist. In 1947 it had been very debatable whether the United States and Great Britain and France would want to try to stay in Berlin, and many had predicted that the Western powers would liquidate their investment in the enclave at the first opportunity. The crisis of 1948 had to some extent consisted of proving one's resolve and one's interest here.

The second lesson was a trifle more cheering, however, in that a basically "peaceful" approach had succeeded in holding the line, not so drastically contradicting the mix of approaches that Kennan thought appropriate. While the Russians had been given a reminder of American willingness to use nuclear weapons, the armored column thrust down the Autobahn had not needed to be tried, as technology applied imaginatively, in another demonstration of American ingenuity, had offered a nonviolent way around what had at first seemed to be a military problem. In the rest of Western Europe, similarly nonmilitary approaches began to win victories for the West, as deliveries of American economic assistance in the Marshall Plan buoyed up the economies of France, Italy, and West Germany, as the freeing of West Germany from the residues of an artificially restrained inflation tied to the old currency created what was to be the spark plug for a prolonged economic boom all through Europe.

THE MILITARIZATION OF CONTAINMENT

Why then did we see a subsequent shift of the cold war into much more of a reliance on military means, as the centerpiece of containment? We do quite correctly remember the cold war as a prolonged confrontation of arms.

To begin, there had all along been a certain nervous anticipation of what Soviet behavior would be like after economic recovery from the devastation of World War II had been completed. When domestic needs had been addressed, Stalin might be able to assign more manpower and money to his military again, and perhaps then to push forward into more territory even when facing American strategic air power. As noted, the deterrent impact of such strategic air power was substantially in debate, with some Americans very impressed by the nuclear destruction of Hiroshima and Nagasaki, but others noting that the comparable nonnuclear destruction of Hamburg or Tokyo or Dresden had not produced surrenders by the Axis regimes.

Second, much more directly addressing the nuclear question, the Soviet Union was detected in testing an atomic bomb of its own in 1949, surprising Western experts by how early this was achieved, apparently thereby moving toward canceling whatever American advantages had stemmed from the American monopoly. A National Security Council study under the direction of Paul Nitze (NSC-68) thus now concluded that substantial Western investments in conventional military forces might be required to fulfill Kennan's requirements of containment, along with a substantial expansion also of U.S. strategic air forces, for the balance of forces might otherwise not be sufficient to keep the Russians from aggressing. If the A-bomb had deterred Stalin when only the United States possessed it, it might be less plausible as a deterrent when the Russians had it as well, and might remain out of use on both sides, as Soviet conventional forces rolled forward.[26]

Third, seeming to confirm many of such fears, there was a substantial buildup of Soviet and Eastern European satellite ground and air forces after 1949. At whom was this aimed? One possibility, of course, would have been a conquest of Western Europe, the vision that had bothered Americans ever since 1945. A more modest Soviet plan might instead have involved an invasion of Yugoslavia to depose Tito, thus to erase the possibly infectious example of heretical behavior within the Communist world.

Facing these possibilities, we thus for the European case see the beginnings of what its critics would call "pactomania" and what its supporters would think of as "alliance readiness"; the Western European Union Treaty of 1948 signaled the first postwar military alliance clearly aimed at the Soviet threat, and this was rounded out much more fully with the 12-nation founding of the North Atlantic Treaty Organization (NATO) in 1949.[27] Yet the NATO treaty commitment for almost another year might have amounted again to a mere declaratory formalism; it was important, as was the stand in Berlin, for committing American resolve to the defense of territory that otherwise might seem up for grabs, for committing American honor to the defense of Western Europe as part of containment, but it as yet included no actual augmentation of military strength. The hope might still have been that all that was really needed was to remove any confusion in Soviet minds on what territories the United States held dear, on what peoples it was insistent on protecting, on where its line of containment was to run.

The real capstone to the military crystalization of the cold war came then in June in 1950 with the outbreak of the Korean War.[28] The North Korean invasion of the South was a blatant aggression, with very few revisionists even today accepting the Communist version that it was Syngman Rhee's forces that had attacked (so that Kim Il-sung's tank divisions had to defend themselves all the way south into the Korean Peninsula?).

While always entertaining some possibilities of mutual misunderstanding and "prisoners' dilemma" as an explanation for the cold war it is hard to see how the South Korean armed posture here in any way could have posed a threat to the North, since the United States, after withdrawing its own forces in 1948, had left behind only a very lightly armed constabulary force. As North Korean forces pushed rapidly to Seoul and beyond, threatening to overcome all resistance and occupy the entire peninsula, it looked all too much like the German invasion of Poland in 1939; the Nazis had similarly offered trumped-up evidence of a Polish invasion of German territory, with Hitler's Panzer divisions then "defensively responding" in a push all the way to Warsaw.

A short review of the chronology of the Korean War will remind us of why it was sometimes called a "yo-yo" war by American soldiers, full of disappointments and setbacks for each side.[29] The quick North Korean push to the South had threatened a total defeat for the South Korean forces, but American forces were now reintroduced, with UN Security Council blessing, just in time to maintain a perimeter of some 50 miles radius around the southern port of Pusan. General MacArthur then launched a brilliant amphibious end run to the North in a landing at Inchon, close to Seoul, that promised to impose a total defeat on the North Koreans.

Exploiting the victories in the South, MacArthur's forces pushed north past the thirty-eighth parallel demarcation line, occupying the major North Korean cities of Pyongyang and Wonsan, advancing toward the Yalu River boundary with China. A surprise Chinese intervention then routed MacArthur's forces, sending them reeling south, with a Communist occupation once again of Seoul, with South Koreans and the United States and other forces of the United Nations Command then finally putting a stop to the Communist advance at a line to the south of Seoul. The fourth round then came with an American–South Korean offensive pushing the Chinese and North Koreans back north of Seoul again, approximately to the current truce line.

A number of mysteries remain on the origins of the Korean War. As noted, the attack was so blatant that very few analysts would see it as an inadvertant outbreak of conflict. Why did the attack come, however, while Soviet delegates were boycotting sessions of the UN Security Council (in protest of the failure to seat the new Peking regime in the Chinese seat), thus allowing the United States to escape a Soviet veto in getting Security Council endorsement of the American defense of South Korea?

One possibility was of course that the Russians had sincerely not expected the United States to resist the Communist military attack, seeing this as one more "reunification" of mainland territories, similar to the Communist total defeat of Chinese nationalist forces on the mainland of China. Public statements by Secretary of State Dean Acheson and by General Douglas MacArthur had late in 1949 and early in 1950 seemed to omit Korea from the perimeter of territories the United States was committed to defend.[30]

A second possibility was that the Korean attack had been unauthorized by Joseph Stalin, launched simply on the authority of Kim Il-sung. It is sad to reflect that we may never know for certain how the decision process in the Communist capitals was functioning in 1950.

Uncertainties about Communist motivation leave us with uncertainties about the real significance of the Korean War. One result in any event was to push the world now into an enduring pattern of high military expenditures, a pattern that may have been less inevitable than remembered. Would Stalin or Kim Il-sung have launched a tank attack if they had known that Truman would resist? While Korea was seen as a menacing pattern for the future, there were to be no more Communist tank attacks in the 1950s or 1960s. Was this because this had never been Moscow's plan? Or was it because the United States and its allies proved themselves determined to resist?

Since this had now looked all too much like confirmation of the worst American and West European fears for the future, the response was a massive U.S. investment in military forces. American defense expenditures now climbed to a new plateau, from which they would never again come back down; as substantial American forces were dispatched to Korea in what became a successful effort to rebuff the North Korean attack, substantial forces were deployed to Europe as well, and the military-government forces in the American Occupation Zone of Germany were augmented and transformed into six combat divisions poised for a possible attack from the East. The European NATO allies of the United States were encouraged to make matching augmentations of their own ground forces, in preparation for deterring or repulsing the Korean kind of aggression.

The Korean War thus also now produced a general tidying up and extension of containment to Asia as well. Even before the Communist Chinese intervened in the Korean War, President Truman, in response to the initial attack on South Korea, had committed U.S. naval forces to the defense of Taiwan. In time, this was to include a corollary commitment also to the Nationalist garrisons remaining on some tiny islands just offshore of the mainland, most importantly Quemoy and Matsu.[31]

Various future tensions and complications were buried in these commitments. Taiwan might be reasonably easy to defend without crises in the future, but the offshore islands were not, being (like West Berlin) a position to which the adversary could always fairly easily apply geopolitical and military pressure. The American commitment to Taiwan (again analogous to West Berlin) amounted to a disparagement of the sovereignty of the Peking Communist regime, leaving the United States in the ongoing position of particularly much challenging the legitimacy of two Communist regimes, Peking's and Pankow's.

Closing the trap on the other side, the initial American commitment to Taiwan again made it more difficult for the United States to renounce such a commitment gracefully in the future. Never to have declared a commitment to Taiwan (or to West Berlin) would have put fewer other American commitments into doubt if these positions were renounced. Finally, as yet a fourth analogy to the American commitment to the Berlin enclave, the American government and public now began to discover likable attributes again in the Kuomintang regime, as it demonstrated an ability to achieve substantial economic progress for Taiwan, greater than that accomplished by the Communists on the mainland, and at a lower sacrifice of personal freedom. Just as the United States had begun its defense of West Berlin while still viewing most Germans as Nazis, and then had come to view them instead as democracy-loving partners, so the commitment to Taiwan was destined to move out from strategic considerations to a new round of genuine human identification, making any American decoupling from the situation less likely.

In a direct link again to the Korean War, the United States also now reluctantly began offering support to the French in Indochina, anticipating future wars in Laos and Vietnam on the model of Kim Il-sung's tank attack in Korea.

Finally, to pull U.S.-Chinese relations most tightly into the cold war, the optimistic pursuit of a total victory in North Korea had then by December pulled U.S. forces into open warfare with the Chinese. The sight of American and Chinese troops shooting at each other, with the United States persuading the United Nations General Assembly to pass resolutions condemning the Peking regime, was to poison relations on both sides now for two decades, postponing for the same two decades any seating of the Peking regime in the Chinese seat at the United Nations.

THE MATURE COLD WAR

With the settlement of the stalemated Korean War by a truce in 1953, we can then at last contemplate an analysis of the cold war as a steady state. The United States now plunged fully into what was afterward to be attacked as a "pactomania," as the Southeast Asia Treaty Organization (SEATO) and the Central Treaty Organization (CENTO) and a series of other mutual-defense treaties were added to NATO. John Foster Dulles, secretary of state in the Eisenhower administration that assumed office in 1953, was often accused of a silly pursuit of illusory grandeur here, for many U.S. "mutual-defense" alliance partners looked quite venal, and quite weak, hardly capable of helping to defend the United States, only needing to be defended.

Alliances in the old days, prior to 1914, had been meaningful exchanges of promises, whereby Great Britain and France, or Great Britain and Japan, were swapping contingency commitments of genuine aid and assistance for any future war. Neither side to such an alliance particularly much wanted to have to join in someone else's war, but each wanted very much to have a committed partner, and each thus entered into a mutual defense contract feeling that it was gaining in the net. These were the kinds of alliance that the United States had chosen to avoid until the initialing of NATO. If NATO was perhaps now genuinely appropriate to American national interests, given the changes in the international scene after World War I and II, were not American contracts with Pakistan or Thailand much more to be ridiculed, as offering nothing in exchange?

Yet much of such criticism misses the mark. Alliances in the nuclear age have to be something different from what they were in 1907. For the United States, a mutual defense treaty with a state in Asia now amounted mainly as a way of making it credible that we, as a stronger but more distant power, would indeed intervene if the weaker local state were attacked. The treaty commitment was something the United States would in fact *want* to be tied by, unlike the older form of alliance where this was simply the price one had to pay for someone else's promise in return. By tying one's own hands, one made deterrence more credible, given that Americans were globally viewed as taking their treaty commitments seriously. The intent was straightforwardly now to prevent misunderstandings on the other side, to prevent repeats of the armed attack on South Korea.

This changed nature of alliances indeed now applied almost as much to NATO as to SEATO. The United States did not need Belgian help to shield Hawaii, or Thai help to defend Massachusetts. Rather the United States wanted to give a unilateral military commitment, phrasing it in terms of "mutual defense" merely for the sake of tradition and international appearances.

Other critics of American foreign policy, after the Korean War, were to interpret this pactomania as a sign of American lust for world empire and craving for expansion. Yet some interesting counterevidence is offered in public opinion polls taken over these years, in particular, in a question on "who is winning the cold war." If Americans had seen the establishment of SEATO and CENTO as an expansion of their empire, they might have been expected to describe their side as "winning." Yet the answer here is typically the opposite, much more consistent with an American self-interpretation here of holding the line, of "containment," of trying to prevent expansion by the other side, and having only some uneven success at it.[32] Americans may well have believed that they were defending a position, rather than assaulting an opposing position.

With the cold war settling in as a steady state, crises now came to be interpreted less as changes, or as the initial discovery of hostility, and more as periodic renewals of American proof of commitment. In these years we began to see an extended analysis of the issues of resolve, with John Foster Dulles suggesting that a taking of risks in "brinkmanship" was needed, to keep proving to the other side that the United States indeed meant to prevent Communist expansion.[33]

How, according to such theories, would the Communist challenge to U.S. resolve come? The potential aggressor would begin by trying minor insults to see if the United States would respond, applying "nickle and diming," or "salami tactics." How would one then prove his resolve in resisting such aggressions? It could be shown by signing treaties, as has just been discussed as pactomania, or by "jawboning" and "eyeballing," i.e., by making public statements that sounded resolute, something at which President Eisenhower may have been particularly good. Resolve moreover could be shown by moving troops around, by deploying them to Europe, or to Korea, or later to

Vietnam. Finally, American resolve in the defense of the free world could be proved in actual fighting, not merely by the deployment of troops forward, but by letting them be used in combat.

Such a logic led after a time to a particularly resigned and callous view of crises, almost that crises would be normal and essential. Just as one could not be a good parent without spanking his children once in a while, or could not be a good policeman without making some arrests to prove that the law was being enforced, one could not preserve the defenses of the non-Communist states without there occasionally being a war, or at least a major threat of war, wherein the United States would prove its determination and willingness to make sacrifices.

By this logic, the Berlin crises of 1948–49 and 1958–61 played this role, as did the Quemoy and Matsu crises of 1954 and 1958, and then the Cuban missile crisis of 1962. Some sort of Soviet threat of blockade or attack or aggressive deployment would have to come along every so often, to be rebuffed by a firm American resistance, after which the "winner" in this contest of brinkmanship could coast along again for a time thereafter, on the basis of the resolve that had just been proved.

The chronology of the Cuban missile crisis illustrates this reasoning fairly well.[34] Periodic rumors of a Soviet deployment of nuclear missiles to Cuba had emerged through the spring and summer of 1962, usually discounted as long as anti-Castro Cuban emigres were the source. Perhaps for domestic reasons, in light of the coming congressional elections, perhaps because of more serious international considerations, President John F. Kennedy now took a stand against any deployment of "offensive missiles" to Cuba. The Russians nonetheless then proceeded to try to sneak such missiles into Cuba, on the assumption that they would be allowed to stay once they were in place, with humiliating implications for the American resolve in analogous cases elsewhere.

U.S. reconnaissance overflights of Cuba detected the move, and a blockade was imposed on the island, labeled a "quarantine" for sake of international appearances. The threats were further conveyed that any firing of such missiles from Cuba would lead to a full American World War III retaliatory response, and that a failure to move the missiles within a reasonable length of time might bring air or ground attacks on Cuba itself.

Khrushchev's response to the threats was to back down, in what everyone then labeled as Kennedy's finest hour. While Dulles had been criticized by the Democrats for brinkmanship, the same Democrats took pride here in "crisis management." Very few Americans at the time questioned the wisdom or even the necessity of the entire exercise. Was the prevention of such a Russian deployment to Cuba (which would only bring Soviet medium-range missiles within range of targets that could already be hit by Soviet intercontinental-range rockets) really worth risking a World War III?

By winning a concession on Cuba, just as it had earlier won a concession on West Berlin, the United States became more tied to retaining this position in the future, lest giving it up might suggest too clear a diminishing of U.S. resolve. Was the concession by the Russians not likely to become embarrassing in future decades, as the Soviet leadership could always needle the United States by "nickle and diming" the ban on missiles in Cuba?

Could it even be that the magnitude of the apparent American success in the Cuban missile crisis too much emboldened and energized the American government afterward, as for the first time a feeling emerged that the United States might be "winning" the cold war? The years after the crisis saw the beginnings of what is regarded as detente with the USSR, and then with China, but it also saw the American plunge into the Vietnam War. As yet another kind of cold war conflict, the United States in the mid-1960s entered into a substantially different confrontation with the Communist world, guerrilla insurgency. It was not so much this time a game of "chicken," as in the 1962 threat of a thermonuclear holocaust, but rather a "tug of war," whereby each side was simply threatening the other with a continuation of the mutual agony. World War III was hardly even to be in question as the Vietnam War was fought out; but very high costs were nonetheless borne by the two sides.

THE ALTERNATIVE OF DISENGAGEMENT

George Kennan, already reknowned for having formulated the concept of containment in 1947, came forward with an alternative to it in the mid-1950s with "disengagement."[35] Rather than holding back the spread of Communist regimes by confronting them all around the globe along a defined line, this alternative approach would have relied in some sectors (in Kennan's proposal even in a location as valuable as Germany) on the leaving of a space between the two zones of military alliance.

The advantages would be several. To begin, this might facilitate the reunion of countries that had been divided into Soviet and Western zones at the end of World War II. National unity would be something valued in its own right by the Germans, or Austrians, and indeed by

Koreans or Vietnamese. If, in exchange for the United States forswearing any military use of the national resources involved, the Russians would agree to withdraw from their half of such a country, a net gain for American national goals might well have been attained.

Second, even where an issue of national unity was not in question, the creation or maintenance of such a buffer zone of disengagement might lessen military tensions between the United States and the USSR, putting each less on its guard lest the other make some quick offensive move, perhaps reducing the likelihood of war, at least reducing the costs of continuous military expenditures.

This second accomplishment however depended on achieving some internal strength and viability in the countries of the disengaged zones. If they merely amounted to a vacuum of political or military strength, susceptible to overthrow and conquest with ease from either of the sides, they would increase rather than decrease the mutual tensions and apprehensions of war.

The countries within a zone of disengagement thus did not have to be strong enough to be treated as some sort of "third force," as a balancer in the traditional balance-of-power model (this kind of mechanism was to come into play in the Soviet-American relationship considerably later, as Europe recovered all of its prosperity and political and economic room for maneuver, as China made clear its independence of Moscow). But such countries of disengagement would have to be reasonably secure in their own political base, such that the supposed gains of winning their space would not tempt either of the alliances to race the other to intervene.

Such a disengagement scheme indeed seems to have worked successfully for some locations along the iron curtain since 1945. Sweden together with Finland perhaps amounted to this in Northern Europe, Finland in effect being able to maintain the kind of political democracy that the United States seeks for all countries, without in the same move directing any military menace at the USSR. The ability of the Finns to escape the fate of the Poles or the Bulgarians has importantly depended on the leverage provided by Sweden, which in effect may have abstained from NATO membership in exchange for seeing Finland spared a Marxist dictatorship.

On the southern flank, the status of Yugoslavia may have amounted to the same buffer of disengagement, although the early years of Tito's independence from Stalin caused concern that Yugoslavia would rather become a victim of aggression, and the years after Tito's death in the future raise similar worries here. Moscow has presumably all along been annoyed enough by the example of "Titoist" independence in communism to be more than a little tempted to put an end to it.

Closer to the central front, the Austrian Peace Agreement of 1955 added another zone of disengagement. As in the Finnish case, the Austrians were able to achieve the kind of political system that the United States values, in exchange for rigorous pledges that it would not become a member of an alliance such as NATO.

Until 1977, Afghanistan may have provided another such buffer area, wedged between the USSR and such United States allies as Pakistan and Iran. The fall of Afghanistan to forces declaring their loyalty to the USSR suggests the long-run fragility of such arrangements, and (unless Turkey moves into some sort of new neutralist role) it has not been replicated along any of the other points of contact between the Soviet bloc and the allies of the United States.

Neither side might thus have wanted such an empty zone if it were to become a constant temptation to battle, rather than a cushion against such temptation; much thus depends on the local distribution of strengths, as we try to predict whether this approach will reduce or increase tensions and costs, as compared with containment.

Yet other factors also always come into play besides the contribution to peace. In the Austrian and Finnish case, the United States achieved extensions of political democracy, at a very bearable price. The NATO military position might be stronger if it included Sweden and "West Austria," but the political gains of having free elections and a free press through all of Austria and all of Scandinavia outweigh this. Happily for the strength of the arrangements, the Russians have had accommodating preferences; even if it must be ideologically galling for the Soviets to see Vienna and Helsinki governed by the "bourgeoisie" rather than the "workers," the net exchange of keeping all of Austria and Sweden nonaligned has been worth it.

Why then did the same approach not get applied to Germany?[36] The gains of doing so might have been considerable. Germany would have been reunified, presumably under a politically democratic government, producing substantial satisfaction to the United States. The rearmament of West Germany and East Germany might have been avoided, producing satisfaction for Europeans and for others with memories of World War II, and generally reducing military expenditures and tensions in the European area.

Yet the very considerations outlined above suggest why doubts had to emerge about the feasibility of such accomplishments. Germany was perhaps too valuable as a prize of industry and population for the two sides ever to be ready to do a deal on the Austria pattern; i.e., it was more of a prize than a barrier. Would the USSR really have stood for the elimination of the Marxist regime over East Germany, or would it instead have insisted on conditions endangering and undermining the free political process for all of a unified Germany? Would the West not have been tempted to slide into a de facto military alliance with a unified Germany, despite any treaty agreements, if a democratic unification had actually taken place?

The United States cares a great deal about the denial of a free press and free elections in East Germany. But the USSR may care a great deal on the same issues, feeling very strongly the opposite way; free elections in East Germany almost assuredly would bring back much of the market capitalism that Moscow had taken pride in stamping out.

THE CONTEST IN VIETNAM

As suggested at many points in this book, the American involvement in the Vietnam War became the acid test of American resistance to the expansion of Marxist regimes, in an apparent struggle against a monolithic one-party dictatorship stressing economic equality, in a defense instead of what looked like a more politically pluralistic system that did not give such total priority to economic equality. It was a test that the American commitment in the end did not pass, as the war was lost, as the defense of South Vietnam failed, as Americans were more profoundly and deeply driven to reexamine all their priorities on foreign policy.[37]

In some ways, the historical fact that Vietnam became the focus is surprising and bizarre, since American commitments to defending an alternative regime to communism did not begin as strongly here as in Europe, or even as elsewhere in Asia. With regard to South Korea, Americans could bring themselves to believe after 1948 that they had left this former possession of Japan as a political democracy, and the same held true in the Philippines, where the regime winning independence from the United States seemed to pass this test, as opposed to the Marxist-oriented Hukbalahap guerrillas. Japan might now become a democracy, and thus would be worth defending, as were obviously Australia and New Zealand.

The relatively straightforward American commitment to political democracy was shown well in the attitudes of Franklin Delano Roosevelt during World War II, vehemently opposing any return of French rule to Indochina, an attitude obviously causing great distress to Charles de Gaulle.[38] American Office of Strategic Services (OSS) agents indeed worked closely during the last year of the war with the Communist leader Ho Chi Minh, as part of the general anti-Japanese effort, for a time seeing him possibly as a nationalist ready to base his rule on popular election, rather than as a Marxist of the Stalinist mold, ready to suppress all alternative political forces by the power of secret police arrest and assassination. After the death of Roosevelt, American enthusiasm for a return of French colonial rule did not increase; as with the Dutch in Indonesia, the net impact of American pressure was toward getting the European colonial power to abandon its claims, to let an indigenous regime emerge.

Indochina thus amounted to another confusing case for the extension of American containment doctrine to Asia, as had been the Kuomintang regime on the mainland of China. American doubts about the Chinese Nationalists after 1945 had been based on whether the regime could survive and hold its own, and perhaps in equal part on whether it was not too corrupt to qualify as the kind of representative government the United States wished to support. In the case of Indochina, the earlier qualms were not so much about whether the French might be able to establish a regime after the Japanese had been driven out, but whether such a restoration of European colonial rule could in any sense be morally justified.

Even with the more general commitment to military containment that took shape after the Korean War, the United States government was not willing to deploy its defensive resources seriously into Indochina until the French government had at last made a major commitment to local independence, until American officials and the American public then concluded they had found a local leader and local forces that were both anti-Communist and patriotically and nationalistically anti-French. The embodiment of this seemed to come after 1954 in the person of Ngo Dinh Diem. Diem's apparent personal strengths and potential popular appeal very much impressed John F. Kennedy, when Kennedy in the United States was years away from running for the presidency.[39] But the same impression was registered on a fair number of other important Americans, ranging from left to right across the middle of the spectrum, most of them not sharing Diem's and Kennedy's Roman Catholicism as a religion.

What is then illustrated by the strong subsequent American commitment to the defense of the rest of Indochina against Communist advances, after Vietnam north of the seventeenth parallel had been surrendered to Communist rule by the peace treaty of 1954? It of course in many ways exemplifies the straightforward national-political focus of American attitudes toward colonialism and dictatorship, the stress above all on retaining the possibility of political democracy, of republican rule, of self-government. Correspondingly, there was a relative inattention to things like the economic relationships of landlords and peasants, the exact degree of poverty or of nonmarket economic relationships in the countryside, the social and economic significance of the Asian traditions that had survived under French rule, which had even been utilized and exploited under that rule.

It is very difficult, despite the best efforts of the radical and revisionist attack on American foreign policy, to prove that American economic imperialism was the prime mover now in the American commitment to the defense of South Vietnam, for the amount of such investment by American firms was continually small; the primary investment had remained French, and the prospect was later that it would become Japanese.

It is more plausible to indict American motivation here for a certain economic blindness by which the economic grievances and unhappiness of the Vietnamese peasants was underestimated, along with the likely appeal and fighting power of forces like the Vietminh and later Vietcong. Yet "blindness" can sometimes be an issue of relative attention, and a real sorting out of the facts on the issues and grievances of Vietnam after French rule may take a long time into the future. Were Americans really so indifferent to poverty and economic injustice here, or were they simply and necessarily distracted by something else that was much more worrisome, the threat of an outright Communist police state, a dictatorship that might never be overturnable, no matter what the degree of popular discontent.

The possibility of a Communist takeover of the south of Vietnam, and of the rest of Indochina, beginning as it did when the cracks in the Communist monolith had not really surfaced, when communism still looked like a far more cohesive and disciplined (and therefore potentially more dangerous) force than fascism had been, thus posed the specter of Communist conspiracy.

This threat of monolithic conspiracy was then exacerbated and reinforced by the prospect of a continuous Communist exploitation of treacherous methods, which Ho Chi Minh's rise to power in the north of Vietnam had illustrated all too well. The Communist approach here consisted of nothing less than ensuring their own popularity by killing off all possible alternative popular candidacies, by assassination, midnight arrests, and other forms of terrorism. In the north as in the south, there had been other forms of nationalist opposition to the French, other forces that might have been able to win substantial shares of the vote, if French rule had been surrendered and freely elected systems of self-governance had been at last installed. Yet such movements in the north had been ruthlessly suppressed, as Ho and his Communist Party apparently felt that the rightness and appropriateness of their own economic program justified the sacrifice of anything like the voter choices of a political democracy. Among the alternatives that thus were liquidated were various Trotskyite factions, religious sects, nationalists patterned on the model of the KMT in China, and voting movements based on the Roman Catholic church where it had won adherents.

In the south, the tactics thus became the same after 1955, in what Americans indeed now came to see as the worldwide technique of guerrilla warfare, disrupting and terrorizing the system until it falls to the more disciplined and fanatic cadres of the Communist movement.[40] The essence of the terrorist guerrilla attack was to make it impossible for a regime like Diem's to function. Targets for assassination included the best and the worst of what the government had to offer. Tax collectors were killed, in what might always seem a more popular action among the peasants. Also killed, however, were any individuals who might bring credit to the regime by offering truly useful services, such as schoolteachers, malaria-control experts, and agricultural experts.

All too analogous with West Berlin, and the Italian elections, and the Korean War, and the Cuban missile crisis, the conflict in Vietnam thus came to look again like a contest of resolve. Who could best stand the pain of the prolonged endurance contest of a guerrilla war, who cared the most about the issues at hand?

For both sides, however, there was one important deviation from earlier contests of resolve, for it would not just be the United States and the Communist military forces that were accepting sacrifices as part of staking out barriers of containment; there would be a great deal of suffering as well among the innocent parties caught in between, indeed among the very people to whom one side wanted to offer free elections in the end, and to whom the other side wanted to offer an economically satisfactory situation. For the American strategists here, and very possibly for the other side as well, the entire exchange had become an elaborate extension of hostage theory. If one is not at least a little bit callous about those who are kidnapped and taken hostage, the kidnappers of this world will have a field day, feeling free to apply such tactics again and again. By taking some chances with the safety of kidnap victims, while vigorously pursuing and attacking those who have done the kidnapping (those who are threatening the hostages), we conversely can hope to reduce the incidence of this form of attack in the first place.

Without such callousness, whoever cares the least about the welfare of the innocent might thus continually win control over them. To protect the Vietnamese, or at least to protect the Thais against a similar form of attack, Americans in effect girded themselves to fight a major war in which a great number of Vietnamese would be killed and wounded. The entire moral picture was simply the opposite of the wisdom of Solomon, where the strong king had awarded the baby to its real mother because she proved herself by being willing to surrender the baby rather than see it harmed. In real-life international relations, and a foreign policy trying to save people from dictatorial rule, there is no such superior Solomon to render justice.

One tried to protect the victims up front if he could, but would have to be ready to sacrifice them if one would be endangering others by the precedent of conceding the first contest too easily and peacefully. This is the current Israeli attitude on situations where Arab terrorists seize Israelis as hostages. It is the official attitude of the State Department when American diplomats are taken hostage (although the department has apparently stuck to such a tough line less rigorously than have the Israelis). It was in effect the attitude that was meant to justify all that was brutal and destructive about U.S. policy in "defending" South Vietnam; the U.S. contesting the possession of South Vietnam was partially intended to protect the place, but was above all intended to show that such areas could not be seized or kidnapped without serious retaliation against the aggressor.

All of this was thus rounded out on a global basis in what became "domino theory." The United States allegedly fought in Vietnam because it cared about Vietnam itself, caring about all the Vietnamese, but perhaps having to sacrifice some in order to save the rest.

If Vietnam were not contested and perhaps defended, moreover, it would be usable as a base against Cambodia and Laos, and later against Thailand and Malaysia; since the United States cared about these places also, it would feel driven to fight brutally in Vietnam, lest they become geographically exposed.

Even apart from the contiguous links of geography, moreover, American foreign policy makers were to feel concerned about the *precedent* of Vietnam, for a weak resistance to such insurgent tactics might encourage guerrilla forces elsewhere, all around the globe, to believe that they could take power merely by threatening to hurt the innocent and to destroy the normal functions of society; a strong and vehement resistance to such tactics—even if the defense did not work in the end—might discourage similar guerrilla movements in the future by a deterring fear that the costs of such victories might be too high.

The same callous policy of "sacrifice the hostage if necessary" that had been espoused for the domestic kidnapping situation was thus in effect projected up to the level of nations as well. If Americans could not hold on to a part of Indochina for the U.S. notion of the free world, the United States might have to devastate it to keep it from becoming too effective a base against other dominoes down the row, or at least so that a further offensive against such countries as Malaysia and Indonesia would be delayed until defenses could be prepared. Aside from disrupting the bases for further offensives, the United States moreover would at least have proven itself to be a "bad loser" in such contests where it did not have the resources or perseverance to become a "winner."

Just as West Germany had earlier been worth contesting for three different kinds of reasons, the same reasons applied in Vietnam. Germany and the Germans were worth defending for the people themselves, for the position they offered as a buffer for the defense of other peoples, and for the precedent of proving American resolve. In West Germany the United States succeeded in holding on to all three, in South Vietnam it did not.

Was this attitude toward Vietnam and the Vietnamese callous and brutal? Of course it was. Was it therefore devoid of all altruism? Just as clearly it was not, for it is logically quite analogous to the attitude of Israeli governments toward the fate of Israeli hostages, or of the U.S. State Department toward its diplomats. Because the United States cares deeply about all the people, it may be cruelly driven to sacrifice some to save others; it may have to override its concern for the very most vulnerable, lest this be used as a stepping stone to make all the others vulnerable.

As compared with the Cuban missile crisis, or the Berlin blockade, Vietnam was thus to be a somewhat different kind of contest of resolve, by its very nature, by the intentions and strategies of the human beings engaged with it. It was more of tug of war than a game of chicken; it had very little of the ploy of "get out of the way, or there'll be a disaster," and much more of "don't expect us to quit first."

Is there any way that the defenders of such a callous and draconian form of defense could justify the costs? Is the double-standard morality of such a strategy not too much for a people such as Americans to bear?

The defenders of such a policy might have a try at justifying it, if only because (in their dream of dreams) there would be no costs. There had been no direct costs in the confrontation over Cuba because the adversary saw a clear American willingness to accept and impose costs, and thus surrendered in the prospective contest of resolve. In the same way, the advocate of "counterinsurgency" could have contended that all would be well if Americans only maintained an image of being willing to sacrifice hostages, for then the hostages would never be taken in the first place. "If we all hold firm together, betraying no lack of resolve, the enemy will quit, and we will come out ahead on all fronts."

What were the flaws then with this approach? A few Americans may have been incapable of bluffing on such questions, incapable of hiding their horror at seeing Vietnamese villages burned and people killed. Another few, as noted throughout this book, may have now settled into supporting the opposite from the start, wanting Ho Chi Minh to succeed to power instead of Diem, simply because they felt that economic democracy came ahead of political pluralism. With this much of a crack in the facade of American resolve, guerrilla forces in a place like Vietnam would thus at least be tempted to probe and test American resolve further, to impose somewhat higher casualties on the Vietnamese, and thus higher costs on the United States as well.

A multiplier effect then sets in whereby another layer of Americans become opposed to trying to defend Vietnam at these higher costs, as American boys engaged in infantry operations in Vietnam join the victims, as the damage to the lives of ordinary Vietnamese grows. The defection of this next slice of Americans, induced by the previous escalation of costs, of course then encourages the insurgent side still more, and raises the costs still more, then disaffecting another slice of American opinion, and raising the costs still more in yet another encouragement of the guerrilla side.

The final total of the costs of trying to win this tug of war thus becomes much larger, as succeeding layers of individuals become convinced that the gains cannot be worth such costs. Can the difference between a Marxist and a traditionalist regime in Thailand, or a Marxist and a relatively democratic regime in Singapore, really be worth the suffering of such costs by the Vietnamese or by Americans in Vietnam? The overwhelming American answer came to be "no," even among the majority of Americans who perhaps would still have believed, in the absence of threats of warfare, that the Thai or Singapore regimes were more conducive to the happiness of Southeast Asians than a regime like Hanoi's.

But this same agony on costs, and the apparent ineffectiveness of the regime the United States had been supporting in Vietnam, now also induced strong second thoughts among many Americans about whether the reverse preference might not be generally appropriate, a preference for the style of Hanoi.

NOTES

1. Useful surveys of the major events of the outbreak of the cold war are to be found in Herbert Feis, *From Trust to Terror* (New York: Norton, 1970); John L. Gaddis, *The United States and the Origins of the Cold War* (New York: Columbia University Press, 1972); Adam Ulam, *The Rivals* (New York: Viking Press, 1971); Daniel Yergin, *Shattered Peace* (Boston: Houghton Mifflin, 1977); and Paul Y. Hammond, *The Cold War Years: American Foreign Policy Since 1945* (New York: Harcourt, Brace and World, 1969).

2. Examples of such analysis of the cold war very much reflecting the changes in American opinion emerging during the Vietnam War can be found in Stephen Ambrose, *Rise to Globalism* (New York: Penguin, 1976); Gar Alperovitz, *Atomic Diplomacy* (New York: Simon and Schuster, 1965); and Walter LaFeber, *America, Russia and the Cold War* (New York: Wiley, 1967).

3. Some representative examples of this more traditional liberal interpretation of the cold war are John Spanier, *American Foreign Policy Since World War II* (New York: Praeger, 1977) and Louis Halle, *The Cold War as History* (New York: Harper & Row, 1967).

4. On the end of World War II in Europe see John L. Snell, *Wartime Origins of the East-West Dilemma Over Germany* (New Orleans: Hauser Press, 1959).

5. See Gabriel and Joyce Kolko, *The Limits of Power* (New York: Harper & Row, 1972).

6. See Richard J. Barnet, *Roots of War* (Baltimore: Penguin, 1973), pp. 18-19.

7. George F. Kennan, "The Sources of Soviet Conduct," *Foreign Affairs* 25, no. 4 (July 1947): 566-82.

8. On the possibility of a United States loan for Soviet postwar recovery, see George Herring, *Aid to Russia 1941-1946* (New York: Columbia University Press, 1973).

9. See Alperovitz, *Atomic Diplomacy*.

10. The Anglo-American issue on nuclear secrecy is fully detailed in Richard Hewlett and Oscar Anderson, *The New World* (University Park: Pennsylvania State University Press, 1962).

11. See Charles de Gaulle, *The Complete War Memoirs* (New York: Simon and Schuster, 1964), pp. 657-59.

12. See Winston S. Churchill, *Triumph and Tragedy* (Boston: Houghton Mifflin, 1953), p. 235.

13. The pattern in Czechoslovakia before the Communist takeover is chronicled in Joseph Korbel, *The Communist Subversion of Czechoslovakia* (Princeton: Princeton University Press, 1959).

14. The explanation of American judgments on the Communist takeover of China is outlined extensively in Tang Tsou, *America's Failure in China* (Chicago: University of Chicago Press, 1963).

15. On Finland, see Max Jakobsson, "Substance and Appearance: Finland," *Foreign Affairs* 58, no. 5 (Summer 1980): 1034-44. On Austria, see William B. Bader, *Austria Between East and West: 1945-1955* (Stanford: Stanford University Press, 1966).

16. See Herbert Feis, *Churchill, Roosevelt, Stalin* (Princeton: Princeton University Press, 1957).

17. See Herbert Feis, *The Atomic Bomb and the End of World War II* (Princeton: Princeton University Press, 1966).

18. David Irving, *The Destruction of Dresden* (New York: Holt, Rinehart and Winston, 1963).

19. Speech before House of Commons, January 23, 1948.

20. Kennan, "The Sources of Soviet Conduct."

21. See "Interview with George F. Kennan," *Foreign Policy*, no. 7 (Summer 1972), pp. 5-21.

22. See George F. Kennan, *Memoirs 1925-50* (Boston: Little, Brown, 1967), pp. 363-67.

23. See Samuel Huntington, *The Common Defense* (New York: Columbia University Press, 1961), pp. 33-46.

24. On the 1948 culmination of the cold war, see Frederick H. Hartmann, *The New Age of American Foreign Policy* (New York: Macmillan, 1970), especially pp. 175-86.

25. For events in Berlin, and in Germany generally, see W. Phillips Davison, *The Berlin Blockade* (Princeton: Princeton University Press, 1958).

26. The text of NSC-68 has been reprinted in *U.S. Naval War College Review* 27, no. 6 (May-June 1975): 51-108.

27. The foundation of NATO is discussed at length in Robert E. Osgood, *NATO: The Entangling Alliance* (Chicago: University of Chicago Press, 1962).

28. The continuing uncertainties surrounding the outbreak of the Korean War are outlined in Allen Guttmann, ed., *Korea: Cold War and Limited War* (Lexington: D. C. Heath, 1972). See also I. F. Stone, *The Hidden History of the Korean War* (New York: Monthly Review Press, 1962).

29. See Allen Whiting, *China Crosses the Yalu* (New York: Macmillan, 1960) for detailed chronology on the course of the Korean War.

30. The U.S. statements on Korean defense are discussed in Glenn D. Paige, *The Korean Decision* (New York: Free Press, 1968), pp. 68-69.

31. The commitment to Taiwan, and to islands otherwise held by the Nationalists, is discussed in O. Edmund Clubb, *20th Century China* (New York: Columbia University Press, 1964), pp. 340-41, 369-73.

32. See public opinion polls cited in Helen Gaudet Erskine, "The Cold War: Report From the Polls," *Public Opinion Quarterly* 25, no. 2 (Summer 1961): 302.

33. The most important Dulles statement here emerges in an interview in *Life*, January 16, 1956, pp. 70 ff.

34. A useful overview of the events of the Cuban missile crisis appears in Elie Abel, *The Missile Crisis* (Philadelphia: Lippincott, 1966) and in Robert F. Kennedy, *Thirteen Days* (New York: Norton, 1971).

35. Kennan's clearest presentation of the argument for disengagement appeared in *Russia, The Atom, and the West* (New York: Harper, 1958), a reprinting of his Reith Lectures on BBC Radio.

36. The partition of Germany into two members of two hostile camps, rather than any reunification with neutralization, is discussed in John W. Keller, *Germany, The Wall and Berlin* (New York: Vantage Press, 1964).

37. For discussions of the Vietnam War, see Leslie Gelb and Richard Betts, *The Irony of Vietnam: The System Worked* (Washington, D.C.: Brookings, 1979); Robert Galucci, *Neither Peace Nor Honor* (Baltimore: Johns Hopkins University Press, 1975); and George McT. Kahin and John W. Lewis, *The United States in Vietnam* (New York: Dial Press, 1967).

38. Franklin Roosevelt's attitudes on the future of French Indochina after the end of the Japanese occupation are discussed in Russell H. Fifield, *Ameri-*

cans in Southeast Asia: The Roots of Commitment (New York: Thomas Y. Crowell, 1973), pp. 37–43.

39. The impression Diem made on John F. Kennedy and on other Americans is discussed in Ernest Gruening and Herbert Wilton Beaser, *Vietnam Folly* (Washington, D.C.: The National Press, 1968), p. 139.

40. Analyses of the political and military nature of guerrilla war are offered in David Galula, *Counterinsurgency Warfare* (New York: Praeger, 1964); Nathan Leites and Charles Wolf, *Rebellion and Authority* (Chicago: Markham, 1970); and Sam Sarkesian, ed., *Revolutionary Guerrilla Warfare* (Chicago: Precedent, 1975).

8
Detente or Disarray?

Parallel with the three conflicting interpretations of the outbreak of the cold war could be at least three interpretations of what has followed, for a time typically labeled "detente," increasingly now viewed instead as a period of disarray and confusion.

If one had concluded that the cold war was caused primarily by the preemptive incentives and temptations of the situation after 1945, he might then trace a detente to some sort of elimination of this by a more generous Mother Nature. The power politics interpreter might thus uncover some new stabilizing tendencies and factors making it easier for the two superpowers to avoid conflict. Greater inclinations toward defense instead of offense around the globe, and firmer foundations for the various small-nation regimes in between, might have combined to make everyone feel less threatened, and less able to threaten. This would then have allowed more of a balance-of-power multipolar arrangement to settle into place, instead of the rigid bipolar alliance systems so typical in the years of the full-fledged cold war.[1]

This chapter will therefore first discuss the outlines and plausibility of this kind of power politics interpretation for a detente. The power politics analyst would have blamed most of the original cold war on a prisoners' dilemma situation in the international system itself, and would then have credited the relaxation of cold war tensions in a detente to a removal of this prisoners' dilemma situation. If the world is now backsliding into some increased tensions again of a "new cold war," perhaps the realpolitik school would then simply attribute this to a new twist of the international situation, once again suggesting opportunities and fears in the military, political, or economic offensive.

Yet many of the Americans who have been confused or disappointed about trends in world politics are now not so ready to see
this simply as a detente where international problems tended to solve
themselves. Some additional explanations will be needed for all that
has happened since 1967, pulling us straight back to the questions
raised at the beginning of this book. Whether or not the need to defend places against attack has declined, Americans, after the debacle
of the Vietnam War, had indeed become less inclined to defend such
places.

The radical and the liberal might thus both have to agree that the
American people became less willing to commit themselves to the
jungles and deserts and mountains of the world, to the support of
what used to be called the "free world"; these two viewpoints would
then sharply diverge in the lessons they drew from this.

The radical second view would see the 1967 shift inward as a
correct reassessment by Americans, reflecting on previous error in
the cold war and before, realizing at last that it had been the United
States which had borne the brunt of the fault for conflict in recent
decades, rather than the USSR or Communist China, or North Vietnam, or Marxist regimes in general.[2]

Some radicals would concede Communist aggressiveness in the
distant past, but deny it for recent decades; others would express
skepticism about such aggressiveness more generally, seeing it all as
an illusion of the American capitalist system. Perhaps Khrushchev
was more moderate than Stalin, and then Brezhnev was more reasonable than Khrushchev. Or perhaps the Soviet Union was never aggressive at all, this being the grand fiction of the peak of the cold war. If
the cold war was begun by American imperialism, rather than by
Soviet imperialism, perhaps truth has at last won out, perhaps detente can be explained by an unmasking of a false American vigilance
here.

The radical view, as noted at the outset, would thus treat an
American turning inward as an altogether appropriate alternative to
the misguided and evil foreign policy commitments of the past. Once
the experience of awakening an American conscience had been completed, the radical would want the "new isolationism" to end, of
course, as the United States exported its energies again in an active
foreign policy, but this time on the correct side, liberating South
Africa, ending economic oppression in El Salvador.

Yet it is probably easier to establish that the attitudes of many
Americans have changed, than to establish that such a change of attitude is well founded. Whether the Soviet Union has changed so much
from the 1950s to the 1980s is debatable. The fault of who began

the cold war remains debatable. The more certain fact is that a significant number of Americans, in coming to doubt the wisdom of American foreign policy goals during the Vietnam War, had switched sides on these debates, and on the grander question of which they are a part.

The third viewpoint of the American liberal would thus return to the central point that this book has noted several times, that much of the change in foreign policy interactions in the 1960s is specifically due to a fundamental crisis of self-evaluation within the United States, as Americans have become unsure of whether they wished to defend the same causes and allies as in the past.[3]

The third interpretation of the confusion in American foreign policy since 1967 would probably regard this change in American attitudes as largely regrettable, as a loss of self-confidence where self-confidence might indeed have been appropriate. The radically oriented forces endorsing rule without the blessing of elections are still obnoxious forces in this third view, and they are still aggressive forces. A detente produced by confusion in the United States about the priorities of political democracy and economic democracy, when paired off against the resolve of the Marxist regimes, does not amount to a picture of international problems solving themselves, but a rather more troubled future.

As has been the case all through this book, the threats and opportunities of the international arena, as stressed by the power politics school, explain a portion of American foreign policy, but only a portion, with the radical and liberal schools then arguing about how to interpret the rest. To call the years since 1967 a time of detente is to rest heavily on the power politics school of analysis. To find some worrisome gaps in this optimistic picture is to shift into one of the others.

POWER FACTORS CONTRIBUTING
TO MULTIPOLARITY

It would be wrong to deny that the international military and political power factors of the 1960s contributed toward reducing international conflict and tension: The issue is rather how much. How indeed would we outline the nature of the contribution here?

In important part, we must begin again by reversing the explanations introduced as reasons for the cold war. In the 1960s there was generally less of offensive potential around the areas of the globe that mattered to the two sides. Instead of being an economic wreck and a political power vacuum, ripe for military conquest or political subversion, the Europe of the 1960s was prosperous and politically stable. The North German plain that had always looked so suitable for a tank attack had instead, as a result of the very prosperity of the Federal Republic, become congested with traffic and urban sprawl.

With the construction of the Berlin Wall in 1961, the stability of East Germany was conversely no longer so menaced by the existence of West Berlin, which before had served as an escape hatch for the most productive young workers in the East. This in turn meant that the Communists no longer had to direct as much of a threat against West Berlin.[4] The enclave, besides ceasing to be a menace to East German economic and political stability, had also ceased to be any kind of economic asset in its own right. While an East German Communist leader might still have liked to absorb it to remove an ugly blotch from his country's map, the stakes were much smaller now, so that the threat of economic reprisals by West Germany and Western Europe might suffice as a deterrent to any new blockade of access to Berlin.

The progress of the decolonization of Africa and Asia in the 1960s moreover hinted that there would be fewer power vacuums here as well, fewer instances where the two sides would be tempted to intervene, each in fear that the other side was about to intervene first. If Vietnam had seemed like a contest of rival capabilities for guerrilla insurgency and Green Beret counterinsurgency, it was possible at the start of the 1970s that this case would turn out to have been exceptional, with most newly independent countries being far less vulnerable to outside influence.

We should not exaggerate the new defensive strengths of the various fronts here, and one explanation now for the disappointment and pessimism of the postdetente era may indeed stem from such exaggerations. Yet the new stability may indeed have been present, at least for the 1960s, in most of the situations cited.

As such stabilizing influences took hold, they were reinforced and multiplied by an ensuing loosening of alliances. Because the nations of the West felt less menaced by the Communist bloc, they chose to be less cohesive, and thus perhaps posed less of a threat to the bloc. Because the nations of the Communist bloc felt less menaced by the West, they also chose to be less cohesive, and thus in turn again posed less of a threat to the West.

We are quite accustomed today to seeing very vivid examples of intra-Western and intra-Communist political antagonisms. The French withdrawal from the military structure of NATO in 1966 was perhaps more symbolic than substantive, but it nonetheless showed that there were important issues on which Paris reserved the right to refuse to follow Washington's lead.[5] Many U.S. allies felt free to denounce the American presence in Vietnam, and/or to vote against U.S. positions at the United Nations. At the Free University of West Berlin, a university established through American contributions during the Berlin blockade after the suppression of academic freedom at East German universities, students now regularly take part in the most vitriolically anti-American demonstrations.[6] American relations with Japan have similarly often been less than cordial, producing serious embarrassment for Tokyo by the American opening to Peking, and by sudden embargoes on the sales of some commodities.

Before an American became too discouraged at this picture of the fractionation of the West, however, he would have to absorb the parallel news that a very similar process has been occurring in the East as well.

The first example of a break in the Communist world's total subordination to Moscow was noted earlier with the 1948 assertion of Marshal Tito's independent line for Yugoslavia, a case long regarded as so unusual and special that all possibilities of such assertions of independence were referred to as Titoism."[7]

Far less successfully, one saw efforts by local Communist leaderships in Hungary and Poland in 1956 to achieve some greater independence from Moscow. The Hungarian Revolution was crushed by the armed might of Russian tanks, after the new Hungarian leadership had declared its intention to withdraw from the Warsaw Pact. The situation in Poland also came close to blows, but agreements were reached short of actual fighting between Polish and Russian forces.

Despite the violent suppression of the Hungarian uprising, and the apparent bringing into line of the Polish Communist leadership, the longer-run adjustments in these two countries were quite important. First, the new governments installed by Moscow (Kadar in Budapest and Gomulka in Warsaw) proved to be surprisingly liberal and accommodating to the expressed wishes of the two peoples. Kadar soothes the situation in Hungary by declaring that "who is not against us is with us," exactly the opposite of the more demanding pressures for conformity and submission that had characterized most Communist appeals in the past. Second, the lesson for the future was that the loyalty and military cooperation of such countries would moreover not be assured even when there were Communist Parties securely in power, since the local parties inevitably tended to become somewhat responsive to the feelings of their own nationality. Who would now ever count on Hungarian or Polish troops to fight loyally by the side of the Russians if a war erupted in Europe?[8]

The more major break then occurred at the beginning of the 1960s, as increasingly tangible evidence began to emerge of a dispute between Communist China and the USSR. For a time, the evidence here was almost bizarrely esoteric, as the two Communist powers, which had all through the 1950s striven to avoid showing even the slightest differences of opinion, now slowly and most roundaboutly began to fire insults at each other. For the years from 1960 to 1962, this came most indirectly in Russian attacks on Albania (seen as a surrogate for Peking), and in Chinese attacks on the "revisionism" of Yugoslavia.[9]

Americans could clearly have been hoping for a Sino-Soviet split ever since 1949, and had just as clearly been guarding against falling into any wishful thinking here. The straightforward evidence, as noted earlier, suggested that the Chinese party, like almost all the other Communists in the world, was intent on marching in perfect step with the Russians, no matter how often Moscow changed its direction.

The earliest form of a Chinese separation from the Russians did not come then as so very good news, for in important aspects it did not match the Titoist model. Tito, although he had been somewhat stridently anti-American before the 1948 break, fairly quickly thereafter warmed to an accommodation with the West, as all concerned felt a need to cooperate in the face of the common Russian enemy. The Chinese in the early 1960s seemed by contrast to be basing much of their disagreement with the Russians on opposition to Moscow's moves toward detente with the United States, in effect sticking to a purer and more vehement prediction of inevitable conflict between communism and capitalism. The news of a Sino-Soviet split in the 1960s was thus good news for the United States, in that the adversary coalition was fragmenting, but bad news in that one portion of that adversary seemed to be turning more hostile than ever before. One of the most bizarrely illuminating exercises for any student today would be to compare back issues of *Peking Review* (now *Beijing Review*) for three-year intervals starting in 1955. In the 1960s one found almost not a word that was complimentary about the United States. Today the same would be true instead of the coverage of the Soviet Union.

The Chinese break from Communist solidarity was thus clearly the most important break, in that it made it easier for other Communist states and Communist Parties to move down similar tracks. A country of 800 million cast more of a shadow, and created more of a precedent, than Tito's Yugoslavia.

Since the Chinese break, several other moves have come in similar directions. The Rumanian example is particularly interesting, for it has combined a very repressive (almost Stalinist) domestic political regime with a reaching for independence in economic policy, and then in foreign policy. Under the leadership of Nicolae Ceausescu, the Rumanians have thus far escaped Soviet armed intervention, despite some fairly direct insults to the leadership and policies of the USSR, and the close geographical proximity of the two countries.

Events in Czechoslovakia went down a different road, however, more parallel to those of Hungary in 1956. Here, unlike Rumania, the move for independence from Moscow included substantial drives toward domestic political liberalization and reform, i.e., toward a restoration of political democracy, the kind of regime that Americans would tend to approve of. Greater independence in economic and foreign policy would probably have emerged along with such reforms of the domestic policy process, but Moscow's decision to send in troops in 1968 may thus have arisen because of the domestic reforms themselves.

The Soviet leadership apparently has been willing to tolerate the insolence of the Rumanians, because that regime at least does not tinker with a restoration of free elections at home, with all this would portend. While the Czech and Hungarian cases may not have amounted to any greater assertions of national prerogatives and national independence, they had opened the possibility that the Communist Parties involved would not always retain power, but might actually step down after losing an election, perhaps an unforgivable heresy in Moscow's eyes, a heresy that Tito or Mao never tolerated.

As an immediate event, the invasion of Czechoslovakia had to be seen as a setback for detente between East and West, and the Soviet-American strategic arms limitation talks (SALT) were postponed because of it. As a symptom of background factors, however, it amounted to a reinforcement for detente, in that it once again showed some weaknesses in the ability of Moscow to control all that goes on behind the iron curtain.[10] Would a Russian soldier advancing into Germany be pleased to have a Czech battalion next to him?

Assertions of independence have also come from various of the Communist Parties not in power, in countries outside the Soviet bloc, and in recent years this generated the interesting new concept of Eurocommunism. The term is misleading if it implies that there is a great deal of agreement among the Communist Parties of Western

Europe, in particular those of France, Italy, Spain, and Portugal. Yet it does serve as a meaningful reminder that Communist Parties in these western countries now feel some substantial freedom to ignore what Moscow might want, a freedom that they surely did not feel in the 1930s, or even the 1940s.[11]

The Italian Communist Party has indeed had a longer tradition of criticizing Russian decisions, the most important early instance coming in denunciations of the 1956 invasion of Hungary. The French party, by contrast, has always tended to be somewhat more Stalinist in style and international orientation. Yet, tempted by the prospect of winning other parts of the French Left into a Popular Front approach to electoral campaigns, it has also felt inclined to show some independence from Moscow.

The Spanish Communist Party has perhaps been the wildest of all these European parties, with its leader derisively comparing Moscow's ideology to Roman Catholic theology, and Moscow's alleged centrality to that of the Pope. The Portuguese Communist Party by contrast has been very loyal to Moscow. An example of what such independence and splits can lead to was shown then in the contest for power in Portugal in 1975 and 1976, when the Italian and Spanish Communist Parties were seen lending assistance to the Portuguese Socialists, in opposition to the Portuguese Communists.[12] Some other Western Communist Parties, for example the Icelandic Party, have become so independent that they have even ceased to attend international party gatherings in Moscow. The Swedish Communist Party has similarly been characterized by great independence in the policy stands it takes.

Is it just the physical remoteness of countries like Italy from the USSR that explains the increasing independence of their Communist Parties? A more complicated explanation is surely required, for such parties had everywhere marched in virtual lockstep with Moscow in the 1930s and the early 1940s. Rumania is physically as close as one can get to the reach of the Soviet armed forces, but has nonetheless in the 1960s and 1970s embarked on the perilous course of defying solidarity with the USSR on issues of world politics.

AMPLIFICATIONS FOR MULTIPOLARITY:
THE DECLINE OF THE DOLLAR

Other factors, besides military formations and political alliances, can play a power role for shaping the international arena, and we must take some note here of the impact of changes in the international economic system. The loss of cohesion in the West was demonstrated strikingly in the 1970s by two major economic developments: the loss of central role for the U.S. dollar, and the emergence of a world-wide energy shortage, as shown in major increases in the prices charged for petroleum.

Let us first digress a little into the role played by the dollar. What have been some ways of keeping trade moving across international boundaries in the past?

We have memories of the gold standard, the system by which gold was once moved from country to country in the settling of gaps in international trade, reducing the currency supply in one country and expanding it in another. There are many reasons why this system would no longer be found acceptable, including the depressing impact of decreasing any particular country's money supply and the general inability of gold to grow in quantity sufficiently to keep up with the world's need for currency and reserves.[13]

A second alternative has then been to rely on a major reserve currency as the medium of international exchange, as the entire world keys on the national currency of this one central industrial and trading partner. This was the role of Great Britain before World War I, and it has been the role fulfilled by the United States since World War II.

To show the relative merits of this second solution and the reasons it was so widely accepted after 1945, despite any centrality and possible power it accorded the United States, we must note a third alternative that indeed gripped the world from the Great Depression up to the outbreak of World War II, a system of inconvertible currencies and simple barter, as nations sought economic autarchy in place of a dependence on trade. The years of such striving for autarchy were the years that produced Hitler's Germany, and Americans in 1945 were not alone in believing that greater international trade and international interdependence would have political value for making fascism and the extremes of nationalism less likely.[14]

It would thus again be misleading to conclude that the establishment of the U.S. dollar as a world reserve currency at the end of World War II was something Americans sought for selfish reasons of strategic power or material advantage. Foreign use of the dollar of course gave the United States an elementary advantage or "free ride" in terms of trade, since the United States had to sell less and could afford to buy more, with the world's wish to acquire dollar reserves making up the difference. Yet the reliance on the dollar did more than give Americans an extra slice of the world's products, for it very much speeded European economic recovery after the devastation of World War II.

Descriptions of the years of the dollar exchange system as a "regime" may thus too much echo the premises and presumptions of the power politics analyst, while references to this as "dollar diplomacy" similarly echo too much the premises of the radical. The United States and the world more or less stumbled into the exchange system based on the dollar, and if Americans were pleased with it, this was in important part because of the foreign prosperity it seemed to be fostering.

The United States in the postwar world was in a position analogous to that of the richest man in a small town, whose IOUs after a time come to be used as money, thus making trade possible. Since the rich man's store is always crammed full of high-quality merchandise, his IOUs are accepted in transactions among other citizens, and indeed are sought after. Since the town is itself composed of people anxious to expand their liquid assets, the total demand for IOUs grows over time, such that the rich man is encouraged to go deeper and deeper into debt, in effect buying more of his fellow citizens' goods and services each year than would have been warranted if he were living on a balanced budget, and selling fewer of his own goods and services. The rich man is thus able to consume more, and needs to work less; while his debt to his fellow citizens grows, it is a debt that he may never have to repay, as long as his reputation for being able to pay goes unquestioned.

It was not inevitable that this system would come under challenge at the end of the 1960s, but it was likely. To begin, there would be some resentment of this "free ride," even among U.S. allies, a feeling that it was not proper to give Washington a privilege in dispensing so valuable a commodity as the central means of exchange for international trade. Whether the United States was spending most of the windfall on foreign aid, or on its own consumption choices, might make some difference; the United States was for long quite generous in giving out amounts of foreign aid in excess of the balance of payments deficit. When the balance of payments deficit became tied to the costs of the Vietnam War, however, a war not at all popular in Europe, then it became more resented.

Beyond resentment of a free ride, moreover, the time was also to come when other currencies, as a result of the very trade that the U.S. dollar had made possible, would challenge it in terms of future promise. (The analogy to our richest merchant in a small town would come when the use of his IOUs had made it possible for other merchants to prosper and grow.) In time the currency (the IOUs) of the United States would diminish in value compared to those of West Germany and Japan and other American partners, and the central role of the dollar could not be continued, even if U.S. partners had wanted it.

The world's economy is thus no longer willing (or perhaps no longer able) to let the U.S. dollar serve as its unit of exchange, having now to rely rather on uneasy arrangements of flexible exchange rates, and of "market baskets" of mixtures of currencies in national reserves.[15] The consequences of such new arrangements have surely not been disastrous, but some costs have nonetheless been borne in the process, as the daily uncertainty of exchange rates has probably discouraged international trade somewhat, and a worldwide monetary inflation has to some extent been facilitated by relaxation of the international constraints that used to be imposed by the reliance on the dollar.

The attempts to establish a single currency unit for exchanges just within Western Europe shows that some clear advantages might still be found in maintaining such a standard, wherever this is possible.[16] If the U.S. dollar has outlived its usefulness as a global currency, nothing else as yet has come along to replace it. That the dollar was ever able to play this role may have been an accident of history, just as was the similar role played earlier by sterling. Yet the impact on the world in the net may well have been quite benign, just as American intentions about this impact were benign.

The loss of central role for the dollar can certainly be viewed as a blow to American prestige and influence. Yet it was not nearly as much a gain for the Soviet Union, and hence again fits less well with the bipolar model of a cold war. It may, as suggested, have been a blow of sorts for all who desire an orderly flow of world trade. If it enhanced the relative prestige and influence of the countries of Western Europe, it provides the kind of multipolarity and confusion that fits not badly with detente.

AMPLIFICATIONS FOR MULTIPOLARITY: ENERGY SHORTAGES

The worldwide shortage of energy, as signaled by the dramatic rise in oil prices achieved by the Organization of Petroleum Exporting Countries (OPEC) after 1973, is a second major economic change now dividing the non-Communist world.

Why should a cartel have been successful in oil when such arrangements have always failed in other commodities?[17] There is usually a great deal of double crossing within any cartel. Driving up prices by holding back output puts each of the producers into a position of great temptation, for they can reap a large profit by secretly again adding to their output. As each partner suspects the others of doing this, and is strongly tempted to do so also, the result is normally that total production soon enough slides back to what would have been produced by an unrestricted market without a cartel, and the price again falls.

But the oil case is special because too much of the oil comes from a few countries, most prominently from Saudi Arabia, a country that now can collect so much in oil revenues that it might be embarrassed by them, so much that it would actually prefer to keep its oil production down, and hold its oil reserves for the future time when the foreign exchange would be more immediately useful.[18] In effect, we may have a backward-bending supply curve here, shown in Figure 8.1, as compared with the more normal situation in graph A, the supply curve in graph B shows less oil will be offered as more money is offered per barrel.

Americans have trouble in understanding this kind of market logic because they are used to the much more normal market situation shown in graph A of Figure 8.1. If Americans want more of any particular commodity in their everyday life, they simply raise the price offered, and additional quantities of the needed commodity turn up soon enough. This is all very closely tied to the American belief in free trade, in "fair exchange is no robbery," in the elementary existential choice by which partners are more or less allowed to negotiate contracts as they will.

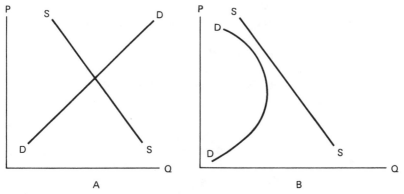

FIGURE 8.1

As the price goes up, the quantity demanded falls somewhat, while the quantity offered normally rises. The price continues to be bid up until an equilibrium point is at last reached, where as much of the commodity is offered as will be purchased. Without any coercion by either side, demand has been curtailed and product production has been stimulated, so that there is no unsatisfied demand left around.

The special problem of oil, however, in light of the particularly rich position of the Saudi nation, is that supply and demand might conceivably never meet here, as more could be demanded at any price level than would be produced, thus generating a very strong challenge to the voluntaristic assumptions of American commercial practice and American foreign policy.

When else have we ever seen such a peculiarly contorted supply curve? As one thinks of a few parallel cases, the Saudi attitude on oil may seem a little less bizarre. The use of a compulsory draft to assemble an armed force may be very parallel; no matter how much the military offers in pay, it may prove impossible to get enough young men to enlist to bring the army to the strength the public desires. As the wage was pushed up, a few more people would enlist; but those who were paid much more for their first enlistment might by then have so much money in the bank that they saw no need to stay in the service, and the net supply of labor would again fall below what was demanded.[19]

Looking again at an international situation, one might also see an analogy with British trade with China in the early nineteenth century. Anxious to buy tea from China, the British were dismayed to find the Chinese indifferent to Western products, such that it would be impossible to get as much tea produced as international commerce demanded. The British solution was of course a relatively shameful form of international coercion, forcing the Chinese government in the Opium War to tolerate the importation of narcotics, thus to stimulate a demand for this import among Chinese, thus to develop an incentive for the Chinese to sell tea.[20]

It is at least possible that this has been the Saudi situation since 1973. And even if the supply curve for the Saudi oil producer has not yet been bent backward in the mid-1970s, the observation is certainly valid that it may bend in this direction at some point in the near future. Such an attitude about oil revenues may also apply to Norway as it faces the prospect of oil riches, or to Canada, or to Mexico. The memory of what an inundation of oil revenues did to Iranian political stability adds a political dimension to the simple finiteness of demand for foreign purchases here; regimes now have one more reason to want to postpone their inflow of oil revenues until some later time, instead of producing at full capacity.

In a world of perfect fidelity to financial commitments, the Arabs or the Norwegians or Mexicans could simply accept burgeoning oil revenues at the early stage of great demand, and deposit or invest them around the world, bringing the fruits of such revenues back to the homeland later after a carefully designed development program has been arranged. But we noted earlier that the world does not provide such perfect guarantees of wealth from one decade to the next. Keeping the oil under the deserts of Arabia might thus be a much more reliable means of storing such well-being for the future, rather than leaving money in New York bank accounts, or buying business firms in the United States or Europe.

One wiser and safer use of such revenues is obviously to invest in the industrialization of the oil-supplying country, acquiring the capital goods that will provide new flows of income in the future. But such investment cannot be arranged instantaneously, and efficiency often entails delay here, "learning to walk before beginning to run."

Such a straightforwardly economic disinterest in increasing oil production in Saudi Arabia is complicated moreover by the political considerations that influence the Arab states, in particular the hatred for Israel and the resentment of U.S. support for Israel. It is a historical fact, of course, that the OPEC cartel crystallized just at the time of the October 1973 war between Egypt and Israel.

Even if oil supplies would thus somehow be delivered in sufficient quantity under normal conditions (even if the backward-bending supply curve had not yet materialized), the United States in its dependence on energy imports would thus still have to steer the difficult passage between two more fears relevant to the goals of its foreign policy.

The next fear, after the insufficiency of supplies at *any* price, would be that the price would simply go too high, even as it reached an equilibrium of supply and demand, producing unprecedented wealth in states such as Abu Dhabi and Saudi Arabia, extreme poverty in places like India, and a relative poverty and economic slowdown in the United States and Europe.

But a third fear will be that oil supplies would be cut off as a political lever whenever some portion of American foreign policy comes to displease one of the crucial suppliers. Americans would thus presumably have to face waiting in lines for gasoline whenever there was another war between Israel and an Arab state, or whenever the Arabs felt the United States had been assisting the Israelis too much or pressuring them too little. Similar lines are in store when-

ever the government changes in an oil supplier like Iran, amid re-
criminations about past U.S. support of the ousted regime.

The United States, in all of its history, has not experienced so
total a dependence on a resource imported from abroad, complicated all the more now by the prospect that natural market forces
might not suffice to bring the resource home by free market methods, or at least that foreign political considerations would suffice to
override market preferences, and thus cut American consumers off
from their supply.

The United States gets all its bananas from abroad, but if a crisis
hit, it could do without bananas at breakfast. The political issues of
the Caribbean and the shape of the banana market are, moreover,
not likely to hold back supplies.

The same has more or less been true for all the other commodities upon which the United States depends, ranging from coffee to
chromium and bauxite. The fear is occasionally raised that a Communist conquest of all of Africa south of the Congo would leave the
United States in dire straits with regard to certain critical metals.
Given the political and military rivalries between the United States
and the Soviet Union, this is a threat that has to be taken seriously.
Yet, while Moscow might have the political will (as do some Islamic
forces) to hold back exports to the United States, it (unlike the
Islamic states) is never very likely to become averse to (or even indifferent to) earning hard currency from the West.

To what extreme might the United States be pushed by its need
for oil? Great Britain, in its dependence on tea, had once resorted to
force in the Opium War, and the United States, as the leader of the
politically democratic portion of the fully industrialized world,
might thus find itself also considering a recourse to force, if the
necessary supplies of oil remained unavailable in voluntary exchange.
The possibility was indeed discussed openly in the immediate aftermath of the 1973 OPEC price increase,[21] and the subsequent Arab
embargo on oil shipments to the United States, but was generally
rejected by Americans as contrary to the free and voluntary trade
arrangements the United States has historically tried to maintain
with foreign countries.

Americans thus remember themselves (rightly or wrongly, depending on the analyst's point of view) as opposed to naked selfish
aggression. "We never start wars" accords very well with the U.S.
historical memory. While Secretary of Defense James Schlesinger and
Secretary of State Henry Kissinger released some occasional statements about how the use of force could not be ruled out, if the
economic plight of the free world became desperate, such state-

ments basically drew no more American public endorsement than the private journal articles advocating such military intervention.

The increased dependency of the United States and Western Europe and Japan on oil imports (with a similar dependency soon to come for the Soviet Union and Eastern Europe) again is not good news for the United States, but has also not been bad news of a cold war variety. It hardly seems plausible to attribute Saudi Arabia's decisions to hold back oil production to Communist influence, when the USSR has not even had an embassy in Riyadh. Rather the energy crisis had been one more possible reinforcement for detente, making the world more complicated and less bipolar, burdening both sides of the iron curtain; amid a host of new problems, it at least suggested a hope that some old problems of East-West military confrontation would subside.

THE SHIFT IN CHINA

As the West became fragmented by economic and other issues, the Communist world did not apparently become cohesive and monolithic, at least on the evidence of continued alienation between Moscow and the Chinese Communists. Analysts of the Chinese turn against the Russians could thus look forward to a return to a multipolar balance of power, taking much of the tension out of the old bipolar cold war.

How much of the improvement in Sino-American relations would we want to credit to the emergence of antagonism between Peking and Moscow? Americans have indeed indulged themselves in a certain amount of straightforward balance-of-power amusement here. When President Nixon first startled observers by referring to the Peking regime as the "Peoples Republic of China," rather than the normal "Communist China," the Soviet ambassador was quick to call Henry Kissinger to ask what was going on. Kissinger's glee could hardly be contained as he asked how there could be any problem, since Moscow had always used that title to refer to Peking.[22]

Chinese forces on the borders with the USSR presumably tie up some Soviet armored divisions that could otherwise be deployed in Europe facing NATO, just as the forces of NATO tie up some forces that might otherwise be facing the Chinese. Communist Chinese spokesmen have made their awareness of the linkage all too clear in recent years, with regular calls for NATO vigilance and skepticism about the Mutual and Balance Force Reduction (MBFR) negotiations in Vienna that have been rather fruitlessly underway for years.

The Chinese indeed endorse the cynical witticism that MBFR actually stands for "much better for the Russians."

Yet there are definite limits to how Machiavellian the United States can afford to be in exploiting any balance of power mechanisms here. At the outer limit, an American surely could not look forward with any equanimity to a war between the Soviet Union and China, this being perhaps the clearest illustration of the obsolescence of traditional balance-of-power mechanisms. In the days before nuclear weapons, such a war would simply have worn down the military strength and political appeal of two U.S. adversaries, and might have been welcome. The threat of the use of nuclear weapons against Chinese or Russian cities would be extraordinarily menacing to the United States itself, however, since such an attack would destroy the very hostage upon which it relies for deterrence, for the maintenance of good behavior by the Russians and Chinese.

One can also never be certain that anything about the Chinese or Russian situations will be all that durable, and the possibility of a Sino-Soviet rapprochement or detente can hardly be ruled out. As Kissinger was fond of noting, too visible an American exploitation of the split might lead each of the Communist powers to feel that it was being manipulated, and might then make their reconciliation all the more likely, for fear of being used.[23]

If it was only an exercise in power politics, the American warming to China might thus have to be somewhat more cautious and limited. Yet this warming may indeed have reflected more than power, stemming rather from the alleviation of some deeper misunderstandings between Peking and Washington, in particular on the question of how to interpret guerrilla warfare versus counterinsurgency (on whether revolution was for export or had to be indigenous),[24] stemming also from some older and deeper identifications between Americans and Chinese.

While Russians seem to have always admired Americans, Americans have not so typically reciprocated the sentiment through the years, at least as their hierarchies of affections for foreign nationalities go; memories of the tyranny of the czars and the pogroms against Jews were followed all too quickly by the Bolshevik seizure of power, as Kerenski's interregnum did not last long enough to produce the warmer identification it might have. By contrast, as noted earlier, the American identification with the Chinese people had been stronger, fostered by years of missionary activity, and by the example of the hardworking Chinese wherever he appears around the globe.

The warmth and enthusiasm of the American public response to

President Nixon's opening to China surprised virtually all concerned, as Nixon expected to draw more opposition at home, as the Peking regime had expected less positive responses from the American community at large. Some of this was of course extraordinarily superficial and faddish, as Chinese food and acupuncture suddenly became major topics of interest; but some of it was at least a little more substantial, as Americans now convinced themselves that China somehow was a different kind of communism, less bureaucratically burdened than the USSR, less centrally watched by a secret police, less rude and inefficient. Theories gained acceptance that Mao's philosophies were somehow more Chinese than Marxist.

If China was extracting cooperation and hardwork by the use of its traditional social pressures, rather than by brute threats of arrest and deportation to labor camps, this might have been just as totalitarian as the USSR, or even more so, as the straitjacket would be all the more binding in being so closely fitted to the individual. Yet the straitjacket was less visible and ugly, with fewer explicit "human rights violations" in the process.[25]

Critics of U.S. foreign policy attitudes, and of U.S. attitudes on life in general, can of course accuse the United States of being dominated just as much by such a totalitarian web of social consensus, all the more binding because we are not even aware of it. Are Americans somehow socially totalitarian themselves, in their respect for consensus, so as to make it all the more likely that they would like the Chinese form of Marxism more than the Russian?

The internal political arrangements of China are clearly so complicated that such straightforward warm or cold feelings among Americans cannot hope to suffice as interpretation. Also insufficient, grounded more directly in the evaluation of foreign policy behavior and threats is any dichotomy of "hawks versus doves" (a dichotomy equally to be avoided in analyses of the Soviet Union).

China, like the USSR, is influenced by a host of factions and interests that group and regroup depending on the immediate issue at hand, and may in the net contribute to a warming of relations with the United States at one point and to a cooling at another. Among such groups, one must at least include the following: the Communist Party, the bureaucracy of the government, the professionals of the army, the navy, and air force, and the internal purists, those who perhaps most faithfully reflected Mao's desires during the Great Cultural Revolution, putting ideological purity ahead of technological competence or simple material accomplishment.[26]

The "choices" of Chinese foreign policy have thus never been only whether to be anti-American or anti-USSR, but also have included some important options of simply avoiding foreign policy involvements altogether. The kinds of nonreliance on professional competence advocated by Mao, and by the Gang of Four, might indeed have made American foreign policy ventures easier by making China less of an active participant in international affairs. Yet what Americans might desire where the welfare of the Chinese people was the issue might be very different from what would be desired for China if only U.S. national power or prospects for economic trade were at stake.

As part of the grand circularity in the explaining of detente, one additional possibility thus merits some attention. As cold war tensions decreased, some old intrabloc conflicts came to be renewed, allowing the Chinese to widen and open their conflict with the Russians because their fear of the United States had somewhat abated. But some old positive possibilities were renewed as well, and some old potentials for friendship were unblocked.

Given this array of causes and effect, someone might yet have asked whether the world had accomplished so very much with detente. Had the United States perhaps simply improved its relations with some former enemies, at the price of reducing closeness with former allies? Was U.S. closeness to China matched by some estrangement from Japan and France? Are the USSR's better relations with West Germany balanced out by worse relations with Rumania?

A poll of American public opinion taken in 1972 generated the bizarre response that U.S. relations with China and the USSR were better than with France and Germany.[27] Did this simply amount to a greater fragmentation all around, amid more cross-cuttings of bitterness and disagreement, with hardly anything thus to be particularly pleased about here?

There might be more to the good news here than this. The most important consideration, in this nuclear age, is presumably the likelihood of war, and it was very possible that the fractionation of the two alliances in the 1960s made war less probable. War requires close coordination on both sides, close alliance cohesion, in effect bipolarity. As Madison's *Tenth Federalist* suggests how to avoid civil war at home, the same kind of multipolarity of cross-cutting cleavages might have allowed a very stabilizing form of balance-of-power politics to take hold abroad. The earlier rigid alignments of bipolarity had focused and intensified the hostility between the two major systems of politics, and in the process may have pushed it closer to the critical mass needed to induce a war.

The fuller explanation for the easing of the cold war, for the emergence of detente, was thus bound to be somewhat circular, with different background factors reinforcing and overrunning each other.

It could be that the members of the Western alliance simply came to dislike each other more in the 1960s, just as the Chinese and the Russians drew further apart. Or it could primarily be that the Western and Soviet blocs found less to fear, and more to like, in each other. Yet there may be no need for so clear a choice between those two models. Did the United States fear the Russians less because the alliances were fractionated? Or were the alliances fractionated because the United States feared the Russians less? Each of these tendencies supported the other in a complicated cycle that in the end may have amounted to detente.

As alliance threats are lessened, one feels more free to indulge some of the intraalliance hostility that had been put onto the shelf; and by doing so, one again lessens fears in the opposing alliance, thus allowing their members to indulge more in their intraalliance hostilities, thereby again reducing fears on one's own side, and so forth.

DETENTE IN BLACK AFRICA

Through most of the period remembered as the cold war, a special quiet hung over the continent of Africa, such that the area was hardly associated at all with this intense period of Soviet-American confrontation.

For several reasons, the continent did not seem threatened by the expansion of communism. Most obviously, it was not adjacent to any bases from which Soviet power could be extended; the USSR's 1945 demand for trusteeships in Libya and the other Italian colonies had been rejected, and the Russians basically lacked any naval power at this time. The postwar years also saw a general lack of guerrilla insurrection in Africa, Algeria being the principal exception. The term "Africa" indeed has typically been used to refer to sub-Saharan Africa, black Africa; the area to the north of the Sahara is often seen instead as part of the Mediterranean world, sharing its particular trends and problems.

The earliest ringing of the cold war alarm bell for Africa indeed came only in 1960, in the wake of the sudden and badly planned Belgian surrender of control in the Congo (today's Zaire). As the Belgians tried to retain a mineral-rich portion of the territory by a secession of the Katanga province under the rule of Moise Tshombe, the possibility of Soviet influence over the rest of the Congo emerged in the person of Patrice Lumumba.[28]

In a heavy application of U.S. influence, the country was reunited by an intervention of military forces under United Nations auspices, in the process leading to the deposition and ultimate execution of Lumumba, with a seemingly pro-American Col. Mobutu ascending to power. The pattern thus far of course looked a great deal like a Guatemala or a Laos, an initial quashing of Communist sentiments, by the means of a military dictatorship or an American puppet, but worrisomely thereafter likely to boil up in a protracted wave of guerrilla wars by which the Marxist side would gain strength.

Yet the ensuing 15 years for Africa indeed did not so much resemble events in Southeast Asia, but rather took a quite different form. Mobutu in many ways did not function now as the instrument of American foreign policy. The decolonization process was, meanwhile, handled with moderation and skill for the great bulk of French and British Africa, thus offering much less opportunity for penetration by forces aligned with the Soviet Union. By the middle of the 1970s, the remainders of white rule in Africa consisted solely of Rhodesia and South Africa and the Portuguese colonies, as the bulk of the continent had been steered into a government which, if not based on a system of free elections, was at least indigenous enough to avoid tempting the Communist states into ambitious programs of intervention.

As the United States, after the short 1960 burst of anxiety about the Congo, thus relapsed again into a relatively less excited stance about Africa, what did this show about U.S. general foreign policy attitudes here? Does this overall lull show some sort of decline in American opposition to colonialism?

Franklin Roosevelt, as mentioned, had been vehemently opposed to a French return to Indochina in 1945, and the United States similarly frustrated Dutch efforts to hold on to Indonesia in 1948 and 1949. Yet the United States objected far less to French efforts to hold on to Algeria, or the British stand in Kenya, or even to the later "unilateral declaration of independence" in Rhodesia.

As stipulated earlier, the difference may reflect a sort of racist inattention. Most Americans typically have not felt as close to Black Africans as to Poles or Czechs.[29] The result may thus be that our hearts have not been in the struggle one way or the other. Clearly there has been no American emotional backing or support for the Rhodesian–South African side, and there was none for the Portuguese in Mozambique and Angola. But the racism of White Americans, by this view, would show up in that there was not much strong feeling on the other side either.

Yet we must also introduce a very different kind of explanation for the lower intensity of American feelings here, the ratchet effect noted earlier for the workings of the Monroe Doctrine, whereby political self-government would be rallied to by Americans when it had once been established, but not before that.

The wartime Japanese occupation of the European possessions in the Far East had made a tremendous difference from the American standpoint because it allowed local regimes to assert themselves, against which any renewal of European rule would have to look like a reversal of self-government, just as would any European return to Latin America. The American tradition had been to challenge any efforts to overturn a status quo of self-government, and to be patient otherwise, where that degree of self-government had not yet emerged. In Asia it would have taken armed action to restore European rule, and the United States would oppose it. In Africa, no such armed action was in question, since the continuity of European rule had by and large not been broken.

How consistent does this leave Americans? Should Americans thus be against all forms of colonialism as part of being in favor of political democracy? At the plane of absolute logic, the answer of course was yes. In terms of simple ability to lift an issue into view, however, there would be more attention paid to political feelings already expressed, as in Europe or Asia. For Africa, the American policy was more to tolerate and bet on "smooth transitions" and "gradual evolutions."

Perhaps the most serious accusation to be leveled against the American policy for black Africa prior to 1975 was thus not that there was any real commitment to maintaining a colonialist and racist status quo, but rather a general inattention. The United States had a certain amount of leverage to deploy here to favor one side or another, but elected largely not to use it; it bought coffee or bauxite from regimes very much dependent on such sales, without making any serious effort to exploit this on behalf of its political causes. The distractions of European defense, and then of the struggle to try to keep South Vietnam from falling under Communist rule, may simply have rendered the American public and government incapable of sorting out the opportunities for interference and intervention here.

Paradoxically, the most supportable radical criticism of U.S. African policy might then well be that Washington did not intervene *enough*. In a period when critics of U.S. foreign policy may have come to expect that American intervention was automatically bound to be damaging, damaging to the happiness of peoples abroad, or damaging to the happiness and well-being of the United States itself, some would thus have responded with a sigh of "Thank God for American neglect"; but others would not.

It is a fair challenge of the purity of anyone's advocacy of isolationism to see whether he would oppose *every* possible deployment of American influence and power abroad. A standard example here has thus turned to South Africa. Would an American radical really object to a U.S. government effort to overturn the white regime that has imposed the system of apartheid on the black majority there? A genuine isolationist would respond that this is just as much to be avoided as trying to keep Italy from falling under Communist rule. A few radical commentators might try to avoid the question by explaining that the United States was somehow congenitally incapable of taking the black side in this basic dispute, forgetting earlier American policy with regard to the British in India, and the French in Indochina, and the Dutch in Indonesia. Most such radicals might however admit that they would have to welcome *this* kind of deployment of American power, if it were to be offered.

The years until the Portuguese collapse in Africa in 1975 might thus be summarized as follows. American policy was characterized more by neglect than by positive mistakes. Africa was not very much pulled into the discussions of containment of Soviet expansion, or of domino theory, because it was geographically not on the road to anything else of importance to the United States. The cold war basically did not seem to have gotten to Africa in the years when detente replaced cold war as the dominant theme of Soviet-American relations.

To add to a general relaxation here, the newly independent African countries now did not appear likely to be taken over by Communist Parties or armed forces, but rather seemed extraordinarily adept at playing the superpowers off against each other, while retaining their own freedom of action. The first deployments of Communist strength on the continent themselves seemed quite non-monolithic, with pro-Chinese and pro-Russian and other versions apparently checking each other.

Detente more generally has been traced to the resurrection of local strength and viability in regimes (leaving them all less obvious targets for attack or subversion) and to the multiplication of disputes and cleavages along varying axes, thus producing more of a balance-of-power system again (in place of the old bipolar array where each alliance had huddled under the shelter of its superpower's nuclear umbrella). This combination of impacts now indeed seemed very applicable to the African case, as most of the new regimes seemed to have a strong local base, as the split in the Communist world seemingly made balance-of-power mechanisms work here as well.

DISILLUSIONMENT ABOUT DETENTE

Everyone would probably agree that the cold war shifted into something different at some point in the 1960s. If we called what came afterward detente, is this detente now shifting back in the 1980s into something resembling the cold war again?[30] Or did the post-cold war period at its best never amount to a genuine detente, something one could so much rely upon, something one would wish to maintain?[31]

Americans certainly may have lost some of their militance about the cold war because the Communist world was no longer so monolithic and cohesive, having rather fallen into squabbling within itself, as the Communist-governed states now even directed military threats against each other. But Americans may have lost as much of this militance because they had become confused during the Vietnam War about whether a moral opposition to communism was even appropriate in the first place.

This explanation of the change in international relations in the 1960s might thus be considerably less reassuring than the first. A world in which neither side sees opportunities for moves forward is nicer than a world in which one side continues to press forward, while the other has ceased to resist.

Americans are thus no longer enthusiastic about detente. A portion of their loss of enthusiasm for detente might of course simply go back to the original, more precise, definition of the concept, namely as a *relaxation* of tension, a *change* in the level of counterproductive activity from high to low. Having gone through one such change, its novelty and good feeling may well have worn off, as Americans might be asking "what else is new," or "what have you done for me lately?"

But the deeper concern about detente might be that any stabilizing changes in the international system were not so deep or so lasting as to be counted upon. If the cold war ended mainly because Americans lost their ideological consensus, rather than because local regimes became more secure and more stable, the term "detente" might hardly be appropriate to describe what followed.

DOUBTS ABOUT DETENTE IN BLACK AFRICA

A number of the premises for African detente were badly shaken in the years after the 1975 Portuguese collapse, coinciding indeed with the broader disillusionment with detente that followed the Egyptian attack on Israel in the 1973 Yom Kippur War, and the growth in Soviet strategic force strength in the same years. The departure of the Portuguese from Mozambique saw a very rapid takeover of the territory by perhaps the most explicitly Marxist regime now to be established on the African continent. Even more disturbing were events in Angola, the other major Portuguese colony, where the Organization of African Unity (OAU) had advocated a coalition of the three major insurgent movements that had opposed the Portuguese: the MPLA (backed by the USSR), the FNLA (which had backing from both China and the United States), and UNITA (also drawing backing in the end from China and the United States). When coalition talks broke down, in important part because of the attitudes of the MPLA, a civil war ensued, with large numbers of Soviet weapons and Cuban troops being flown in to have an ultimately decisive impact on the outcome. The United States and the Chinese surreptitiously supplied some aid to the factions opposing the MPLA, but memories of the costs of the Vietnam War kept down the possible level of American support, and precluded the use of any actual American troops. The U.S. government at this point made the major blunder of encouraging an intervention by South African troops on the side of UNITA, a step which led the Chinese to adopt a low profile and to cease their support, a step that led the OAU to cease insisting on a coalition. Instead of supporting all the sides evenly, the OAU now endorsed the claims of the MPLA.[32]

Several disturbing lessons thus seemed to emerge from the Angolan and Mozambican episodes. At the military-geopolitical level, the fear might now be that Communist forces would no longer be so effectively divided; the Chinese confrontation with the Russians might count for much less when the Russians had the air transport to move large numbers of Cubans around, and the Chinese did not have a capability or inclination to counter this with any similar numbers of Cambodians, and so forth.

At the basic domestic political level, the parallel fear emerged that communism might now indeed be more able to install itself, to settle in to grab a hold in Africa comparable to the Communist regimes in Bulgaria or Cuba or Vietnam, applying all the techniques of ideological orthodoxy and secret police that Americans had feared since 1945.

Many such fears were then to be repeated when the center of African political turmoil and military activity shifted after 1975 to the Horn of Africa in the dispute between Ethiopia and Somalia.[33] Would the Russians and the Cubans again come in by the use of their new troop carrier aircraft, reversing whatever the normal outcome of the local military and political processes would have been without such intervention? Would the Ethiopians, after the deposition of Emperor Haile Selassie, go totally Marxist, generating yet another regime with no more tolerance than Bulgaria's for political liberty or pluralism?

As we enter the 1980s, two very different interpretations thus vie to explain recent events in Africa, one still consistent with the prediction that power considerations can nourish superpower detente, the other suggesting instead that the West will be hard-pressed to defend its interests against Communist expansion.

Predictions of multipolarity and balance-of-power and detente still have some plausibility. Cynics about Africa, in the wake of the earlier Congo experience, used to sneer that African governments "could not be bought, but only rented." The comment was intended to be derogatory, but was inadvertently a compliment, being consistent with a pattern where political trends are mostly shaped locally, by which balance-of-power mechanisms can be counted upon to prevent any one faction (or either of the superpowers) from too much getting its way; this over the longer run could ease any temptations or fears that might pull the superpowers in for races of power and influence here.

What if black African political factions have thus not really been pro-Communist and anti-Communist, but have only been sounding that way to seduce Moscow and Washington into supplying arms assistance? This may thus be an exaggeration of the ideological aspects of such conflicts, if factions based mainly on local ethnic considerations deliberately stress either a Marxist or a pluralist coloration as a way of acquiring material and weapons support from the outside. The ideological differences between the MPLA and FNLA and UNITA in Angola were virtually nonexistent, by some accounts, or at the least were very much exaggerated, as each side girded itself for the defense of a particular "way of life" in the former Portuguese colony.

The dramatic reversal in whether Somalia or Ethiopia was to be seen as the more "leftist" similarly suggests how reflections of the outside world may color in the picture. Prior to the overthrow of the pro-American government in Ethiopia, to be replaced by a "pro-Soviet" regime in Addis Ababa, Ethiopia's ethnic arch-rival, Somalia, had also been pessimistically painted as a Soviet satellite and military base in the American press, for substantial amounts of Soviet military equipment had indeed been delivered to the Somalis. The sudden swing of Ethiopia into an alliance with the USSR thus caught observers by surprise with regard to both sides of the confrontation. The officers of the Ethiopian junta that now so enthusiastically identified with Moscow had virtually all been trained in the United

States. Moscow's decision to accept their identification came despite Ethiopia's look of a loser in its 1976 border conflict with Somalia, and in Eritrea's struggle for independence.

Such a view of the Soviet Union and the United States as being hoodwinked by the local African factions would, *if true*, be good news for detente and for the world. Yet what if some of the black African Marxists of the 1980s are not just pretending, but are more seriously committed to Moscow's leadership, and more adept at establishing permanent dictatorships?

The world will watch the future of domestic and international behavior in the former Portuguese colonies, and in Ethiopia, to see which theory holds best. If Soviet influence is as clearly circumscribed in such places as it was in Egypt and Somalia, if the Cubans flown in by Soviet transports do not become an irresistible military instrument in the continent, some of the premises that were normally associated with the prediction of detente will seem to have been reconfirmed. But what if they are not?

The world will similarly watch the accords reached in Rhodesia as it became Zimbabwe in the clear election victory of Robert Mugabe in 1980.[34] If the electoral system is maintained, or if the regime at least seems to be more indigenous than controlled from the outside, the Western world will relax somewhat. If Zimbabwe instead falls as much under Soviet control as Ethiopia, then the worry about falling dominoes will again rise.

THE ROLE OF YOUTH AND EDUCATION

The United States did little to prevent the imposition of a Marxist regime in Angola. It has made less of a contribution to newly "anti-Communist" Somalia than the Russians and Cubans made to newly "Marxist" Ethiopia. The United States did nothing with its military forces to prevent the final tank attack on South Vietnam by Hanoi in 1975, or to prevent the incursion of Soviet military forces into Afghanistan in 1980.

It would have been altogether nice if American "neoisolationism" had simply turned out to reflect a lack of need to defend foreign areas against attack. Yet the pace of events since 1967 and the indications of American public opinion polls suggest that more than this has been involved here, including a troublesome new unwillingness to defend many places even when a need for help is perceived.

The cold war thus may not have ended entirely, or even mainly, because opportunities for aggression and crisis had disappeared. It may have ended, in as large part, because Americans have become unclear as to whether the radical or liberal interpretations of their past are correct.

How are Americans to interpret the trends since 1967, as compared with U.S. foreign policy attitudes before 1967? How much of American blood and treasure will the United States be ready to commit to overseas efforts in the future, and on behalf of what kinds of causes? Throughout this book, the concern with the past has been primarily for the clues this can offer for the interpretation of American foreign policy in the present, and for predictions about the future.

One possible source of confusion in analyzing the trends of such American opinion has stemmed from the role of youth and education. Anyone who has been on an American campus would come away with the impression that young people since 1965 have been much more opposed to foreign commitments than their elders; by the natural replacement of one generation by another, one would thus have to conclude that the United States was destined to become less and less interventionist, and more and more self-critical of its purposes in ever having extended a military defense of its allies.

Yet public opinion polling, until the mid-1970s, typically showed an almost exactly opposite distribution of opinion from age-group to age-group. The older the American, the more opposed he was to the Vietnam War, to foreign entanglements in general, and to preparations for military engagement with the Communist powers, as is seen in comparing the three age-groups in Poll 5. Given this distribution, would one instead have to make an inference that the United States was likely to turn more interventionist, rather than less, as the younger voters replaced the old? Was the wave of the future to be a greater support for the defense of places like Berlin and Yugoslavia and Vietnam?

In Poll 5, one should note how the "refuse to get involved" response draws greater support with greater age of respondent for every contingency but two, Yugoslavia and Taiwan (where the 21–29 age-group comes out slightly ahead of the 30–49 age-group, but where the over-50 age-group is still the leader). On the response of "send troops," younger respondents again seemed uniformly more willing to endorse this than older respondents (with the exceptions of the contingencies of Turkey, Israel, and Taiwan, where over-50 respondents were still least willing, but where the 30–49 group was slightly more willing to send troops than the 20–29 group).

A compilation of questions related to war published in *Public Opinion Quarterly* supports this intuition that there was indeed a trend toward greater pacifism among the young, but again steers us into the paradoxical finding that the young are only belatedly catch-

POLL 5

In the event a nation is attacked by Communist-backed forces, there are several things the United States can do about it. As I read the name of each country, tell me what action you would want to see us take if that nation is actually attacked—send American troops or send military supplies but not send American troops or refuse to get involved at all.

| | | National | Age-Group | | | Level of Education | | |
			21–29	30–49	50–over	College	High School	Grade School
West Germany	Send Troops	28%	33%	32%	20%	36%	28%	17%
	Send Supplies Only	41	45	41	40	45	41	37
	Refuse to Get Involved	42	18	19	27	12	22	33
Turkey	Send Troops	10	13	14	5	11	11	6
	Send Supplies Only	36	46	37	29	44	35	30
	Refuse to Get Involved	37	29	34	44	35	36	40
Israel	Send Troops	11	14	15	6	13	13	7
	Send Supplies Only	44	50	45	40	53	43	37
	Refuse to Get Involved	33	29	30	37	27	32	40
Japan	Send Troops	17	23	20	9	23	16	11
	Send Supplies Only	34	41	37	29	42	33	29
	Refuse to Get Involved	38	29	33	48	29	40	44
England	Send Troops	37	51	44	24	41	38	24
	Send Supplies Only	33	28	32	25	33	33	31
	Refuse to Get Involved	19	15	15	26	13	18	29

India	Send Troops	7	13	8	3	7	9	5
	Send Supplies Only	40	50	44	32	48	40	33
	Refuse to Get Involved	39	30	35	46	37	37	43
Mexico	Send Troops	45	52	52	36	35	46	33
	Send Supplies Only	26	25	24	27	28	24	27
	Refuse to Get Involved	19	14	15	25	11	19	28
Thailand	Send Troops	11	17	13	6	11	13	7
	Send Supplies Only	36	43	41	29	45	35	30
	Refuse to Get Involved	38	30	34	44	36	36	42
Brazil	Send Troops	16	22	18	10	18	17	10
	Send Supplies Only	36	41	41	30	46	36	29
	Refuse to Get Involved	33	27	27	41	28	32	40
Yugoslavia	Send Troops	7	10	7	4	7	8	4
	Send Supplies Only	51	50	49	53	29	27	25
	Refuse to Get Involved	51	50	49	53	52	51	50
Nationalist China	Send Troops	11	13	15	5	11	12	8
	Send Supplies Only	30	35	22	27	38	30	25
	Refuse to Get Involved	45	44	41	49	42	45	47

Source: Albert H. Cantril and Charles W. Roll, Jr., *Hopes and Fears of the American People* (Washington, D.C.: Potomac Associates, 1971), pp. 86–89.

ing up with their elders in this regard:[35]

	Before 1965	1965– 67	1968 and After
Percent of questions on which the young exceeded the old in pacifism	38%	49%	75%
Average percentage point gap between young and old in degree of pacifism	-2.3	+1.0	+6.0

When the questions related to "pacifism" were specified, more-over, the young even after 1964 still seemed less opposed to foreign interventions than their parents:[36]

Specific Pacifist Attitude	Percent of Questions on Which Young Were More Pacifist than Old
Favor antiwar demonstrations	100%
Favor greater or speedier withdrawal of troops from Vietnam	88
Unwilling to utilize nuclear weapons	86
Consider themselves doves rather than hawks	83
Oppose bombing raids	82
Unwilling to declare a war or to escalate a war	67
Oppose compulsory military service	58
Disapprove of sending U.S. troops abroad	35
Consider specific wars have been a mistake	8

Yet the paradoxes here may not be so difficult to disentangle. The crucial comparison for predicting the future has all along not been how young voters compare with old, but how young voters to-day compare with young voters in the past. The United States may all along have been governed by a normal aging process in which voters became somewhat "alienated" and "isolationist" and anti-foreign policy venture as they grew older. Youths in the United States might normally feel more capable and optimistic than their disenchanted elders. A failure in the fight for the upper rungs of the economic ladder may well take the shine off the visions inculcated in American grade schools and high schools, visions that all Americans have a chance at success, that the United States as a whole has a chance at success where reforming the world is concerned.

Respondents aged 51 might thus always have been more pessi-mistic or cynical than voters aged 21 on the possibilities of successful altruism in foreign policy; how unsettling it would be to discover that voters aged 21 are now starting out much more cynical than be-fore! If the same processes of further disenchantment through aging were to affect this group, the long-term trend for American foreign policy sentiment might indeed be what one would intuitively have guessed it to be, toward fewer military commitments. (The tip of the iceberg was visible here in the questions cited in Poll 5, where the middle-aged group had been left out on a limb as the most willing to send troops, and least inclined to "Refuse to Get Involved.")

The underlying proposition here is thus that youth has normally felt more power for American dealings with the outside world, while age normally wears down the sense of American capabilities. A related assumption is that higher levels of education normally raise this sense of how much can be accomplished. This might be because the foreign policy courses of American universities have stressed the opportunities for doing good out there. It could rather be simply because greater education has normally produced greater economic success in the United States, and therefore less disenchantment, less sense of being unable to control events.

Returning to the 1971 opinions cited in Poll 5, it is remarkable how well the choices were related to levels of education. In every case, the more education one had, the more one felt a need for the United States to get involved. In seven out of eleven cases, greater education also led to greater willingness to "send troops" (the exceptions being India, Thailand, Yugoslavia, and Taiwan). Further comparisons of political opinion by level of education are found in Polls 6, 7, and 8.

POLL 6

The United States and various North Atlantic countries, such as Canada, England, France, Norway, and Holland, have signed a mutual defense pact—that is, each country has agreed to come to the defense of any of the other countries if it is attacked. Do you think the U.S. Senate should or should not ratify (approve) the North Atlantic Security Pact?

	Should	Should Not	No Opinion
National Total			
May 18, 1949	67%	12%	21%
July 8, 1949	67	15	18
Opinion in May 1949 by education			
College	80	12	8
High school	73	11	16
Grade school	58	12	30

Source: "The Quarter's Polls," *Public Opinion Quarterly* 13, no. 3 (Fall 1949): 549–50.

POLL 7

Do you think that the United States should or should not supply arms and war materials to the North Atlantic nations if they agree to provide us with air bases and any other help that they may be able to give?

Poll of May 18, 1949	Should	Should Not	No Opinion
National total	65%	16%	19%
By education			
College	75	17	8
High school	71	14	15
Grade school	55	18	27

Source: "The Quarter's Polls," *Public Opinion Quarterly* 13, no. 3 (Fall 1949): 549–50.

POLL 8

Some people say that the North Atlantic Security Pact is a plan for the United States and other member nations to get ready for an attack on Russia. Other people say that the North Atlantic Pact is a plan only for defense in case the United States or any member nation is attacked. Which do you agree with? (Asked only of those who had heard or read about the Atlantic Pact.)

Poll of June 5, 1949	Defense	Ready to Attack	No Opinion	Unfamiliar with Pact
National total	53%	5%	7%	35%
By education				
College	79	6	7	8
High school	60	6	6	28
Grade school	39	4	8	49

Source: "The Quarter's Polls," *Public Opinion Quarterly* 13, no. 3 (Fall 1949): 549–50.

Lest one had come to distrust his intuition too much on the basis of the polls cited above, one could confirm an on-campus anti-foreign-policy trend readily enough by the opinions for a Florida campus in 1962 and 1972 found in Poll 9.

By 1973, moreover, to complete the move to full visibility in the overall trends, the polls on appropriate amount of military spending had at last fully reversed from what they had been in the past, with youngest respondents and best-educated respondents now expressing the most opposition to such spending, as shown in Poll 10.

POLL 9

Items in Pacifism Scale	Male Agreement		Female Agreement		Total Agreement	
	1962	1972	1962	1972	1962	1972
1. The U.S. must be willing to run any risk of war which may be necessary to prevent the spread of communism	78%	22%	64%	32%	72%	25%
2. If disarmament negotiations are not successful, the U.S. should begin a gradual program of unilateral disarmament, i.e., disarm whether other countries do or not.	4	30	9	34	6	31
3. Pacifist demonstrations—picketing missile bases, peace walks, etc.—are harmful to the best interests of the American people.	50	17	37	15	44	17
4. The U.S. has no moral right to carry its struggle against communism to the point of risking the destruction of the human race.	30	83	40	90	34	85
5. It is contrary to my moral principles to participate in war and the killing of other people.	15	43	20	66	17	49
6. The real enemy today is no longer communism but rather war itself.	26	65	37	73	31	67
7. Pacifism is simply not a practical philosophy in the world today.	60	41	45	27	54	37

Source: Roger B. Handberg, "The Vietnam Analogy: Student Attitudes on War," *Public Opinion Quarterly*, 36, no. 4 (Winter 1972–73): 613.

POLL 10

There is much discussion as to the amount of money the government in Washington should spend for national defense and military purposes. How do you feel about this? Do you think we are spending too little, too much, or about the right amount?

	Too Much	Too Little	About Right	No Opinion
National	42%	8%	40%	10%
Level of education				
College	48	6	38	8
High school	42	9	40	9
Grade school	36	6	42	16
Age-group				
18–29 years	50	8	35	7
30–49 years	41	8	43	8
50 and over	38	8	41	13

Source: The Gallup Poll, February 1973, cited in *Current Opinion* 1, issue 4 (June 1973): 48.

The American post-1967 turn inward is in the end to be explained not just in terms of changed opportunity, but also of changed desire. This post-Vietnam phase of American foreign policy attitudes may thus be of a very different form from all the other cycles and phrases that have been discussed. It is different, it has been contended throughout this book, because a large fraction of Americans have now for the first time come to doubt the moral desirability of implanting a duplicate of the U.S. political system in foreign countries. If they are thus being turned into some sort of "neoisolationists," it is not so much by the *costs* of having influence abroad, but by doubts as to the appropriateness of such influence.

From where have those doubts then stemmed, doubts that now may be so much upsetting American confidence in the exportability of the American model? Two distinct possibilities need to be discussed, and perhaps to be blended, here.

A U.S. SHIFT LEFTWARD?

A possibility to be considered would be that many United States voters, or at least some of them, had shifted markedly leftward on issues of politics as well as economics. Americans, might (foreign policy aside) now have lost a great deal of their confidence in their historical experience at home, by this view, as the years since the Great Depression at last had caused distrust of capitalism and the economic by-products of political democracy.

Exactly how far this domestic distrust of the traditions of liberalism and capitalism could have gone is not so easy to determine; whether any leftward movement is likely to continue is all the more debatable.

It might have been no surprise in the 1970s if the general drift of the United States had indeed continued to be to the Left, because the trend of the entire world seemed to lie in this direction and the continuing momentum of all the shifts within the United States since the New Deal also had to be seen as giving the state greater influence over the economy, and assigning greater priority to the leveling of economic income. If such a leftward trend were to continue, therefore, it also would be no surprise if more and more Americans thus became prepared to write off the value of political democracy and republican government for many of the poorer corners of the world (in the belief that the need for economic redistribution in such areas, in Greece and Malaysia and Panama, was too pressing to afford the trappings of multiparty elections and an independent press).

A few Americans, of Marxist or other radical persuasion, would find such an analysis of the third world even relevant for the United States itself, dramatically calling into question whether the political processes of the United States are not overrated in value, given the economic inequalities and insufficiencies that also persist in America. If other countries have concluded that free elections and free press are not worth having, because this helps maintain poverty, perhaps the United States should make the same choice, putting economic democracy ahead of political democracy.[37] It might not be unfair to accuse the Students for a Democratic Society (SDS) of having adopted this outlook on American choices.[38]

The overseas rejection of the American model thus fits in with some more general doubts about the American model, even on its appropriateness for the United States. For a certain fraction of Americans (most probably not a majority) the events of the outside world supported a major leftward turn in feelings about life in the United States itself. Seemingly supporting this view, it might be no coincidence that the years of the loss of American foreign policy consensus, the later 1960s, also saw a substantial drop in public opinion statements of confidence in American institutions in general, as seen in Poll 11.

If such a turn leftward at home had gone far enough, it could of course circle back upon itself to produce an altruistic interventionism

POLL 11

As far as the people running these institutions are concerned, would you say you have a great deal of confidence, only some confidence, or hardly any confidence at all in them?

Percent with a Great Deal of Confidence in:	1966	1971	1972	Spring 1973	Spring 1974	Spring 1975
Banks and financial institutions	67%	36%	39%	—%*	—%	32%
Major companies	55	27	27	29	31	19
Organized religion	41	27	30	35	44	24
Education	61	37	33	37	49	31
Executive branch of the federal government	41	23	27	29	14	13
Organized labor	22	14	15	15	18	10
Press	29	18	18	23	26	24
Medicine	72	61	48	54	60	50
TV	25	22	17	18	23	18
U.S. Supreme Court	51	23	28	31	26	31
Scientific community	56	32	37	37	45	38
Congress	42	19	21	23	17	13
Military	62	27	35	32	40	35

*Data not available.

Source: Ben J. Wattenberg, *The Real America* (Garden City: Doubleday, 1974), p. 296.

again in the future, but on behalf of new causes and new allies. Instead of resisting Cuban interventions in Africa, Americans might thus have been joining in the Cuban siege of the white South African redoubt. Instead of supporting free speech and free press in developing nations, one would be supporting the nationalizations of industry, even including the press. Whether or not the United States transformed itself into a Marxist state domestically, it would sharply realign its foreign policy into being more supportive of the Left, perhaps as in the brief fling it had with such associations during World War II, when Americans embraced Ho Chi Minh because he opposed the Japanese, and despite the fact that he opposed the French.[39]

The far left of the American spectrum does not truly favor isolationism, or the total avoidance of an exercise of American power abroad. It may, for tactical reasons, pretend to agree with the selfish isolationists (or with the "iron-law" altruistic isolationists who believe that no good can ever come of such exercises abroad). In reality the Left really favors an altruistic exercise of interventionary power, but simply on behalf of a new cause, much as it was vehemently anti-isolationist after Hitler invaded the Soviet Union in 1941. The Marxist agrees with those Americans who now feel isolationist because they have become unsure of the impact of the U.S. political system on the happiness of humans abroad, but he hopes that such Americans will resolve their confusion, to become backers of very different political systems around the world.

The world and the American public have not yet been ready for the suggestion that the Marines be sent abroad to install Marxist regimes, so the suggestion hardly gets advanced. Principled isolationists—those who accept an iron law that the United States must always accomplish something different from what it intends when intervening abroad—would of course have been as much opposed to a pro-Marxist intervention in Angola as to an anti-Marxist effort. A more serious radical would in truth have to favor such an action, however, even if he for the moment has no hope of getting it.

A U.S. SHIFT RIGHTWARD?

The election of Ronald Reagan as president in 1980, if nothing else, showed that a simple leftward shift in American ideological attitudes could not work as an explanation of the changes and likely future of American foreign policy. If there had indeed been such a steady drift leftward ever since the beginnings of the New Deal, this may well have produced second thoughts in the past decade, as Americans have now more generally lost confidence in the ability of government action to cope with their problems, Keynesian economics no longer seems so applicable to all the necessary outputs of an economy, and the "English disease" and other trends have caused major misgivings about democratic socialism, or any other kind of socialism.[40]

Keynesian economists were once eloquent in explaining how full employment could be achieved at the same moment as stable prices. The contemporary experience of "stagflation" has made the general public much more skeptical and pessimistic here. As the opponents of socialism had predicted all along, some serious costs have emerged, even where no threat to political democracy or freedom appears, as various kinds of waste are induced by a reliance on the state for economic regulation and redistribution, and this can be devastating for individual incentives.

The warning of the ecologists that the world may not be able to sustain continued economic growth, or even current high rates of consumption, moreover in a roundabout way may have made the equality of distribution look a little less important. If we are all going to be richer, perhaps we could all be more generous; but if we are *not* all going to be richer, more and more Americans may resent being taxed for the alleviation of someone else's poverty.

If the drift of the United States were to be back toward the Right, one might perhaps have looked forward again to a greater concern for the defense of political freedom abroad. Old-fashioned liberals favor laissez-faire and an absence of government restrictions only in part because they fear that socialistic controls will destroy initiatives, but in larger part because unchecked state authorities would be able to imprison the opposition party, and thus exempt themselves from ever facing an electoral challenge.

A distrust of socialism, even of the socialism of political democracies, is emotionally consistent therefore with a renewed defense of what used to be called the "free world." Yet, as will be discussed in the next section, even such a rightward shift will produce some ambivalences on how much Americans want to mount this defense, ambivalences compounded where there is still a strengthened left wing in American political life very much opposed to such a defense.

Compared to the 1952 views of Americans on domestic ideological questions, some Americans may have thus moved abruptly leftward, but others to the Right. Americans are less united and consensual than in the past, on domestic as well as foreign policy. As a reflection of their own society, Americans are less in agreement about the outside world, and are therefore less optimistic about their ability to improve it.

A DOUBLE STANDARD?

How do the trends in American political sentiment, as they so much affect foreign policy, then sort out? The percentage of Americans who are now actually far enough left to question even the at-home value of contested elections is not so very great, but it is greater than it was in the past.

If any such significant fraction of Americans has shifted its support leftward from political freedom to economic equality, a larger number of Americans probably still remains true to the old values, convinced that nothing is worth doing in the United States except in a context of elections and press criticism, and convinced that this must also be just as true in India or Kenya or Poland or Burma. These then will be people who still see the termination of contested elections in the third world countries as the insidious machinations of world communism, or as misguided reachings for shortcuts by the leaders of underdeveloped countries.

A third group of Americans must now be counted in, however, before one strikes a balance of votes here, and this would be those who now see a double standard, who would be resolute in defending political democracy first and foremost for the United States and Great Britain and Canada and most of Western Europe, but who would now treat the economically underdeveloped and non-Europeanized portions of the world as governed by different priorities and standards, as being "unsuited to free elections," or "too poor to have a free press."

The out-and-out Marxists were not numerous enough to destroy the American sense of consensus. The last point of view, however, is now much more widespread, so that consensus as we knew it is gone.

The exact boundaries of this "free-world capable" zone will sometimes be ambiguous. Japan is presumably included, which keeps this from becoming what might otherwise be ethnically a totally Caucasian zone. Portugal and Spain may be marginal, depending on whose theory of political development is most persuasive for the American analysts that matter, and depending also on how events break there in the aftermath of Franco and Salazar. Even Italy can come into question, as can Greece.

Canada, Australia, and New Zealand are included without a question, as are Scandinavia, the Low Countries, and Germany, and Israel. France is more likely to be included than not. India may objectively deserve to be included, given its demonstrated attachment to the processes of contested elections, but it may well be left out because too many Americans can no longer bring themselves to hope that any economically developing country can maintain such an attachment.[41]

The explanation for such divisions is an explanation of disappointment. The aftermath of World War II had indeed produced a great pleasant anticipation in Americans, with the prospect of the end of colonial rule in the European domains of Africa and Asia. Self-rule, by freely elected governments, would now at last spread to the far corners of the globe, duplicating the earlier U.S. impact on Latin America and on Europe itself. It was thus not surprising that Americans were thereafter quickly to be appalled, and frustrated, and bothered, and confused by the tendency of one decolonized nation after another to give up the political democracy to which it had advanced, becoming instead one-party regimes with no meaningful elections, a state-controlled press, and a disrespect for elementary personal civil liberties.

The reasoned explanation emerged soon enough that this was not due simply to the personal character defects of the persons overturning elections, but rather to a failure of political democracy to induce economic situations as satisfactory as those in the United States. Forced to choose between political democracy and economic democracy, where the general level of economic accomplishment and progress was so much lower, the newly emerging nations often enough then have made a choice opposite to what Americans would have expected or advised.

Upon digesting such explanations of the various rejections of the American example, a fair number of Americans were thus now to conclude that much of the world might *not* be happier under a Minnesota style of government. This new pessimism might at first look like a simple extension of the old altruistic "iron law" arguments against foreign influence, somehow contending that transplants of American models are bound to become corrupted in the process. Yet the new pessimism and doubt goes further. There are now many Americans who will believe that political democracy would be inappropriate for foreign countries—*even if* it were not corrupted in the process of transmission from the United States, even if the United States itself were not made more authoritarian in the process of projecting itself abroad.

The "iron law of nontransferability" is something that no serious student of politics could accept in its rigid form, for the world abounds with examples of genuine influence by one country on another. The new doubts are thus based less on the *impossibility* of the "Americanization" of the world, and more on a finding that it would indeed not conduce to the happiness of the people involved. To have

Americans believing that other human beings will become less happy as their political structure more resembles that of the United States, it is being argued here, is indeed a new development.

If Americans are thus to resign themselves to a major difference between their own situation and that of much of the world—such that political democracy is desirable for North America and Europe and Japan, but not for the developing world—there is a real risk that the overall altruism of American world outlooks will then be further diminished. We earlier noted a crude and elementary interpretation of human psychology which suggests that much of one's altruism and sympathy is a function of how much one sees other creatures as like oneself. Because dogs somehow resemble humans, while bugs do not, we pass humane laws forbidding cruelty to dogs, but not to insects. A crude materialist would conclude that all of charity and sympathy is simply a way of avoiding pain to ourselves; we sleep better at night, we increase our own "welfare" or "utility," by blotting out the picture of human suffering elsewhere.

One worrisome possibility for the future of American foreign policy is thus that Americans will still rally behind freedom, but no longer behind freedom for all. What comes from the Left as a reasoned explanation of the special priorities that must apply in the Afro-Asian world (priorities placing economic equality ahead of political liberty) will hit people more to the Right as an indication that Afro-Asian peoples are "different" ("inferior"?), and thus not so much to be identified with in any event.

There is thus a nontrivial fly in the ointment for any presumption that a shift instead rightward in American politics could renew the American foreign policy commitment to defending political freedom and republican democracy around the globe. For a series of reasons already mentioned, there is some correlation between the American "rightism" of a distrust of governmental power, and the "rightism" of the elementary racism that decides to see different peoples as differentially suited to political freedom. The same American who might be deeply shocked by a suspension of political freedoms in England or Australia might now revert to an indifference about such a suspension in Zambia or Vietnam or India, on the argument that "those people just aren't suited for Western ways."

We might thus see the emergence of a "right-wing" view that becomes indifferent to the replacement of election systems around the globe by "socialist peoples' republics" because the people involved are Angolans or Vietnamese or Indians or other non-Europeans, people who are "just not like us." At its base, this will be a retrenchment of the defense of political freedom, a "tuning out," which is more racist than based on any class analysis, but with the same out-come. Japanese will qualify as "Europeans" by this definition (as indeed the South Africans classify them so), but the rest of the countries "fit for freedom" will be European, plus the United States, plus the white-populated members of the British Commonwealth.

The bulk of the breakdown of consensus on the purposes of American foreign policy can not be blamed on a simple racism. Much of the breakdown may have begun among people who cared genuinely about the Vietnamese and the Tanzanians, but who then concluded that a two-party system and free press would be bad for these peoples' happiness, because such liberal institutions stand in the way of effective redistribution of economic wealth and power. This is basically a view that arrived from the Left.

Yet Right and Left have a penchant for coming together in embarrassing ways. The advanced social scientist, who patiently cautions Americans against assuming that their system will work for peoples anywhere, finds himself in a funny de facto agreement at the end with the racist, an agreement that at least needs to be explained away.

NOTES

1. Such an interpretation of the emergence of detente might be extrapolated from Seyom Brown, *New Forces in World Politics* (Washington, D.C.: Brookings, 1974).

2. As an example of a radical interpretation of the weakening of cold war commitments, endorsing many of what have been labeled radical premises, see Ronald Steel, *Imperialists and Other Heroes* (New York: Random House, 1971).

3. An interpretation more true to traditional American self-assessments is to be found in James Chace, *A World Elsewhere; Options for the Future* (New York: Charles Scribner's Sons, 1973).

4. For such a view of the Berlin wall as having had effects in the long run see James A. Nathan and James K. Oliver, *United States Foreign Policy and World Order* (Boston: Little, Brown, 1976), pp. 313-14.

5. The real nature of the French "withdrawal" from NATO is discussed in Carl H. Amme, *NATO Without France* (Stanford: Hoover Institution, 1967).

6. The enormous changes in the attitudes expressed by West German youths as expressed in terrorism by a minority, but in many other forms, are discussed in Jillian Becker, *Hitler's Children* (Philadelphia: Lippincott, 1977).

7. For an important discussion of Titoism as a phenomenon, see John C. Campbell, *Tito's Separate Road* (New York: Harper & Row, 1967).

8. Helmut Sonnenfeldt, "Russia, America, and Detente," *Foreign Affairs* 56, no. 2 (January 1978): 275-94 offers an insightful analysis of the continuing tensions in Soviet dominance over Eastern Europe.

9. For early and cautious discussions of the Sino-Soviet split, see William B. Griffith, *Albania and the Sino-Soviet Rift* (Cambridge, Mass.: The M.I.T.

Press, 1963) and Donald Zagoria, *The Sino-Soviet Conflict* (Princeton: Princeton University Press, 1962).

10. For a fuller discussion of the long-run significance of the events in Czechoslovakia, see J. P. O'Grady, "Czechoslovakia Did Not Revive the Cold War," *South Atlantic Quarterly* 70, no. 1 (Winter 1971): 22–33.

11. The phenomenon of "Eurocommunism" is discussed interestingly in B. R. Starogin, "Identity Crisis of West European Communists," *Dissent* 22, no. 2 (Summer 1975): 251–60.

12. The struggle for power in Portugal in the mid-1970s is outlined in Tad Szulc, "Lisbon and Washington: Behind the Portuguese Revolution," *Foreign Policy*, no. 21 (Winter 1975–76), pp. 3–62.

13. A very useful discussion of the complexities of international economics is presented in Joan Edelman Spero, *The Politics of International Economic Relations* (New York: St. Martin's Press, 1977).

14. American attitudes on the postwar political system of alternative systems of money and trade are outlined extensively in Richard N. Gardner, *Sterling-Dollar Diplomacy: Anglo-American Collaboration in the Reconstruction of Multilateral Trade* (Oxford: The Clarendon Press, 1956).

15. Possible successors to the dollar as means of keeping international trade moving are outlined in Richard Cooper, "Prolegomena to the Choice of an International Monetary System," in *World Politics and International Economics*, ed. C. Fred Bergsten and Lawrence B. Krause (Washington, D.C.: Brookings, 1975), pp. 63–98.

16. See R. Ball, "Layman's Guide to the European Monetary System," *Fortune* 98 (December 31, 1978): 88–90.

17. The special opportunities of the OPEC cartel are discussed in Steven Krasner, "Oil Is the Exception," *Foreign Policy*, no. 14 (Spring 1974), pp. 68–84.

18. For a discussion of possible Saudi indifference to the earning of additional foreign exchange, see James E. Akins, "The Oil Crisis: This Time the Wolf Is Here," *Foreign Affairs* 51, no. 3 (April 1973): 462–90.

19. A helpful discussion of the complexities of voluntary military service can be found in Steven L. Canby, *Military Manpower Procurement* (Lexingon: D. C. Heath, 1972).

20. For an analysis of the background motives of the Opium War, see Peter Ward Fay, *The Opium War* (Chapel Hill: University of North Carolina Press, 1975).

21. Robert W. Tucker, "Oil: The Issue of American Intervention," *Commentary* 59, no. 1 (January 1975): 21–31.

22. Marvin Kalb and Bernard Kalb, *Kissinger* (Boston: Little, Brown, 1974), p. 233.

23. See Henry A. Kissinger, *The White House Years* (Boston: Little, Brown, 1979), pp. 163–94, 684–732.

24. Chinese attitudes on guerrilla war are outlined in John S. Pustay, *Counterinsurgency Warfare* (New York: The Free Press, 1965).

25. For a very critical interpretation of totalitarian aspects of the Chinese Communist regime, see Simon Leys, *Chinese Shadows* (New York: Viking Press, 1977).

26. For an analysis of the complexity of factions and considerations in Chinese decision making, see Maurice Meisner, *Mao's China* (New York: The Free Press, 1977).

27. Poll reported in William Watts and Lloyd A. Free, *State of the Nation* (New York: Universe Books, 1973), pp. 201, 205, 206.

28. The political struggle in the Congo at the beginning of the 1960s is outlined in Conor Cruise O'Brien, *To Katanga and Back* (London: Hutchinson, 1962).

29. American popular attitudes toward black Africa are discussed in Rupert Emerson, *Africa and United States Policy* (Englewood Cliffs: Prentice-Hall, 1967).

30. For an analysis seeing detente as real, but now eroding, see Strobe Talbott, "U.S.-Soviet Relations: From Bad to Worse," *Foreign Affairs* 58, no. 4 (Spring 1980): 515-39.

31. For an analysis seeing detente as never real, and always illusory, see C. Gersham, "The Rise and Fall of the New Foreign Policy Establishment," *Commentary* 70, no. 1 (July 1980): 13-24.

32. The final collapse of the anti-Marxist position in Angola is discussed in John Stockwell, *In Search of Enemies* (New York: Norton, 1978).

33. The Russian and Cuban arrival at the Horn of Africa is described in F. Shams, "Conflict in the African Horn," *Current History* 73, no. 432 (December 1977): 199-204.

34. The possibilities and fears of American observers for the future of Zimbabwe are discussed in C. Palley, "What Future For Zimbabwe?," *Political Quarterly* 52, no. 3 (July-September 1980): 285-382.

35. Polls cited in Helen Gaudet Erskine, "The Polls: Pacifism and the Generation Gap," *Public Opinion Quarterly* 36, no. 4 (Winter 1972-73): 616.

36. Ibid., p. 617.

37. As an illustration of such a substantial reexamination of American values, see Michael Parenti, *The Anti-Communist Impulse* (New York: Random House, 1969).

38. For a description of the outlook and appeal of SDS, see Robert A. Goldwin, ed., *How Democratic Is America?* (Chicago: Rand McNally, 1971).

39. The ties between Ho Chi Minh and the U.S. government during World War II are discussed in Jean Lacouture, *Ho Chi Minh: A Political Biography* (New York: Random House, 1968), pp. 94-95.

40. For discussions of Reagan's victory as a sign of a rightward move in American political feeling, see Norman Podhoretz, "New American Majority," *Commentary* 71, no. 1 (January 1981): 19-28.

41. For a discussion of American attitudes on India and the possibility of political democracy, see Francine R. Frankel, "Things Fall Apart: India's Promise," *Foreign Policy*, no. 38 (Spring 1980): 51-66.

9
Where We Stand

How could we now summarize what has happened to the United States in its comparisons of itself with foreign countries since the nineteenth century? The outside world has caught up with the United States in developing the option of political democracy, in shaking off the aspects of traditional and ascriptive rule that all along struck Americans as such an anachronism. Having in effect "copied the American model" here, this outside world has however not been able to match the American success on the economic side (or had not seen the American model as such a success). This lower level of economic accomplishment thus perhaps explains a greater concern for economic equality, for what some might style "economic democracy"; or perhaps this difference in values emerged for other reasons.

The result, in any event, was to find the outside world no longer seeing the United States as any kind of model for the future, but rather as a model of the past. And Americans are having to take this into account, in a mood of frustration and confusion and disappointment. Having been offered the essence of political democracy—free contested elections with a free press—country after country around the world has chosen to give this up, in many cases on the argument that it was inconsistent with the achievement of economic equality and progress.

The major presumption of an overwhelming number of Americans has been that any foreign nation attaining a republican form of government, joining the "free world," would want very much to retain this achievement. A minor American assumption was that economic problems could be solved in this political atmosphere, just as they seemed to have been "solved" in the United States. Few Americans had confronted how they would have chosen, if forced to choose, between political freedom and economic progress; most, by their own experience, would have seen no need for choice. If a choice were to seem more distressingly necessary, moreover, more Americans would have listed themselves as opting for the political freedom, as the more precious of the achievements, as the logical first step toward any other form of progress.

The news that the outside world (in particular the third world) has moved up to—and then simply passed by, without long stopping at—the American achievement of political democracy, has thus produced something genuinely new and different for Americans to find consensus on.

IS THE UNITED STATES STILL THE NEW WORLD?

The common terminology is very revealing here. The United States once heard itself normally described as "the new world," as compared with Europe and its dominions, "the old." Today one rather speaks often of the former colonies as the third world, with the Communist bloc turning out to be the second world, and the United States lumped together with Europe and Japan as the first world.

Is this foreign rejection of the American political model such a new shock? Some might point to historical instances that could have produced a moment of truth much earlier. Yet such historical forerunners were not the same.

When the United States had been disappointed by the seeming failure of others to adopt the American model in earlier times, at least this could still always be rationalized as a rejection from the past, because traditional and ascriptive aristocratic practices continued to hold sway over men, barring any full duplication of the American experience. The change in form of the German unification—from what had been proposed in 1848 to what was realized under Bismarck in 1871—could be seen as being of this nature; even the coming of the Nazis to power (despite some discussions of fascism as "the wave of the future") could be seen as a resurgence of German traditions of autocracy and dynastic rule, literally expressed as the Third Reich.

The Latin American failures to implement constitutions clearly republican in form—constitutions often virtually exact copies of the United States Constitution—could similarly be viewed as the dead hand of a tradition carried over from authoritarian Spanish rule.

It has thus not been in pre-1945 Europe or pre-1945 Latin America that the American model has been so directly challenged by forces other than tradition. Rather it has been in Asia and Africa, and in Latin America since 1945, that the American model has been rejected by those looking very much like spokesmen for the future, hence with a much more devastating impact on American self-confidence.

The American sense of priorities could thus still be very clear for a place like Czechoslovakia or East Germany or Poland, where no degree of "economic democracy" might justify the repression of political freedom that has occurred; but the tendency for many Americans, on campus and off, may now be too much to lump Vietnam and China and Tanzania and Nicaragua together with Cuba as places where economic sharing may have to take priority over the maintenance of this press's freedom to criticize government, as places perhaps "unsuited to freedom."

The American attitudes toward the Castro regime in Cuba may very nicely show the tendencies outlined here.[1] Prior to winning power in 1959, Castro had promised a straightforward return to political democracy, to the constitution and the free elections and free speech that Batista had suspended; there is thus still general indignation that Castro, upon winning power, soon abandoned all of this, establishing the same kind of political dictatorship one sees in Moscow or Sofia. At the same time there has been a growing recognition among another slice of Americans that some kinds of economic improvement, or at least leveling, have occurred under Castro, a kind of Cuban economic democracy where the poorest are less poor, less deprived of medical care or basic housing. If the average lifespan in Cuba has gone up under Castro's rule, this is an accomplishment most Americans could not care to deny.

The new double standards of Americans toward the outside world (and some flaws in this new double standard) are very much illustrated in the responses to Indira Gandhi's declaration of an "emergency" suspending all civil liberties in the summer of 1975. While the American governmental and public reaction in earlier years might have been much more severe, a widespread attitude emerged in the United States, on campus and off, that political democracy had been too much for the Indians to afford, that the Indians had discovered, just as virtually every other developing and poor nation, that contested elections and a press free of governmental control were incompatible with the eradication of poverty or equalization of wealth. Indians presumably would be happier now under the new regime, since it was only Western naiveté and the vested interest of some capitalists that had supported the transplanting of elected government to India.

Indira Gandhi, in part because of the Western press criticism she drew, and in larger part because of some bad tactical advice she received, surprisingly decided to allow one last free election in 1977. To the delight of still many Americans, but to the surprise of those who had written off political democracy as a commodity meaningful to Asians, the voters of India then took the opportunity to defeat her party overwhelmingly.

As Americans were thus dividing the world into sectors in which political democracy is worth defending, and those in which it is not, the Indian case confused the dividing line almost immediately. Indira Gandhi, overwhelmingly defeated in 1977, was to win reelection in 1980. Patrick Moynihan's 1977 comment that "The Free World has doubled in size" clearly blurred all the complexities of the Indian situation, and all the tensions between considerations of political democracy and economic democracy that have begun to confuse and disarm many Americans.[2] Yet his comments at the same time raised a question that should not yet be swept away; will Indians or Chinese or Guineans, or any other people, even when they are beset with economic deprivation and inequality, really have become so indifferent to the pluralistic political freedoms Americans themselves cherish? Will Americans be ready to be so indifferent to such concerns?

The new geographical limitations Americans seem to be placing on their concern for liberty abroad may thus be the basis for a "new isolationism," but it would be a very different isolationism from what is remembered historically. The United States in earlier years intervened in Asia, and avoided interventions in Europe, not because it cared more about one area than the other, but because in simple power terms it had more of a chance to exert influence. The balance of power might keep European states from threatening the United States in the nineteenth century, but it also largely negated the possibility of the United States being able to intervene effectively in Europe. Just the opposite was true in Asia, where the balance-of-power system might not be able to shield China against a takeover, but where American military or naval force deployments could make a difference.

The isolationism of the 1970s promised to be the reverse geographically of what it was in the past, with the United States showing interest still in Europe, but less in Asia. It was the reverse because the limit is now American motives, more than capabilities.

Some realpolitik advocates of a "selfish isolationism" for the United States urge that Americans avoid worrying and caring about the happiness of others, contending that U.S. isolationism of earlier times was based on just such a power-oriented tough-mindedness.

The general argument of this book is that history contradicts this, that Americans have always cared about others, and have only felt limited or isolated by the shortcomings of their abilities to pursue such cares. The future may fall into yet a third pattern.

Rather than a materialistically selfish isolationism, Americans now are really more inclined to a substantively selective isolationism, sorting situations into "free world prone" and "non-free world prone." They may be readier to intervene to defend political democracy in the former than the latter, not because this fits with any selfish master plan, but because it corresponds more to what Americans will want their world influence to be.

THE TRENDS AND THE CARTER ADMINISTRATION

Yet this view, even if it were accurate, might present too static a model of American foreign policy, when it is obviously buffeted by dynamic trends. The losses of Vietnam may thus have swung Americans away from concern with developing countries, such that they prematurely shrugged off the suspension of political freedom in India, where earlier they might have been more indignant. Any American president concerned with foreign policy might have wanted then to shape his policy choices in terms not only of where American policy should be, but also of where it has swung to, and of how one achieves momentum in the correct direction. It is in these terms that we might want to sort out what caused a great deal of comment in President Carter's time in office, his stress on the theme of "human rights."[3]

Carter's statements criticizing disrespect for human rights in foreign countries were one of the more distinctive aspects of his foreign-policy style, and were the object of some substantial disquiet among more experienced foreign policy practitioners. In many ways, this focus on "human rights" has merely been a return to the American stress on political democracy, for it has been framed almost entirely in terms of civil liberties, intellectual freedoms, and free elections and press criticism, rather than a bending in addition toward any new economic rights. Yet the entire spirit of detente had in effect been to deemphasize such distinctions as unduly reflective of the cold war, and too much reflecting the unwitting ideological predilections of Americans toward laissez-faire in politics, if not also in economics.

The presumable cost of such a stress on human rights seemed obvious. As additional embarrassments and discomforts were directed at the Soviet Union, it might cause a more beleaguered Polit-buro leadership to feel less able or less willing to pursue detente and international cooperation with the United States. The costs might come in a loss of progress on the SALT negotiations, on trade agree-ments, or on arms control negotiations for Europe, or on the final defusing of the Berlin situation, or on any mutual restraint with re-gard to Africa or the Middle East or the Indian Ocean.

If prices as substantial as these might have to be paid, what did the president of the United States think he was up to in so indeli-cately calling a spade a spade? While his predecessor Gerald Ford had passed up inviting Aleksandr Solzhenitsyn to the White House to avoid affronting the Soviet Union, President Carter seemed eager to remind the world of what was obvious, that the USSR was a country which delivered little if anything at all in the way of political freedom.

One theory of course was that the president was simply a deeply religious man, continuously reading the Bible, thus regarding blatant falsehood as a sin in and of itself, even apart from its practical con-sequences. It would be deceitful to pretend that people were not mistreated in the USSR and Eastern Europe, and a moral American president would be quick to say so, just as Americans in general would have been quick to say so in earlier times, before they became saddled with so much military power, and with it so much responsi-bility. It may be impolite to be moral and honest about the way a foreign country represses dissent—about how it stays in power de-spite, rather than because of, the feelings of its intellectual and ordinary citizens. But one cost of electing a religious president may simply have been that absolute substantive considerations were put ahead of practical procedural results, with American foreign policy thus indulging itself in a costly return to the Bible.

Yet this interpretation would place too much stress on Carter's religiosity, for one can develop at least one explanation of the human rights emphasis which, while altruistic and world concerned, would have been altogether more practical. In the aftermath and momen-tum and pendulum swing of the American defeat in Vietnam, Carter may have been intent on galvanizing Americans into being ready once more to intervene somewhere, rather than succumbing into a real isolation. The alternative theory will thus be offered that the human rights campaign was a subtle attempt to reengage Americans with the outside world, because of the president's fears now of excessive American disengagement, to reengage them on the basis of a renewed confidence in the relevance of their own model.

As noted, the Vietnam defeat saw extensive speculation about a new realpolitik whereby Americans committed themselves only in pursuit of material interests at home, what in practice might produce very little foreign commitment indeed. Carter's insight may have been that Americans by their very nature were inclined to deploy their military and political power more selflessly than this, but that the reassertion of this propensity would now require a focus on basic and flawless cases meriting such intervention. A country that had become confused by whether there were any "good guys" or "bad guys" in Vietnam might become inclined to confusion everywhere; but the confusion might clear again, the "good guys" and "bad guys" might become identifiable again, if the focus were shifted to the USSR or Poland or East Germany. "Tough cases make bad law," and much of the economically and politically developing world might thus have to be avoided for a time as a tough case; but the corollary is that "easy cases make good law," and the human rights situation of the Soviet Union and its Eastern European satellites makes for easy cases.

The nature of the shift is easily seen by comparing what American folk wisdom would be on Poland and China. In the case of China (or Vietnam) the American man on the street might now have been inclined to conclude that "they don't have much freedom, but the important thing is that no one is starving anymore." By contrast the Polish (or Russian) situation would rather be "the people lost their freedom, and have no economic gains to show for it." The confusing dilemma by which the loss of political democracy is justified by greater accomplishments in the areas of economic democracy cannot be made relevant for the Russian case, or for communism in Eastern Europe—not on Main Street in the United States, not even on campus. While many students will be sympathetic to Marxist movements and Marxist solutions in Asia and Africa, and even in Spain and Italy, very few will want to think of themselves as apologists for Brezhnev and his crowd.

Carter's explicitness vis-à-vis the Soviet Union, when joined with campaigns launched earlier by people like Senator Jackson and linked with the special indignation felt about Soviet restrictions on the exit of Russian Jews, thus had the possible price of reducing Russian agreement to detente, but it could have had the other consequence of making Americans more ready for foreign engagements again, working out from the model of Eastern Europe rather than the model of Southeast Asia. Proving that this was Carter's intention would not be easy. But one can try matching up the actual set of policies with what would have been appropriate to such intentions.

The Communist-governed portions of Europe thus will strike

many Americans as an extension of the rest of Europe, i.e., as still a part of the world that is naturally suited to political democracy. If this "clear case" for some sort of concern and intervention can be brought to the forefront, Americans may shed some of the hang-ups about intervention left over from the Vietnam War, and may begin reexamining the case for an altruistic exercise of power throughout any other part of the world.

If Carter's commitment to human rights were a simple honest reaction to the defects of the outside world, it would of course have entailed calling a spade a spade anywhere on the globe. As such, it risked some peculiar feedbacks, as other countries besides the Soviet Union (including some past allies of the United States) can be found equally lacking in political democracy. When political democracy is so blatantly missing in Brazil and El Salvador and South Korea, and in many other states that had assisted the United States in the opposition to an expansion of the Marxist-controlled zone, a stress on the lack of such democracy in the USSR might not take long to come around the circle. In terms of practical power politics, U.S. alliance possibilities would look confined indeed if all of such regimes were disowned, since perhaps only some 18 countries in the world now pass muster as political democracies, maintaining their citizens' right of dissent and political contest, the essential core of "human rights."

Does this paint Carter again as straightforwardly religious, rather than as a practical politician? Perhaps not. Even a very practical-minded Carter administration might have concluded that American enthusiasm for cooperating with or defending such regimes had now diminished anyway, if only because they were poor non-European countries. If a president of the United States thus had to begin his term with popular backing only for the defense of Western Europe and Canada and Japan, he could not lose so much thereafter by hammering away on human rights. One or two "nondemocratic allies" of the United States might respond to the pressure by reforming their domestic political systems enough to fall again within the sphere of political democracy; this is what happened in Greece and Spain, and what American officials might hope for in South Korea or the Philippines. If others persisted in avoiding elections and press freedoms, however, there might have been no way of engaging American involvement anyway.

A second kind of complication about the human rights campaign might have loomed a little more serious, namely where it might cycle back into other parts of the Communist world, to stand in the way of letting the United States cooperate with one Marxist state against another. There is simply no political democracy to speak of in China, and perfect consistency might thus have required that Carter become just as critical of the situation in Beijing as in Moscow. If this were to become so pronounced as to anger the Chinese leadership into distancing themselves again from the United States, the result would be a serious loss indeed.[4]

Several factors made this less likely. To repeat the point made above, Americans may now be more adjusted to, and tolerant of, political dictatorship in Asian countries and poor areas on the new assumption that a special exception has had to be made where historical processes have not proven political freedom to be consistent with economic quality and progress. Second, for cultural reasons, the lack of political freedom in China and in some other Asian Marxist regimes will not be as visible or blatant; strong social pressures serve the same purpose in China that a secret police interrogation accomplishes in the Soviet Union, but the American spectator is less likely to notice or be appalled by the latter. There has been an altogether remarkable tendency of American visitors and commentators to see no evil in Communist China, and this is likely to continue, even in face of some disquieting second-thought comments at last reaching the press.

THE ELECTION OF REAGAN

Ronald Reagan's defeat of President Carter's bid for reelection in 1980, accompanied by the defeat of senators such as George McGovern and Frank Church, and the achievement of a Republican majority in the U.S. Senate, does not relieve the uncertainty of where American foreign policy is headed.

Reagan began his campaign on an ideologically right-wing tack, implying that he wished to recommit the United States to much of what it had renounced after 1967, indeed referring to the Vietnam War in one early campaign address as a "noble cause."[5] In a fashion quite normal for the American two-party system, each of the candidates then however trimmed toward his best guess of the midpoint of voter sentiment as the campaign rolled ahead, with Reagan deemphasizing some of this specificity of ideology and Carter showing increasingly tougher stands in commitments to defense spending and opposition to Soviet foreign policy adventures.

By the time of the actual balloting, the two candidates had thus naturally come again to look much like "Tweedledum and Tweedledee." the principal issue becoming their comparative competence.

Reagan looked less than all-powerful here because of his age, and because of his tendency toward slips of the tongue in campaigning; but Carter clearly looked worse because of the apparent vacillations in his own decisions through his four years of administration, and all the "bad news" that had to be delivered during his incumbency, not the least of this being the continued plight of the hostages held in Teheran.

As Americans went to the polls, the election looked much closer than it actually was to turn out. The vote seemed mainly a referendum in comparative personal competence, rather than any major indication of American feelings about ideology and foreign policy. It was not clear how much it could settle about the continuing appeal of Lockean concepts of political democracy and free choice, as contrasted with Marxist concepts of economic democracy and material justice.

This is not to say that there were no divisions about such foreign policy issues to be noted in the election. Rather the divisions were within the Democratic Party, instead of between the final stands of the two presidential candidates. The internal divisions of the Democrats, reflecting some of the internal division of the entire country, surely contributed to their defeat. Frank Church and George McGovern and Elizabeth Holtzman were thus probably further away from Jimmy Carter on the issues of foreign policy than Carter was from Reagan, and certainly further than Reagan was from either Gerald Ford or Jesse Helms.

To put it starkly, the Democrats were divided on whether Ho Chi Minh was an example of good or evil in the world. The old McGovern supporters basically disagreed with Carter now on whether it was more important to avoid any "repetitions" of Vietnam, or more important to recover the American resolve lost in that war, a resolve for defending what used to be called the "free world."

Carter, in losing to Reagan, thus did not speak for the radical view at all, having himself tried to get Americans again into the mood to defend political democracies around the globe against forces describing themselves as Marxist. Yet the size of Reagan's victory, and the number of left-of-center congressmen who were defeated, suggests that the 1980 election delivered more of an ideological test than it had promised. McGovern and Church and Culver were made targets in the campaign precisely because they had, since 1967, spoken for the radical view of American foreign policy outlined in this book, a view that has a considerable number of adherents around the country, even while the traditionally self-congratulatory American view also has a great number of adherents.

The country that lost its consensus when a portion of its voters swung to the Left has thus not regained it in this swing back to the Right; rather the gap in the consensus remains open, as the supporters of a Ronald Reagan continue to share very little in their foreign policy outlook with the supporters of a George McGovern or Bella Abzug or Elizabeth Holtzman.

Some of Carter's inability to win reelection was undoubtedly caused by his own political ineptitude, by apparent and real vacillations of foreign policy and domestic policy in his four years of office. Some of it, to repeat, was caused by a simple "bad news" effect, which may now make it difficult for any president to be reelected, as the events of foreign policy and domestic policy deliver disappointment after disappointment to the American public, disappointments for which they will always tend to blame the incumbent.

But a portion of the apparent disarray and disappointment of Carter's foreign policy must also be directly traced to the loss of consensus in American foreign policy thinking that we have been discussing throughout this book. Precisely because Americans now disagree so much among themselves, not only about the means and approaches of foreign policy, but also about the very ends such policy is meant to serve, all of such policy will be a little more prone to disarray, and therefore will be a little less effective in the execution.

The Reagan administration came into office having run in opposition to detente. No great hope was to be entertained now that international problems could be counted upon to solve themselves. And no weight would be given to the view that all of such problems were caused by American imperialism and aggressiveness in foreign policy, so that continued retreat from the world would be appropriate.

But it is always easier for an incoming administration to spell out what it is against, than what it is so precisely for. Ronald Reagan's description of the Vietnam War as a "noble cause" was not repeated in the rest of his election campaign because such specificity was bad politics, and in part because even some of his more right-wing supporters might not have seen Vietnam as the model of positions the United States now needed to defend.

Unlike the Democrats, who were more openly divided between the liberal and radical perspectives outlined in this book, the Republicans were more subtly divided on whether their proposed increases in defense spending were intended solely to protect American material interests or also to shield Thailand and Malaysia against Ho Chi Minh's successors. It was hence difficult to tell, and will remain difficult to tell, whether they would move more toward power politics or more toward a renewed defense of liberty. As noted earlier, some of the shift rightward in American thinking does not include the broader liberal commitment to defending freedom everywhere (a commitment that indeed was expressed most eloquently of all in the Kennedy administration), but rather can fall into a more racist syndrome of concluding that only a few European-style countries are really "cut out" for freedom.

Ronald Reagan's very explicit disavowal of Jimmy Carter's human rights policy showed elements of this strand of thinking. Some of Reagan's comments were sensible enough, that there was no point to having a double standard by which the transgressions of a South Korean regime were condemned while those of a North Korean regime were overlooked, by which an undemocratic regime in Brazil is attacked, while the one in Communist China or Poland is assisted by benevolent silence.[6]

Yet the likely Reagan shift goes beyond avoiding the double standards of the Carter administration, double standards into which it was pushed by the needs of power politics or by the radical elements of Carter's Democratic Party constituency. Implicit throughout is a tone that power considerations may have to be given higher weight now, that any "ally" of the United States can thereby hope to escape American criticism of its domestic practices simply in exchange for the help it has offered the United States in the general global political arena. Implicit also is some suggestion that political liberties are not so serious a matter for Latin America or Asia, again that the United States would have to take such human rights seriously only if they were threatened in Great Britain or Australia.

The incoming administration was clearly committed to expanding the strategic nuclear forces of the United States, and inferentially all the military forces; but skeptics wondered whether such great expenditures would really be possible in light of Reagan's commitment to a tax cut as well, amid a suspicion that some parts of the military spending increase would be shelved so that others might proceed. But different forms of military spending translate very differently into abilities to defend friends and allies overseas, so that it was still not clear whether a more resolute defense of political freedom everywhere could be seen as the mandate of 1980.

A moderate shift rightward from the American sentiments of the 1970s might thus have brought us back more surely to worldwide support of the possibility of democratic political systems against the Marxists. A larger shift rightward might instead bring about a more racist sorting out of who to defend and who not to defend, with stronger backing for Europe, and little or none for places like Thailand.

The simple swing of the pendulum suggested by the Klingberg model therefore does not fit so very well here. By Klingberg's own predictions, we should have had to wait until the 1988 election to reestablish an American commitment to manning barriers against the advance of totalitarian communism. By this time, but only really in about such a length of time, the memory of Vietnam would have faded, and with it the American horror (often felt just as much on the right of the spectrum as on the left) at the idea of a war in an Asian jungle.

The major argument of this book is that the pendulum of American feelings (if this was ever the proper analog) has broken into pieces, now swinging at different rates, very much at odds with each other. The doubts that emerged during the Vietnam years about United States ability to contribute to the welfare of others in this world have not suddenly receded by the swing of some classic pendulum, but rather remain convincing to one portion of Americans, even while they are anathema to another.

And, in a curious way, some of such doubts are accepted in the Reagan camp, by those who endorse the more traditional selfish-isolationist model of the power politician. George McGovern would have been opposed to any American defense of Thailand on what he regarded as moral grounds, on the premises that U.S. duty was rather to root for those invading Thailand; the Reagan camp now probably includes some Americans who were ready to write off Thailand as "Asians unsuited to free elections anyway."

SOME CONCLUSIONS

Three interpretations of American foreign policy have been pitted against each other throughout this book. These are not merely the abstractions of the academic analyst; they are the core of a debate that has left Americans unsure of themselves in foreign policy, and thus unpredictable for the outside world. What Americans will do in the future will depend importantly on what they conclude they have been doing in the past. As Americans remain undecided and in disagreement about their past, they remain so about their future.

As has been pointed out several times, the power politics interpretation is not really so much of an alternative to the liberal or radical views, for it mainly wishes to talk about opportunities, and to ignore ultimate values, while the radical and liberal perspectives disagree precisely about ultimate values. Considerations of opportunities are very important, and the power politics interpretation thus has an important contribution to make, but this contribution ends past a certain point, when the debate shifts to what would truly make people happier around the globe.

The power politics interpretation assumes that every political actor is interested in power. The liberal would deny this for himself, but often would accuse the radical Marxist of being thusly power-minded. And the radical would deny this for himself, but at times will accuse the American liberal and his historical foreign policy similarly of being a lust after power. An acceptance of power considerations thus can make either the radical or the liberal look less high-minded and pure, and more hypocritical, but such an accusation can be very unfair.

The aftermath of the Vietnam War has seen some Americans reproaching themselves for having ever begun moving down the slopes of expediency here, for having ever begun the hazardous calculus of tolerating dictatorships as a means to maintain liberties, or of "using death as a means to preserve life." Such expediency can be made to look outrageously paradoxical in retrospect, or simply hypocritical, or simply foolish.

Was this all pure nonsense, the kind of thing we must rigorously avoid in the future? Or is it instead an inevitable part of the international political process?

It is surely erroneous to say that one can never use a bad means in politics to a good end. One has to do his bookeeping very carefully, of course, to ensure really coming out ahead in the net in terms of our values, to guard against misleading ourselves into seeing gains where there are none. Yet to stay out of every morally complicated situation, for fear of somehow erring on the bookeeping, would be to relinquish most of the power and influence a nation could have for good in the world.

How clear was the U.S. altruistic commitment to political freedom in the earlier years before everything was shaken in the Vietnam defeat? Skeptics here would be quick to point to all the right-wing dictatorships with whom the United States has had friendly relations in the past (one could also point to its friendly relations with Stalin in World War II, or with Tito since 1948, or with the Beijing regime today).

But was this ever at the level of ends rather than means? The United States, it has been argued here, has as a nation been unusually prone to treat foreign peoples and countries as ends in themselves in its foreign policy, rather than as means. Yet no one ever can serve his optimal ends without husbanding some means, without giving some concern to power.

The difficulty with the analysis of Morgenthau and the realpoliticians is that their analysis at times suggests that one should *only* be concerned about power, as if power were an end in itself. A naive idealist might by contrast be accused of *never* being concerned for the power and means to further his ends. American foreign policy has not been naively unaware of the demands of power, but it has been inclined to use a great deal of this power for what it is believed (rightly or wrongly) would work in the end for the happiness of the peoples involved.

Roosevelt's comment about Trujillo that "He may be an s.o.b., but he's our s.o.b." does not suggest that Americans were perfectly content to leave Trujillo in office for as long as he cared to hold it.[7] Support for a Somoza or a Stalin thus hardly demonstrates that the United States would not have preferred democratic electoral systems in place of either of them, but rather shows that each of them was needed at the moment.

The U.S. government rationalization has been that the post-1945 alliances with the Francos and Somozas and General Parks of this world have just been alliances of convenience, as the Communist alternative was a more serious worldwide threat, as Communist dictatorships show signs of becoming permanent, while those of the army or of the right-wing do not. Franco's decease produced elections (with substantial American approval) in Spain, and the Portuguese successors to Salazar (after a near miss with a Communist Party control with the clearest of Stalinist overtones) are installing the same.[8] The colonels in Greece were forced to bow out of office.[9] Where has a Communist dictatorship been similarly deposed, once it got control of the Ministry of the Interior?

Everyone in the world who compromises his ideals about ends, to serve as means to an end, can thus be accused of rationalizing, of really having less noble ends than he professes. Some of this is pretense, but some is simple accommodation to the limits of one's influence. The viewer must in the end be left to decide. Would Americans, if they had been able to, not have replaced Trujillo in the Dominican Republic with the constitution of the state of Minnesota? Until very recently, they most plausibly would.

The United States obviously cannot thus claim to have enlisted only political democracies as allies. In a Machiavellian world, it has often had to be instrumental enough and Machiavellian enough to use less savory partners. The United States however can make another claim that revisionist critics should face. It has had no such political democracies as enemies. So sweeping a claim would include the Britain of 1776 and 1812 (close calls, perhaps), and the Spain of 1898 and Germany of 1914 (by today's standards, also not so far off the mark). Santa Anna may or may not have been a popular dictator, but he was clearly a dictator. One would not want to claim that U.S. conflicts with Mexico were intended to win self-government for Mexicans; in a sense, however, they were intended to win this for the populations of Texas and California, which had so much changed character in the years after 1821. For World War II, the claim is perhaps salvaged only by U.S. failure to declare war on Finland;[10] the semialliance with Pakistan against India provides another close call. Yet the claim is still not really compromised.

If any country around the world wanted to get along with the United States, let it merely, regardless of what economic course it chooses to pursue, have made a complete and unconditioned commitment to free elections and free press and the rest of the attributes of political democracy. This is what Castro promised but did not deliver, and this was more of a promise than Allende could bring himself to offer. Perhaps one cannot prove that such a domestic stance would assure good relations with the American public and government. But one could claim that no instance has yet emerged to prove the opposite.

Was the intervention in Vietnam thus caused by an American selfishness? The case is strong that it was not, that such intervention would never have occurred if many Americans had not sincerely and altruistically identified with the future happiness of Vietnamese and Thais and Malaysians. However much one decides that Americans may have done harm in Southeast Asia, it very probably happened because they wanted to do good.

In conclusion, the realpolitik analyst of foreign policy would yawn in boredom at any such discussion of "doing good" in the world.

The radical would doubt that the United States, with its "bourgeoisie liberalism" has had much to offer the world, and would deny that American foreign policy, in Vietnam or elsewhere, has been guided by any such generous considerations. Such denials can not be dismissed out of hand, even if an author or reader were to disagree with them, for they have persuaded a significant number of Americans, and they have thus influenced the future of American policy by tearing apart what was consensus.

The traditional American liberal finally might join this author in still accepting what almost all Americans used to accept as consensus, that the far corners of the world would become happier places if they were governed in the same basically republican manner as Minnesota. Political democracy could be just as globally appropriate as literacy or penicillin. The loss of consensus in American foreign policy may be a loss to be regretted.

NOTES

1. American feelings toward Castro and Cuba are analyzed in Hugh Thomas, *Cuba: The Pursuit of Freedom* (New York: Harper & Row, 1971).

2. For the Moynihan statements, see the New York *Times*, March 23, 1977, p. 12, and March 24, 1977, p. 27.

3. President Carter's emphasis on "human rights" is explored in J. S. Girling, "Carter's Foreign Policy: Realism or Ideology?," *World Today* 33, no. 11 (November 1977): 417–24.

4. For an interpretation urging a different application of human rights standard to China, see Susan Shirk, "Human Rights: What About China?," *Foreign Policy*, no. 29 (Winter 1978-79), pp. 109-27.

5. The New York *Times*, August 19, 1980, p. 1.

6. For an analysis of Reagan's intended departure from Carter's policies on human rights, see Ronald Steel, "Are Human Rights Passé?," *The New Republic* 183, no. 26 (December 27, 1980): 14-15.

7. Franklin Roosevelt's comment on Trujillo is cited in John Bartlow Martin, *Overtaken by Events* (Garden City: Doubleday, 1966), p. 75.

8. For a discussion of the choices and possibilities for the Iberian peninsula, see Robert Harvey, *Portugal: Birth of a Democracy* (New York: St. Martin's Press, 1978) and Constantine Christopher Menges, *Spain: The Struggle for Democracy Today* (Washington, D.C.: Center for Strategic and International Studies, 1978).

9. The ins and outs of military dictatorship in Greece are discussed in Stanley Harnow, "America's Mediterranean Bungle," *The Atlantic* 235, no. 2 (February 1975): 6 ff.

10. American relations with Finland during World War II are described in John H. Wuorinen, *Finland and World War II* (New York: Ronald Press, 1948), pp. 128-43.

Bibliography

Abel, Elie. *The Missile Crisis.* Philadelphia: Lippincott, 1966.

Adler, Selig. *The Isolationist Impulse.* New York: Abelard-Schuman, 1957.

Almond, Gabriel A. *The American People and Foreign Policy.* New York: Praeger, 1960.

Alperovitz, Gar. *Atomic Diplomacy.* New York: Simon and Schuster, 1965.

Ambrose, Stephen. *Rise to Globalism.* New York: Penguin, 1976.

Amme, Carl H. *NATO Without France.* Stanford: Hoover Institution, 1967.

Bader, William B. *Austria Between East and West: 1945-1955.* Stanford: Stanford University Press, 1966.

Bailey, Thomas A. *Woodrow Wilson and the Lost Peace.* New York: Macmillan, 1944.

Barnet, Richard J. *Roots of War.* Baltimore: Penguin, 1973.

Barnet, Richard J., and Ronald E. Muller. *Global Reach.* New York: Simon and Schuster, 1974.

Becker, Jillian. *Hitler's Children.* Philadelphia: Lippincott, 1977.

Bemis, Samuel Flag. *A Short History of American Foreign Policy and Diplomacy.* New York: Holt, Rinehart and Winston, 1959.

Bergsten, C. Fred, and Lawrence B. Krause, eds. *World Politics and International Economics.* Washington, D.C.: Brookings, 1975.

Blake, David, and Robert Walters. *The Politics of Economic Relations.* Englewood Cliffs: Prentice-Hall, 1976.

Bloomfield, Lincoln P. *In Search of American Foreign Policy: The Human Use of Power.* New York: Oxford University Press, 1974.

Blum, John M. *Woodrow Wilson and the Politics of Morality.* Boston: Little, Brown, 1956.

Bonilla, Frank, and Robert Sirling, eds. *Structures of Dependency.* Stanford: Stanford University Press, 1973.

Bourne, Kenneth. *Britain and The Balance of Power in North America: 1815-1908.* Berkeley: University of California Press, 1967.

Braden, Spruille. *Diplomats and Demagogues.* New Rochelle: Arlington House, 1971.

Brown, Seyom. *New Forces in World Politics.* Washington, D.C.: Brookings, 1974.

Brown, Weldon A. *Prelude to Disaster: The American Role in Vietnam 1940-1963.* Port Washington: Kennikat Press, 1975.

Buehrig, Edward H. *Woodrow Wilson and the Balance of Power.* Bloomington: Indiana University Press, 1955.

Burke, Edmund III. *Prelude to Protectorate in Morocco.* Chicago: University of Chicago Press, 1976.

Burnham, James, ed. *What Europe Thinks of America.* New York: John Day, 1953.

Campbell, John C. *Tito's Separate Road.* New York: Harper & Row, 1967.

Canby, Steven L. *Military Manpower Procurement.* Lexington: D. C. Heath, 1972.

Cantril, Albert H., and Charles W. Roll. *Hopes and Fears of the American People.* Washington, D.C.: Potomac Associates, 1971.

Cantril, Hadley. *Public Opinion 1935-46.* Princeton: Princeton University Press, 1951.

Carleton, William G. *The Revolution in American Foreign Policy: Its Global Range.* New York: Random House, 1963.

Carr, Edward Hallett. *The Twenty Years' Crisis.* New York: St. Martin's, 1939.

Chace, James. *A World Elsewhere: Options for the Future.* New York: Charles Scribner's Sons, 1973.

Chester, Edward W. *Clash of Titans.* Maryknoll: Orbis Books, 1974.

——. *Europe Views America.* Washington, D.C.: Public Affairs Press, 1962.

Chiang Kai-shek. *China's Destiny.* New York: Macmillan, 1944.

Churchill, Winston S. *Triumph and Tragedy.* Boston: Houghton Mifflin, 1953.

Clubb, O. Edmund. *20th Century China.* New York: Columbia University Press, 1964.

Cohen, Benjamin J. *The Question of Imperialism.* New York: Basic Books, 1973.

Commager, Henry Steele, ed. *America in Perspective.* New York: Random House, 1947.

Compton, James V. *The Swastika and the Eagle.* Boston: Houghton Mifflin, 1967.

Cook, Thomas, and Malcolm Moos. *Power Through Purpose: The Realism of Idealism as a Basis for Foreign Policy.* Baltimore: Johns Hopkins University Press, 1954.

Cooper, Chester L. *The Last Crusade: America in Vietnam.* New York: Dodd, Mead, 1970.

Coupland, Sir Reginald. *The Quebec Act.* Oxford: The Clarendon Press, 1925.

Davis, George T. *A Navy Second to None.* New York: Harcourt Brace, 1940.

Davis, Lance E., Jonathan R. T. Hughes, and Duncan M. McDougall. *American Economic History.* Homewood: Richard D. Irwin, 1965.

Davis, Lynn Etheridge. *The Cold War Begins: Soviet-American Conflict over Eastern Europe.* Princeton: Princeton University Press, 1974.

Davison, W. Phillips. *The Berlin Blockade.* Princeton: Princeton University Press, 1958.

deConde, Alexander, ed. *Isolation and Security.* Durham: University of North Carolina Press, 1957.

de Gaulle, Charles. *The Complete War Memoirs.* New York: Simon and Schuster, 1964.

de Tocqueville, Alexis. *Democracy in America.* New York: Harper & Row, 1966.

Devlin, Patrick. *Too Proud to Fight.* New York: Oxford University Press, 1975.

Divine, Robert A. *The Illusion of Neutrality.* Chicago: University of Chicago Press, 1962.

Dulles, Foster Rhea. *America in the Pacific.* Boston: Houghton Mifflin, 1932.

Duroselle, Jean-Baptiste. *France and the United States.* Chicago: University of Chicago Press, 1976.

Emerson, Rupert. *Africa and United States Policy.* Englewood Cliffs: Prentice-Hall, 1967.

Fanon, Frantz. *The Wretched of the Earth.* New York: Evergreen, 1968.

Fay, Peter Ward. *The Opium War.* Chapel Hill: University of North Carolina Press, 1975.

Feis, Herbert. *The Atomic Bomb and the End of World War II.* Princeton: Princeton University Press, 1966.

——. *Churchill, Roosevelt, Stalin.* Princeton: Princeton University Press, 1957.

——. *From Trust to Terror.* New York: Norton, 1970.

Fifield, Russell H. *Americans in Southeast Asia: The Roots of Commitment.* New York: Thomas Y. Crowell, 1973.

Fleming, D. F. *The Cold War and Its Origins.* Garden City: Doubleday, 1961.

Friedlander, Saul. *Prelude to Downfall: Hitler and the United States 1939–41.* New York: Knopf, 1967.

Fuess, Claude. *Carl Schurz: Reformer.* New York: Dodd, Mead, 1932.

Fulbright, J. W. *Old Myths and New Realities.* New York: Random House, 1964.

Gaddis, John L. *The United States and the Origins of the Cold War.* New York: Columbia University Press, 1972.

Gallup, George H. *The Gallup Polls.* New York: Random House, 1972.

Galucci, Robert. *Neither Peace Nor Honor.* Baltimore: Johns Hopkins Press, 1975.

Galula, David. *Counterinsurgency Warfare.* New York: Praeger, 1964.

Gamson, William, and Andre Mondigliani. *Untangling the Cold War.* Boston: Little, Brown, 1971.

Gardner, Richard N. *Sterling-Dollar Diplomacy: Anglo-American Collaboration in the Reconstruction of Multilateral Trade.* Oxford: The Clarendon Press, 1956.

Gelb, Leslie, and Richard Betts. *The Irony of Vietnam: The System Worked.* Washington, D.C.: Brookings, 1979.

Golay, Frank H., ed. *The United States and the Philippines.* Englewood Cliffs: Prentice-Hall, 1966.

Goldwin, Robert A., ed. *How Democratic Is America?* Chicago: Rand McNally, 1971.

Griffith, William B. *Albania and the Sino-Soviet Rift.* Cambridge, Mass.: The M.I.T. Press, 1963.

Gruening, Ernest, and Herbert Wilton Beaser. *Vietnam Folly.* Washington, D.C.: The National Press, 1968.

Guhin, Michael. *John Foster Dulles.* New York: Columbia University Press, 1972.

Guttmann, Allen, ed. *Korea: Cold War and Limited War.* Lexington: D.C. Heath, 1972.

Halle, Louis. *The Cold War as History.* New York: Harper & Row, 1967.

Halperin, Morton H., and Daniel Hoffman. *Freedom vs. National Security.* New York: Chelsea House, 1979.

Halperin, Morton H., and Arnold Kanter, eds. *Readings in American Foreign Policy: A Bureaucratic Perspective.* Boston: Little, Brown, 1973.

Hammond, Paul Y. *The Cold War Years: American Foreign Policy Since 1945.* New York: Harcourt, Brace and World, 1969.

Hartmann, Frederick H. *The New Age of American Foreign Policy.* New York: Macmillan, 1970.

Hartz, Louis. *The Liberal Tradition in America.* New York: Harvest Books, 1955.

Harvey, Robert. *Portugal: Birth of a Democracy.* New York: St. Martin's Press, 1978.

Hayek, Friedrich. *The Road to Serfdom.* Chicago: University of Chicago Press, 1945.

Heinl, Robert Debs, and Nancy Gordon Heinl. *Written in Blood.* Boston: Houghton Mifflin, 1978.

Herring, George. *Aid to Russia 1941-1946.* New York: Columbia University Press, 1973.

Herring, Hubert. *A History of Latin America.* New York: Alfred A. Knopf, 1955.

Hewlett, Richard, and Oscar Anderson. *The New World.* University Park: Pennsylvania State University Press, 1962.

Higham, John. *Strangers in the Land.* New Brunswick: Rutgers University Press, 1955.

Hobson, J. A. *Imperialism: A Study.* London: Allen and Unwin, 1902.

Hofstadter, Richard, and Michael Wallace, eds. *American Violence: A Documentary History.* New York: Alfred A. Knopf, 1970.

Hoopes, Townsend. *The Limits of Intervention.* New York: McKay, 1969.

Huntington, Samuel. *The Common Defense.* New York: Columbia University Press, 1961.

Iriye, Akira. *Across the Pacific: An Inner History of American-East Asian Relations.* New York: Harcourt Brace, 1967.

Irving, David. *The Destruction of Dresden.* New York: Holt, Rinehart and Winston, 1963.

Isaacs, Harold R. *Scratches on Our Minds.* New York: John Day, 1958.

Jackson, Helen Hunt. *A Century of Dishonor.* Boston: Little, Brown, 1903.

James, Daniel. *Mexico and the Americans.* New York: Praeger, 1963.

Jonas, Manfred. *Isolationism in America.* Ithaca: Cornell University Press, 1966.

Jones, Jesse. *The Fifteen Weeks.* New York: Viking, 1955.

Jungk, Robert. *Brighter Than a Thousand Suns.* New York: Harcourt Brace, 1958.

Kahin, George McT., and John W. Lewis. *The United States in Vietnam.* New York: Dial Press, 1967.

Kalb, Marvin, and Bernard Kalb. *Kissinger.* Boston: Little, Brown, 1974.

Keller, John W. *Germany, The Wall and Berlin.* New York: Vantage Press, 1964.

Keniston, Kenneth. *The Uncommitted.* New York: Harcourt Brace, 1965.

Kennan, George F. *The Decision to Intervene*. Princeton: Princeton University Press, 1958.

——. *Memoirs 1925-50*. Boston: Little, Brown, 1967.

——. *Russia Leaves the War*. Princeton: Princeton University Press, 1956.

——. *Russia, The Atom, and the West*. New York: Harper, 1958.

Kennedy, Robert F. *Thirteen Days*. New York: Norton, 1971.

Kissinger, Henry A. *The White House Years*. Boston: Little, Brown, 1979.

Kohn, Hans. *American Nationalism*. New York: Macmillan, 1957.

Koht, Halvdan. *The American Spirit in Europe*. Philadelphia: University of Pennsylvania Press, 1949.

Kolko, Gabriel. *The Politics of War*. New York: Random House, 1968.

——. *The Roots of American Foreign Policy*. Boston: Beacon Press, 1969.

Kolko, Gabriel and Joyce Kolko. *The Limits of Power*. New York: Harper & Row, 1972.

Korbel, Joseph. *The Communist Subversion of Czechoslovakia*. Princeton: Princeton University Press, 1959.

Krasner, Stephen D. *Defending the National Interest*. Princeton: Princeton University Press, 1978.

Lacouture, Jean. *Ho Chi Minh: A Political Biography*. New York: Random House, 1968.

LaFeber, Walter. *America, Russia, and the Cold War*. New York: Wiley, 1967.

——. *The New Empire*. Ithaca: Cornell University Press, 1963.

——. *The Panama Canal: The Crisis in Historical Perspective*. New York: Oxford University Press, 1979.

Laserson, Max. *The American Impact on Russia*. New York: Macmillan, 1950.

Leites, Nathan, and Charles Wolf. *Rebellion and Authority*. Chicago: Markham, 1970.

Leys, Simon. *Chinese Shadows*. New York: Viking Press, 1977.

Lipset, Seymour Martin. *The First New Nation*. New York: Basic Books, 1963.

Luce, Henry. *The American Century*. New York: Farrar and Rinehart, 1941.

Lumsden, Ian, ed. *Close the 49th Parallel, etc*. Toronto: University of Toronto Press, 1970.

Maddox, Robert James. *The New Left and the Origins of the Cold War*. Princeton: Princeton University Press, 1973.

Martin, John Bartlow. *Overtaken By Events*. Garden City: Doubleday, 1966.

May, Ernest R. *The World War and American Isolation, 1914-1917*. Cambridge, Mass.: Harvard University Press, 1959.

McInnis, Edgar W. *The Unguarded Frontier*. Garden City: Doubleday and Doran, 1942.

McPherson, James. *The Struggle for Equality*. Princeton: Princeton University Press, 1964.

Meisner, Maurice. *Mao's China*. New York: The Free Press, 1977.

Menges, Constantine Christopher. *Spain: The Struggle for Democracy Today*. Washington, D.C.: Center for Strategic and International Studies, 1978.

Merchant, Livingston, ed. *Neighbors Taken for Granted*. New York: Praeger, 1966.

Millis, Walter. *The Road To War*. Boston: Houghton Mifflin, 1935.

Molnar, Thomas. *The Two Faces of American Foreign Policy.* New York: Bobbs-Merrill, 1962.

Montague, Ludwell Lee. *Haiti and the United States.* Durham: Duke University Press, 1940.

Montgomery, John D. *Foreign Aid in International Politics.* Englewood Cliffs, Prentice-Hall, 1967.

Morgenthau, Hans. *In Defense of the National Interest.* New York: Alfred A. Knopf, 1952.

——. *Politics Among Nations.* New York: Alfred A. Knopf, 1967.

——. *The Purpose of American Politics.* New York: Alfred A. Knopf, 1960.

Morgenthau, Hans, and Kenneth W. Thompson. *Principles and Problems of International Politics.* New York: Alfred A. Knopf, 1950.

Moss, Robert. *Chile's Marxist Experiment.* New York: John Wiley, 1974.

Mowry, George. *Theodore Roosevelt and the Progressive Movement.* Madison: University of Wisconsin Press, 1946.

Nadel, George H., and Perry Curtis. *Imperialism and Colonialism.* New York: Macmillan, 1964.

Nathan, James A., and James K. Oliver. *United States Foreign Policy and World Order.* Boston: Little, Brown, 1976.

Neustadt, R. E. *Presidential Power.* New York: Wiley, 1960.

Nicolson, Harold. *Peacemaking 1919.* New York: Grosset and Dunlap, 1939.

O'Brien, Conor Cruise. *To Katanga and Back.* London: Hutchinson, 1962.

Oglesby, Carl, and Richard Schaull. *Containment and Change.* New York: Macmillan, 1967.

Osgood, Robert E. *Ideals and Self-Interest in American Politics.* Chicago: University of Chicago Press, 1953.

——. *NATO: The Entangling Alliance.* Chicago: University of Chicago Press, 1962.

Packenham, Robert A. *Liberal America and the Third World.* Princeton: Princeton University Press, 1973.

Paige, Glenn D. *The Korean Decision.* New York: Free Press, 1968.

Parenti, Michael. *The Anti-Communist Impulse.* New York: Random House, 1969.

Perkins, Dexter. *The American Approach to Foreign Policy.* Cambridge, Mass.: Harvard University Press, 1952.

——. *Hands Off.* Boston: Little, Brown, 1941.

——. *The United States and the Caribbean.* Cambridge, Mass.: Harvard University Press, 1947.

Petras, James, and Morris Morley. *The United States and Chile: Imperialism and the Overthrow of the Allende Government.* New York: Monthly Review Press, 1975.

President's Commission on National Goals. *Goals for Americans.* Englewood Cliffs: Prentice-Hall, 1960.

Quigg, Philip W. *America The Dutiful.* New York: Simon and Schuster, 1971.

Pustay, John S. *Counterinsurgency Warfare.* New York: The Free Press, 1965.

Rapoport, Anatol. *The Big Two: Soviet-American Perceptions of Foreign Policy.* New York: Pegasus, 1971.

Rapoport, Anatol, and A. M. Chammah. *Prisoner's Dilemma: A Study of Conflict and Cooperation.* Ann Arbor: University of Michigan Press, 1965.

Rees, David. *The Age of Containment: The Cold War, 1945-65.* London: St. Martin's Press, 1967.

Rippy, J. Fred. *Latin America: A Modern History.* Ann Arbor: University of Michigan Press, 1958.

Robinson, Joan. "Marx and Keynes." In *Collected Economic Papers.* Oxford: Blackwell, 1951.

Rosecrance, Richard, ed. *America As An Ordinary Country.* Ithaca: Cornell University Press, 1976.

Rosen, Steve, and James R. Kurth, eds. *Testing Theories of Economic Imperialism.* Lexington: D. C. Heath, 1974.

Rostow, W. W. *The Stages of Economic Growth.* Cambridge: Cambridge University Press, 1960.

——. *The United States in the World Arena.* New York: Harper, 1960.

Russett, Bruce M. *No Clear and Present Danger.* New York: Harper & Row, 1972.

Sapin, Burton M. *The Making of United States Foreign Policy.* New York: Praeger, 1960.

Sarkesian, Sam, ed. *Revolutionary Guerrilla Warfare.* Chicago: Precedent, 1975.

Schmitt, Karl M. *Mexico and the United States, 1821-1973: Conflict and Coexistence.* New York: John Wiley, 1974.

Seymour, Charles. *American Diplomacy During the World War.* Baltimore: Johns Hopkins University Press, 1934.

Silberschmidt, Max. *The United States and Europe.* London: Harcourt Brace Jovanovich, 1972.

Sivachev, Nikolai V., and Nikolai N. Yakovlev. *Russia and the United States.* Chicago: University of Chicago Press, 1979.

Snell, John L. *Wartime Origins of the East-West Dilemma Over Germany.* New Orleans: Hauser Press, 1959.

Spanier, John W. *American Foreign Policy Since World War II.* New York: Praeger, 1977.

——. *The Truman-MacArthur Controversy and the Korean War.* New York: Norton, 1965.

Spero, Joan Edelman. *The Politics of International Economic Relations.* New York: St. Martin's Press, 1977.

Sprout, Harold and Margaret. *Foundations of National Power.* New York: Van Nostrand, 1951.

——. *The Rise of American Naval Power 1776-1918.* Princeton: Princeton University Press, 1939.

——. *Toward a New Order of Sea Power.* Princeton: Princeton University Press, 1943.

Stearns, Harold. *Liberalism in America: Its Origins, Its Temporary Collapse, Its Future.* New York: Boni and Liveright, 1919.

Steel, Ronald. *Imperialists and Other Heroes.* New York: Random House, 1971.

——. *Pax Americana.* New York: Viking, 1967.

Steele, A. T. *The American People and China.* New York: McGraw-Hill, 1966.

Stimson, Henry L. *The Far Eastern Crisis*. New York: Harper, 1936.

Stockwell, John. *In Search of Enemies*. New York: Norton, 1978.

Stone, I. F. *The Hidden History of the Korean War*. New York: Monthly Review Press, 1962.

Tannenbaum, Frank. *The American Tradition in Foreign Policy*. Norman: University of Oklahoma Press, 1955.

Tansill, Charles C. *America Goes to War*. Boston: Little, Brown, 1938.

Thomas Hugh. *Cuba: The Pursuit of Freedom*. New York: Harper & Row, 1971.

Thompson, Kenneth W. *Realism and the Crisis of World Politics*. Princeton: Princeton University Press, 1960.

Tompkins, E. Berkeley. *Anti-Imperialism in the United States: The Great Debate 1890–1920*. Philadelphia: University of Pennsylvania Press, 1970.

Tsou, Tang. *America's Failure in China*. Chicago: University of Chicago Press, 1963.

Tuchman, Barbara. *The Zimmerman Telegram*. London: Constable, 1959.

Tucker, Robert W. *A New Isolationism: Threat or Promise?* New York: Universe Books, 1972.

——. *The Radical Left and American Foreign Policy*. Baltimore: Johns Hopkins University Press, 1971.

——. *The United States in the World*. Washington, D.C.: Potomac Associates, 1976.

Ulam, Adam. *The Rivals*. New York: Viking Press, 1971.

Varg, Paul A. *Missionaries, Chinese and Diplomats*. Princeton: Princeton University Press, 1958.

Vernon, Raymond. *Sovereignty at Bay*. New York: Basic Books, 1971.

Wagner, R. Harrison. *U.S. Policy Toward Latin America: A Study in Domestic and International Politics*. Stanford: Stanford University Press, 1970.

Wattenberg, Ben J. *The Real America*. Garden City: Doubleday, 1974.

Watts, William, and Lloyd A. Free. *State of the Nation*. New York: Universe Books, 1973.

Whiting, Allen. *China Crosses the Yalu*. New York: Macmillan, 1960.

Williams, William Appleman. *The Tragedy of American Diplomacy*. Cleveland: World, 1959.

Wilson, Charles Morrow. *Liberia*. New York: Harper & Row, 1971.

Wiltz, John. *From Isolationism to War*. Arlington Heights: AHM, 1968.

Woodward, C. V. *Reunion and Reaction*. Garden City: Doubleday, 1951.

Wuorinen, John H. *Finland and World War II*. New York: Ronald Press, 1948.

Yergin, Daniel. *Shattered Peace*. Boston: Houghton Mifflin, 1977.

Zagoria, Donald. *The Sino-Soviet Conflict*. Princeton: Princeton University Press, 1962.

Index

About the Author

George H. Quester is Chairman of the Department of Government and Politics at the University of Maryland, where he teaches courses on international relations and American foreign policy. He received his undergraduate degree in History from Columbia and, after serving as an officer in the United States Air Force, did his graduate work in Political Science at Harvard. Prior to moving to the University of Maryland, he was a Professor of Government at Cornell University. Professor Quester has also taught at Harvard University, the University of Rochester, UCLA, and the National War College.

He is the author of *Deterrence Before Hiroshima* (1966), *The Politics of Nuclear Proliferation* (1973) and *Offense and Defense in the International System* (1977).

DATE DUE

AP 1 4 '83			